Start Your Own

2ND EDITION

MAIL ORDER BUSINESS

Additional titles in *Entrepreneur's* **Startup Series**

Start Your Own

Arts and Crafts Business

Bar and Club

Bed & Breakfast

Business on eBay

Business Support Service

Car Wash

Child Care Service

Cleaning Service

Clothing Store

Coin-Operated Laundry

Consulting

e-Business

e-Learning Business

Event Planning Business

Executive Recruiting Service

Freight Brokerage Business

Gift Basket Service

Grant-Writing Business

Home Inspection Service

Import/Export Business

Information Consultant Business

Law Practice

Lawn Care Business

Mail Order Business

Medical Claims Billing Service

Personal Concierge Service

Personal Training Business

Pet-Sitting Business

Restaurant and Five Other Food Businesses

Self-Publishing Business

Seminar Production Business

Specialty Travel & Tour Business

Staffing Service

Successful Retail Business

Vending Business

Wedding Consultant Business

Wholesale Distribution Business

Entrepreneur MAGAZINE'S

start*up*

2ND EDITION

Start Your Own

MAIL ORDER BUSINESS

Your Step-by-Step Guide to Success

Entrepreneur Press and Rich Mintzer

Jere L. Calmes, Publisher
Cover Design: Beth Hansen-Winter
Composition and Production: MillerWorks

This publication is designed to provide accurate and authoritative information in
regard to the subject matter covered. It is sold with the understanding that the
publisher is not engaged in rendering legal, accounting, or other professional services.
If legal advice or other expert assistance is required, the services of a competent
professional person should be sought.

Library of Congress Cataloging-in-Publication Data

Mintzer, Richard.
   Start your own mail order business/by Entreprenuer Press and Rich Mintzer. —
2nd ed.
      p. cm. — (Start your own)
   Rev. ed. of: Start your own mail order business/Terry and Rob Adams. c 2003.
      Includes index.
   ISBN-13: 978-1-59918-173-8 (alk. paper)
      1. Mail-order business—Management. 2. New business enterprises—
Management. I. Adams, Terry, 1952–Start your own mail order business.
II. Entrepreneur Press. III. Title.

HF5466.A2173 2008
658.8'72—dc22   2008004713

Printed in Canada

10 09 08   10 9 8 7 6 5 4 3 2 1

Contents

▲

Chapter 4
Packaging Your Business: Choosing a Name and a Structure

Chapter 5
Into the Money Bag: Figuring Your Finances

Chapter 9
Your Business Location and Your Employees 157

Chapter 10
Pushing the Envelope, Part I: Direct-Mail Advertising 175

Chapter 11
Pushing the Envelope, Part II:
Advertising, Promotion and Marketing

Preface

You're holding this book, either in your hands, on your lap, or on your desk—probably dangerously near a spillable cup of coffee—because you're one of those people who likes to live on the edge. You're contemplating starting your own business.

This is one of the most exhilarating things you can do for yourself and your family. It's also one of the scariest. Owning your own business means you're the boss, the big wheel, the head cheese. You make the rules. You lay down the law. It also means you can't call in sick (especially when you're also the only employee), you can't let somebody else worry about making enough to cover payroll and expenses, and you can't defer that cranky client or intimidating IRS letter to a higher authority. You're it.

We're assuming you've picked up this particular book on starting and running a mail order business for one or more of the following reasons:

- You have a background in the mail order field.
- You're an avid fan of The Home Shopping Network, your mailbox is stuffed with tons of catalogs, and you think mail order would be a fun and exciting business.
- You love shopping via the internet and want to share the fun.
- You have a background in sales or distribution and feel that sales is sales, no matter what kind.
- You have no background or fascination with any of the above but believe mail order is a hot opportunity and are willing to take a chance.

Which did you choose? (Didn't know it was a test, did you?)

Well, you can relax because there is no wrong answer. Any of these responses is entirely correct as long as you realize that *they all involve a lot of learning and a lot of hard work.* They can also result in having fun and a tremendous amount of personal and professional satisfaction.

Our goal here is to tell you everything you need to know to

- decide whether a mail order business is the right business for you,
- get your business started successfully,
- keep your business running successfully, and
- make friends and influence people. (That's actually part of Chapters 10 and 11, which are about advertising and public relations.)

We've interviewed lots of people out there on the front lines of the industry—all around the country in order to include some of the details directly from the people who have been in the trenches, so to speak. We've set aside places for them to tell their own stories and give their own hard-won advice and suggestions, a sort of virtual round-table discussion group, with you placed right in the thick of things. (For a listing of these successful business owners, see the Appendix.) We've broken our chapters into manageable sections on every aspect of startup and operations. And we've left some space for your creativity to soar.

We've packed our pages with helpful hints so that you can get up and running on your new venture as quickly as possible. And we've provided a resource section crammed with contacts and sources.

So sit back (don't spill that coffee!), start reading, and get ready to become a mail order pro.

Mail Order
Mania

Mail order is one of the hottest industries right now. It's not new—in fact, it can be traced back more than a century. But it's in demand, by consumers and entrepreneurs alike. Why? Reasons abound, both personal and commercial.

This chapter explores the flourishing business of mail order—a sort of in-your-lap TV news magazine report without the commercials. We'll delve into the steadily rising economic success of the field and dip into the secrets of America's mail order industry.

Wish Fulfillment

Everybody loves to get something in the mail—except, of course, those pesky bills. A letter—or especially a package—delivered to your door is like a birthday gift any time of the year. It's wish fulfillment. Even if the contents are something as mundane as kitchen towels or a car mat, that package makes you feel like you've received something special and exciting. So it's no wonder that mail order is in demand.

The venerable Sears Roebuck catalog, a pioneer mail order piece, was dubbed "The Wish Book" because it gave people the power to choose whatever they wanted and have that wish granted simply by sending off an order form and a payment. Sears, however, was not the first mail order company.

Mail Order's Dad

The title of "Father of Mail Order" goes to Aaron Montgomery Ward, a savvy traveling salesman who, in 1872, decided that direct mail was a terrific way to get quality merchandise to rural Americans who frequently suffered at the mercy of substandard goods. The 28-year-old entrepreneur founded his company—and America's shop-by-mail industry—with a single sheet of paper listing 163 products, the cornerstone of what would become the Montgomery Ward catalog.

Sears, Roebuck and Co., founded by former railway station agent Richard W. Sears and watchmaker Alvah C. Roebuck, came into being about 20 years later. By 1895, the Sears catalog weighed in at a hefty 532 pages, crammed with everything a shopper could want, from shoes and buggies to fishing tackle and furniture. A few years later, you could even buy a house from the Sears catalog.

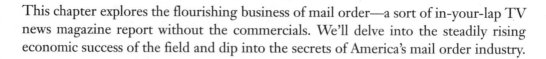

Stat Fact

According to a recent report by the National Mail Order Association, annual U.S. mail order sales have topped the $415 billion mark.

Today, mail order is still an exciting, high-demand source of merchandise. The Direct Marketing Association (also known as the DMA) estimates that each year more than 200 million Americans order a product or service by phone, mail, or the internet.

Why are we including phone sales in our mail order figures? Because mail order is actually an inaccurate moniker for direct marketing, which includes any form of shop-at-home-or-office order placement, from mail to phone to e-mail. Because most people use the term "mail order" to cover these broad bases, we'll continue to do so within these pages.

What makes mail order so hot today? One reason remains the same as when Aaron Ward had his brainstorm—the convenience of shopping from home. Ward, however, based his marketing strategy on the fact that his customers were rural and did not have access to the higher-quality goods available in urban areas. Today, there is a wider range of reasons why people in all areas, including major cities, find that shopping at home is an easy means of buying items.

Off-Duty Shopping

In today's marketplace, most customers can easily access any number of retail stores but don't necessarily have the time. More and more Americans are part of a two-income household, stretched between work and child raising, with scant time for leisure—much less shopping. Single parents, stretched even further to be in several places at once, have reached the conclusion that ordering from home can simply be easier than dragging the kids to the mall.

So mail order fulfills wishes, as well as meets people's needs. It grants consumers the ability to shop in the privacy of their own homes, saving on gas and time spent looking for parking. It also lets you shop at midnight if you so choose.

Yes, you can leisurely browse through the pages of mail order catalogs that offer just about everything you can imagine—with your feet up, a cup of coffee at hand, with the TV on if you so choose, while listening to a CD, or in peace and quiet. Perhaps you prefer cruising the pages of an online catalog on your laptop. However, you choose to browse, you can still do it in the comfort of your own home.

If you have questions, you pick up the phone, key in a number (usually toll-free), and talk to a knowledgeable customer assistant. No more frustration trying to track down elusive store clerks who often don't have the answers anyway. When you're ready to buy, you order by phone, mail, internet, or e-mail in minutes. No more standing in line! And, of course, there's no worry about pickpockets or purse snatchers. No wonder mail order is the modern shopper's paradise!

The Flip Side

What's the flip side to mail order's advantages? Although we'd be lying if we said there wasn't one, mail order's negative points are few. One is that consumers can't handle the merchandise until after they've paid for it. As a buyer, you have to rely on photos and text to give you the full flavor of the goods. You can never be entirely sure of the

▲

size, color, or quality until it shows up at your home. Of course, if you don't like what you get, you can almost always return it, but this takes a certain amount of effort and eliminates most of the fun, especially if you need (or want) the product right away. The socialization of shopping is also lost through mail order, since you are not as likely to get three friends together to browse a catalog as you are to walk through the mall. In fact, many people still enjoy shopping excursions, then come home and order via the internet. Why? Sometimes they find a better price, and other times they just didn't feel like carrying heavy merchandise home.

Another mail order minus is the time element, since you have to wait until the item shows up, whereas if you ran out to the mall, you could have the merchandise in your home the same day. Most mail order companies will ship your goodies overnight by FedEx if you're willing to pay extra for the service, but if you're not, you face a certain lag time. And if those goodies happen to be the wrong fit or the wrong color, there's an even greater delay while you send them back and wait—again—for the replacements to arrive or to receive a credit or refund.

The last mail order negative is a sort of stigma bearing the word "scam." Although many mail order companies, from L.L. Bean to Lands' End to Lillian Vernon have sterling reputations, the idea persists in some minds that mail order is a hotbed of phony merchandise hawkers. Because there were (and still are) some wolves devouring customer lambs, the Federal Trade Commission created the Mail Order Merchandise Rule (now called the Mail or Telephone Order Merchandise Rule) in 1975 to regulate direct-marketing businesses. Let's just say that Big Brother is watching out for mail order customers and that the majority of mail order businesses are legit.

Brain Cell Application

So far, we've examined mail order from the consumer's perspective. Now let's take a look at the industry from the businessperson's point of view. What do we see? An industry that is potentially lucrative for the savvy, hardworking entrepreneur and that has the advantage of requiring relatively little in the way of startup expenses, specialized skills, or intensive apprenticeship—as opposed to, say, professions like medicine, law, high rise construction, or restaurant management.

Bear in mind, however, that this does not mean you can make a fortune without lifting a finger or applying a brain cell. In order to be successful in mail order, you'll need a generous measure of hard work, a concerted and constant study of the industry as a whole as well as your particular niche, and the ability to roll with the punches. You'll also need to be prepared to have a lot of fun!

So let's take a look at the reasons entrepreneurs love mail order. One is that it is as convenient for the direct marketer as it is for the consumer. Since your customers' visits are all virtual, you can work from home—basing your operations in a spare bedroom, at the kitchen table, or even in a corner of the garage, if necessary, until your efforts bear enough fruit to furnish a "real" office. Many of the most successful catalogs, such as Lillian Vernon, began at a kitchen table, in a spare bedroom, or in someone's garage.

Mail Order Moonlighting

Mail order offers the option of starting as a part-time business, which allows you to get your feet wet without jumping into the pool. In fact, many direct marketers insist that moonlighting is the wisest way to go. John Schulte, chairman of the National Mail Order Association (NMOA), believes traditional and internet-based mail order are the last frontiers for the little guy. "You can find ways to make things happen part-time from your kitchen table," says Schulte.

Competition in the mail order biz is tough. But if you start out part-time, you can allow yourself on-the-job training without on-the-job financial anxieties. And if you don't want to sever the ties with your full-time employer until you know you can make it on your own, mail order is an ideal business for you.

What else makes mail order shine for the startup entrepreneur? You don't need a lot of inventory. You can sell merchandise through a drop-ship arrangement. No, we aren't suggesting that you parachute goods to customers like in the Berlin Airlift. Drop shipping is an arrangement in which a third party, such as a manufacturer or wholesaler, sells you the merchandise while keeping it in their warehouse until you make the sale. Then it is shipped from them to your customer. Or you can start out with one product or service, rather than go the L.L. Bean 16,000-products route, and keep your inventory manageable as you grow.

Keep in mind that mail order lends itself to services as well as merchandise. You can offer everything from antique appraisal to

Fun Fact

L.L. Bean Inc., a premier mail order retailer, was born in 1912 when Leon Leonwood Bean, a 40-year-old Maine outdoorsman, decided he'd had just about enough of having cold, wet feet while tramping around in the woods. The resourceful Mr. Bean created the Maine Hunting Shoe, which he not only wore but also sold exclusively by mail, and which became the "sole" of today's 16,000-product mail order operation.

desktop publishing to genealogical research—and for most services, your inventory list will be minimal.

Yet another mail order plus: You don't need to ship the product until your customer's check or credit card clears the bank. Unlike your store-bound retail colleagues, you've got no bounced-check worries.

The Top Contender

What are mail order's minuses from the business owner's viewpoint? Again, there are few, with the top contender being the tough competition from all the other direct marketers out there. As a mail order maven, you'll have to be clever, creative, and persistent—and this book will help.

Another major minus from the direct marketer's side of the fence is the old "scam" stigma we mentioned earlier. Customers who wouldn't hesitate to hand over their money in a retail store can balk at sending it through the mail or giving their credit card information over the phone or the internet. With the increase in identity theft, customers are leery of shopping at places that are unfamiliar. For this reason, you need to work overtime to establish a reputation as trustworthy and have an infrastructure in place that cannot be tampered with by scammers, spammers, or web savvy thieves. Encryption technology and privacy pages explaining that you are protecting your customers right are extremely important today.

Wind Beneath Your Wings

Here's the big secret to keeping the wind in your sails and beneath your wings as a mail order moonlighter: Offer a product or service that appeals to a well-defined market segment—for example, horse lovers or off-road vehicle buffs. Targeting a specific audience rather than the general public keeps you from getting mowed under by the major mail order players who have bigger, splashier catalogs and far larger mailing lists than you'll be working with.

A specific market isn't necessarily a small one. Lands' End began in 1963 as a purveyor of marine hardware and sails—products with a decidedly limited market. Somewhere along the time line (1974 to be exact), the company began adding clothing for the yachtsperson to its merchandise list. Today, Lands' End is renowned for classy casual wear, rather than jibs and mainsails, and boasts annual earnings of more than $990 million.

Counting Your Coconuts

What can you expect to make as a mail order entrepreneur? The amount is entirely up to you, depending only on how serious you are and how willing you are to work for the rewards. One of the entrepreneurs we interviewed for this book brings in annual gross revenues of $150,000; another brings in more than $1 million. Schulte of the NMOA says annual incomes for the industry range from $40,000 to more than $100,000, depending on how long the business has been in operation and how much has been invested in building the business.

By a mail order company's fourth or fifth birthday, Schulte says, about 60 percent will find themselves in the $0 to $40,000 bracket, about 25 percent will fall into the $40,000 to $100,000 category, and a final 15 percent will land in the $100,000-plus range.

The Minneapolis-based direct-mail expert estimates that it takes two to four years to break even with a mail order operation. "Profitability," he advises, "comes at about the same time, in three to five years. You want to start breaking even right away, but the real profits come when you have a solid customer base that buys from you with some frequency. It takes a few years to build up this base."

And while success doesn't come overnight to most, it doesn't come at all to some. "Only about 20 percent make it," cautions Schulte. This isn't a reason to quit before you start, but it's a darn good reason to do your research, plan very carefully and get everything in place before you start. That's why you bought this book!

Crank-Up Costs

One of the Catch-22s of being in business for yourself is that you need money to make money—in other words, you need startup funds. With mail order, you can start off with a much more manageable investment than your peers in retail or manufacturing. Since you can start as a one-person show in your own home, you automatically eliminate expenses like rent and employees. As an added bonus, equipment costs are relatively low; your major outlays will be for a computer, software, two to three phone lines, a digital camera, internet access, and a website. This whittles your other initial expenses down to inventory, advertising (which can be considerable—but necessary) and possibly some other technical accessories. But don't get too carried away with the idea of starting on the proverbial shoestring. There's a downside, which is that starting small can limit your company's potential growth. You need to start with enough funding to give yourself a legitimate chance to succeed. Maxwell Sroge, former president of the mail order consulting firm Maxwell Sroge Company Inc., felt that under

▲

> ⚠ **Beware!**
> You may come across ads from companies purporting to set you up in the mail order business—distributors who will supply you with all the catalogs, advertising copy, equipment, and inventory necessary to get up and running. These are not a good bet. To be successful in mail order, you need your own special niche—not a boilerplate program tailored to nobody.

capitalization was a major reason mail order entrepreneurs would fail.

You can start with a limited investment, but you'll have to be especially creative, and you'll have to really focus your energies on what many experts see as the lifeblood of the successful mail order business: the repeat customer.

For now, let's say you can expect your startup costs to range from about $5,000 to somewhere over the $250,000 mark, depending on what sort of operation you choose to start. If you plan to start small, with a brochure-sized catalog or a print ad, your startup figure will be relatively low. If you decide to start out with a 48-page catalog to rival those of Lands' End and J. Crew and mail it to 100,000 people, you're looking at a lot more money.

To conserve your capital, you can always do a catalog from your kitchen table, design it yourself on a computer, and go with a much smaller mailing. You're not going to go from nothing to Lands' End, with its annual nine-figure revenues, overnight—but remember, it takes time. A successful catalog isn't built in a day.

In this book, we're going to show you how to do things from a variety of perspectives, but the emphasis will be on doing them as reasonably as possible so that you can keep your costs to a minimum. Then, as we've said, the rest will be up to you!

Rock of Gibraltar

Besides startup costs and profits, two other important factors to consider are risk and stability. You want a business that, like the Rock of Gibraltar, is here to stay. Mail order definitely qualifies as a "keeper" business, but choosing a business with a proven track record isn't the key to overnight success.

Even with its relatively long history, mail order's stability rates a "moderate" on the business startup scale. Once you get to the point where you've got a good customer base—which can take a few years—your company should be on a firm foundation.

While everyone's heard tales of somebody who made it rich in mail order overnight, that somebody was either the exception to the rule or an urban legend like the stories of alligators in the New York sewer system—entertaining to hear about, but not necessarily true. As we mentioned earlier, industry experts agree that most direct-marketing businesses don't become profitable until three to five years after the initial investment. Mail order can be lucrative, and you can have a heck of a lot of fun getting there, but you have to be willing to put in lots of time, effort, and startup capital—and you have to be willing to take risks.

The risk factor in starting a mail order business is also considered moderate—less than opening a tofu taco restaurant but more than selling 10-cent cups of coffee to caffeine-deprived commuters. The reason, as we've said, is that the competition is fierce. Unless you've got the right combination of factors—an understanding of your potential customers' wants and needs matched with top-notch marketing skills—you'll have a hard time making it. Not to worry, though. There's a method to the magic of finding that perfect combination, and we'll show it to you in Chapter 3.

Fun Fact

Omaha Steaks first began sending its beefy products by mail in 1952. Since then, the company's steaks have been sent to Presidents Eisenhower and Kennedy and to the governors of all 50 states, and they've been given as gifts to heads of state in Denmark, Norway, and Sweden.

Total Strangers

That hallmark of the upscale mail order industry, the Spiegel catalog, got its start in Chicago in 1865 when Civil War veteran Joseph Spiegel—fresh out of a Confederate prison—launched a home furnishings store. Business flourished and survived the Great Fire of 1871 because Spiegel, whose warehouse was demolished, managed to salvage and store the furniture stock in his backyard.

Although this prudent move allowed the store to bounce back from disaster, it wasn't the company's greatest innovation. First came a retailing concept that was revolutionary in 1892: offering credit via installment plans. Then, in 1905, Spiegel's son, Arthur, got even more radical, suggesting catalog sales backed up by installment credit through the mail. Spiegel Senior initially balked at the idea, claiming it was ridiculous to offer credit to total strangers, but he eventually gave in.

A test catalog sent to Chicagoans met with instant success and thus the Spiegel mail order business was born, giving rise, in turn, to a number of new ideas, including the first Christmas catalog and the use of photography instead of line drawings to show products.

▲

Traits of the Trade

Hey kids! Take this fun quiz, and find out if you've got what it takes to become a mail order maven.

1. My idea of a fun evening is:
   a) watching *The Postman Always Rings Twice* on video.
   b) snuggling up with a hot toddy and a rough draft of my catalog advertising copy.
   c) cruising around town singing "Please, Mr. Postman."

2. Here's how I usually send Christmas gifts to relatives who live out of state:
   a) I wait until December 24, stuff the gifts into old grocery bags with the addresses scribbled in crayon, then rush down to the post office and stand in a huge, snaky line with all the other procrastinators, hoping my gifts arrive in time and intact.
   b) I wrap my gifts carefully in specially selected packaging no later than December 10, call my predesignated FedEx or UPS courier (I've already checked to see which is cheaper and faster), and then follow up to make sure the gifts have arrived on time and intact.
   c) I usually just hope no one notices I forgot to send gifts.

3. Here's how I manage my library books:
   a) I return them as soon as I receive the first overdue notice!
   b) I carefully note the due date and return them on or before that time.
   c) I try to get them out from under the sofa when I get the collection letter from the city attorney's office.

4. When I want to sell my car, I:
   a) write "For Sale" on the windshield in shaving cream and hope the next rain doesn't wash it off.
   b) write a snappy advertisement, call my local newspapers to get the best ad rates, place the ad with the top few, and then determine which ones net the best results before renewing the ad.
   c) hope a tree falls on the car in the night so I can collect the insurance money.

5. I would best describe my self-motivational abilities as follows:
   a) I manage to get things done sooner or later.
   b) I love setting goals and accomplishing tasks!
   c) My self-starter frequently sticks.

Traits of the Trade, continued

6. If asked to sell Girl Scout cookies, I would:
   a) buy ten boxes myself so I wouldn't have to decide how to market them.
   b) sell one variety on one street and a second variety on another, keep accurate records of sales, compare which variety sold the most, and then request more boxes of that one to sell.
   c) politely decline.

Answers: *If you chose "B" for each answer, you passed with flying colors! You've got what it takes to become a mail order maven. You're creative, organized, an efficient time manager, and self-motivated, and you possess a good accounting bent.*

The Right Stuff

OK, you've decided that running a mail order business is potentially profitable. You're willing to invest not only the money but the time to learn the ropes and become established as a pro. What else should you consider? Your personality.

Not everyone is cut out to be a mail order maven. This is not, for example, a career for the creativity-challenged. If you're one of those folks who'd rather undergo a root canal than come up with peppy advertising copy, then you don't want to be in mail order. It's also not a career for the math-phobic. Believe it or not, there's a lot of number crunching involved in the mail order business. It's fun because it tells you how well your creative ideas are doing, but if you're a person who draws the line at working with figures, then you don't want to be in mail order, either.

This is also not a career for the time-management deficient. If you're a star procrastinator who can't seem to send anything out in the mail until it's already overdue, then you should definitely look elsewhere for entrepreneurial satisfaction.

If, on the other hand, you delight in dreaming up advertising ideas, you enjoy calculating how well your plans are paying off, and you're an efficient time manager, then a mail order company is probably a good business for you to start.

Mix It Up

This doesn't mean that only ad agency executives or accountants need apply. Mail order entrepreneurs come from all avenues of life. The ones we interviewed for this book represented a variety of careers: food writer and cooking teacher, mom,

Fun Fact

When Sears launched Allstate Insurance in 1931, the only way you could purchase a policy from the company was through the mail.

computer information specialist, bookkeeper, and romance writer.

The tip here is that all of these entrepreneurs figured out how to make their backgrounds and interests work for them in their new careers. They've taken the skills and enthusiasm they've already acquired and applied them to the mail order business—which is crucial to being a successful direct marketer. Many top mail order experts have long agreed that you can most effectively sell something with which you are familiar. While a minority of sales people can sell "anything," most successful mail order marketers have an interest, even a passion for what they sell. Such familiarity helps not only in selecting merchandise and in dealing with customers, but in following trends in the life of a product – and most products change in styles (and/or technology) often to keep up with the times.

"It's very good for people who have a special knowledge, skill, or interest that they want to share," John Schulte of the NMOA advises, "and who can find a way to contact others who share the same passion." That's exactly what the entrepreneurs we interviewed have done.

Beth H., a food writer and cooking teacher, got into mail order through her knowledge of foods for people on a gluten-free diet. "I started in January of '93," the Connecticut resident recalls. "My son and I are both allergic to glutens, so I started making mixes that I could use for myself. Then I converted them into formulas that I could mix up in large batches and started offering them to people in various support groups around the country. By July, I was so overwhelmed with requests that I couldn't keep up. I had to go to somebody to help me make them. It's really grown from there."

Beth's business has definitely grown. From five products and a small flier sent to support groups, she has expanded to a line of products that fills a 28-page catalog and has mail order sales from around the world.

Hey, Sports Fans

Kate W., whose mail order company caters to a very different market, also notes that it takes some time to learn and to grow your business. "I think that in your first couple of years, your learning curve is tremendous," the Overland Park, Kansas, resident says. Kate began her business two and a half years ago and bases her product line on her alma mater's football team.

"My husband is a huge, huge fan, and he wears [the team's logo on] everything," the Midwestern entrepreneur explains. "He wears the watch, shirts galore, everything.

We're both graduates of the university, so we're big fans."

As Kate discovered, she and her husband weren't the only "expatriate" fans. Graduates from their university had moved all around the country, and they all were eager for team logo products. Kate decided she'd like to start selling team merchandise, but her husband nixed the idea of a retail store because of the costs involved. The former bookkeeper wasn't deterred. She kept thinking about the concept and arrived at a goal: to engage people like herself and her husband, alumni who had moved away from the city where the university is located but still had plenty of team spirit.

Stat Fact

According to The National Mail Order Association, there is a continuous 7 to 9% annual growth rate in the mail order industry, including all types of mail order businesses.

Finally, Kate hit on mail order as the perfect vehicle to reach this large market. "We decided on it because we could keep down the costs of everything associated with a retail outlet, like rent and employees. It could be done on a smaller basis, with just me starting the business. We could also do nationwide distribution, which was ultimately what I wanted to do," adds Kate.

Filling a Need

Caryn O. began her company based on a lifelong knowledge of her products and, like Kate, as a way to fill the needs of people she knew were potential customers. "I didn't have a background in mail order, but I've always been around people in the fabric business," Caryn says. "My grandparents and great-grandparents had all been in the garment and fabric industry. So I was familiar with textiles—the industry, the people in it, and which companies were reputable."

She also knew what people needed within the industry. "I saw a need [among] small manufacturers who are constantly struggling to stay in business and constantly going out of business because they're forced to buy more than they need to get good pricing," the Roswell, Georgia, entrepreneur explains. "I saw a need for people who do crafts to be able to make extra money for their families. They needed to be able to get fabric at a good price. I also saw a [way to help] home sewers who might have children in the home and find it difficult to get out when they need something or find their selections limited to their local stores.

"So, for all those reasons, I tried to create a business that could help these different people fill their needs and help other businesses stay in business and make money."

Caryn has gone on to fulfill her vision. Today, her company employs ten people, and has customers all over the world.

Using Her Expertise

After more than 20 years in the party planning business, which included writing ten books on the topic and traveling around speaking on how to plan all sorts of parties, Patty, from Minneapolis, Minnesota, wanted to spend less time in airline terminals and more time at home.

"I had been hired by Polaroid to introduce a new camera. They wanted me to help them promote it as a life-of-the-party type of thing, showing people how they could have fun with photos. It was great, I did that promotion and worked for them for a couple of years," explains Patty. Along the way, Patty would demonstrate how you could take little white folders and put your photos inside to create souvenir framed photos from parties. Pretty soon, Patty found a lot of inquiries about the folders, which she bought as a local art supply shop.

"I asked a PR firm that I had worked with and they didn't know where to get them. Neither did the folks at Polaroid, so I went online and tried tracking down a vendor… and it wasn't easy to find."

When Patty finally found a vendor, it set off the proverbial light bulb: The idea was to turn this into an online mail order business selling the folders (photo frames). Well versed in the party planning business, Patty expanded on her initial idea. "It was five years ago that I started with a fairly basic website. The next things I know I'm selling Halloween Pumpkin folders, Santa Claus folders; the kind where you take pictures of the kids with a character at malls or at churches or schools," adds Patty, who now has some 100 designs of Polaroid folder frames that could be used as souvenirs, plus a variety designed for digital camera photos as well. In addition, Patty sells party goods on her now revamped and improved website, www.instantphotoframes.com.

Mail Order Passion

While "doing your own thing" is a definite plus in the mail order business, it's not the only thing to consider. The most important factor in mail order success, the one stressed again and again by entrepreneurs and industry experts alike, is passion—for the mail order industry as a whole and for your product line in particular. After all, you're going to be working with this merchandise for a long time, so make sure it's something you love and believe in. It's very difficult to sell a product that you wouldn't want to buy or own, so you need to know about what you are selling and be passionate about it as well.

State of the Industry

If you're still reading, we assume you've decided to take the plunge and forge ahead with your new career. There is, however, one more thing to take into consideration: the industry prognosis. Fortunately, the prognosis is good. As we saw at the start of the chapter, there's a great big, beautiful tomorrow for the direct-marketing industry.

It's always possible, of course, that economic disaster will befall the country, making it difficult for customers to afford retail merchandise of any kind. But history so far has shown mail order to be an industry that has not only survived, but thrived, through every downturn and depression over the past century.

"The latest thing in mail order is, of course, using the internet as a way of showing off your goods," explains John Schulte of the NMOA, referring to electronic catalogs and websites selling a vast range of goods and services. "They give it different names but it's really all mail order. It's just a new medium for delivering your message and submitting orders," says Shulte, recalling that when the 800 phone number became available, mail order didn't turn into the 1-800 business, it was just a new way to take orders. "It's still remote or distance selling. You sell stuff that people don't touch feel or taste before you buy it, it's still delivered by a common carrier," adds Schulte.

According to Schulte, one of the big positives of the internet is that it can help newcomers to the industry by keeping the costs down. The cost of entering the business and maintaining a mail order company with a catalog was becoming increasingly difficult prior to the internet because of the slowly, but steadily, rising costs of paper, printing, and postage.

"Then along came the internet. In the beginning, it was also expensive to get into because you needed an HTML programmer and they were few and far between. There was no such thing as the shopping cart, so everything you wanted to do was expensive and time consuming. But now, the price has gone way down and if you have some patience and a couple of hours to educate yourself, you can build an effective website using templates," says Schulte, noting that web servers cost about $19.95 per month or less.

Fun Fact

That quintessential mail order haven for bibliophiles, the Book-of-the-Month Club (BOMC), sent out its first books in 1926. Less than a century later, the BOMC reported shipping more than 570 million books—enough to supply every American household with five volumes.

▲

Of course, it is not all about the internet. Catalogs today drive sales and, in fact, people will browse catalogs at their leisure and then often place orders online. Companies can offer some of their top-of-the-line products in catalogs and more on the internet, saving money by creating a smaller, more affordable catalog.

Another plus for the industry is the great diversification and specialization of the media today. Mail order mavens no longer have to spend big bucks to advertise in one of a few magazines or on one of a handful of television stations, reaching many people who are not interested in their products. Instead, specialization has proven beneficial to small business owners by allowing them to advertise in magazines and on television stations directed at their target audience. For example, if you are selling small kitchen appliances by mail order, rather than advertise on one of a few major television networks channels, you can zero in on a channel that reaches your specific audience, such as the popular cooking channel. For less money, the modern entrepreneur can reach a smaller, but more highly targeted, audience.

The internet, lower costs when launching and maintaining a mail order business, and specialization in advertising are just some of that which keeps mail order moving forward with a steady growth rate each year in the 21st century.

Mail Order
101

Y ou've decided to take on mail order as your business. Good! The world is your mailbag, with opportunities around every bend. But as is the case with any business, you can't really be successful until you know what you're doing. So step on into the hallowed halls of Mail Order 101, and let's start learning.

It's All About Sales

Before venturing into some of the mail order details, let's look at the big picture. It's important to understand that you are in the business of selling to consumers, whether it is people in their homes or their places of business. Therefore, some basic sales principles apply.

Supply and Demand

It's as basic as a sales principle gets. If no one wants what you are offering, you will not succeed in sales. Therefore, you need to know if there is a market for your product(s) or services. Years ago, much of the mail order business was directed at getting products into the hands of people living in rural areas where such goods were not as readily available. By meeting the demand for such items, mail order flourished in this manner. Today, however, there are few rural areas in which you won't find at least a strip mall selling most of the popular conveniences. The demand for your products or services, therefore, comes from a wider scope of the population, and you need to seek out whether there is such a market and where it can be found. This means not only finding fishermen who will like your new fishing products, but fishermen who are not already receiving catalogs from three other such mail order businesses that have beaten you to the punch. Demand means areas or markets that are underserved. A glut of companies selling the same type of items will reduce or eliminate the demand.

Lower Costs Mean Higher Profits

Again, it's very simple. You need to focus on products or services that will be cost effective. This means spending a reasonable amount to purchase (or manufacture) the products and market/advertise them, leaving you with a decent profit. It's all about profit margin, and punching numbers is crucial before you start any type of sales business. In the world of mail order, this also means factoring packaging and shipping costs into your equation. While you may love glass vases, if the cost of wrapping them for shipping is greatly diminishing your profit margin, then perhaps this isn't the mail order product for you.

Return Customers = 80 Percent of Sales

In sales, you will soon learn that steady customers are your bread and butter. It costs much more money to acquire new customers than it does to keep regular customers coming back. Therefore, you don't want to be the equivalent of the music industry's "one-hit wonder," debuting with one great product, after which you sink into mail order oblivion. Instead, you want to constantly present new offerings after your customers have purchased your initial product or service. For example, if you plan to start with a no-spill coffee mug for car latte aficionados, you'll want to follow up with a no-splootch jelly doughnut. Or how about a fast-food lap tray? Whatever you choose, you'll want a new item that will entice the same customers who bought your first product. Preparing your marketing for product number two, while product number one is selling, is crucial for ongoing success. Remember, repeat customers are the ones who make your business

> **Tip...**
>
> **Smart Tip**
> It's not just offering the right products that keeps people coming back for more. Quality and customer service are essential to customer loyalty, so set these attributes as cornerstones of your business and keep them there.

a success. So much so, in fact, that experts insist you don't make any money at all off your first sale—that it's the return customer who secures your profits. As you'll soon see, a lot of time, effort, and money goes into finding those initial customers. To lose them after a single purchase is bad business.

You Can't Sell What You Don't Have

Whether your inventory is sitting in your home, a retail location, a warehouse, or a drop-shipping location, you need to be aware of what you physically do and do not have in inventory (or have access to) before you can make a sale. In some cases, you will also need to know what you can and cannot sell legally based on federal or state laws. You will also need to know about interstate sales, especially in the mail order business. Finding suppliers that you can count on is a major step in establishing any type of sales business. Learn as much as you can about a vendor before ordering from them. Don't be lured by great prices if the reputation of the vendor is shady—do your research. By joining organizations where you get literature and interact with other mail order business owners, you can find out which vendors are winners and which ones may sell you down the river.

Don't Spread Yourself Too Thin

Specialization has made it very hard in today's marketplace to try to be a one-stop shop for all possible goods. For this reason, you see fewer large department stores and more successful specialty shops that hone in on specific products. Smaller specialty shops are typically run by experts in their fields. The late mail order consultant Maxwell Sroge of Maxwell Sroge Company Inc., was quoted as saying, "If it wasn't for the improved techniques in target marketing, the increases in paper and postage costs would have destroyed the industry a long time ago." These paper and postage cost increases—which have made printing and mailing catalogs more and more expensive

▲

as the years roll by—were responsible, at least in part, for the downfall of two of mail order's most time-honored icons, the Sears and the Montgomery Ward catalogs. Yet, while these two pioneering icons went the way of the Roman Empire, other mail order marketers prospered. Why? They began to specialize and honed in on a target market, offering select groups of products to select clientele. Instead of spending vast sums of money on the mass distribution of booster-chair-size catalogs, they pared down printing and postage costs by sending out smaller catalogs with carefully selected merchandise directed to those potential consumers who were most likely to buy their particular products. The result? They made more profit per dollar spent than the bigger guys, and they're still around! Finding a niche is typically the way to position yourself in a highly competitive market.

Stay In Your Area of Familiarity

Keep in mind that establishing a niche does not mean that you sell only one item, but you do build on one theme, or keep your products in the same "family." For example, a golf pro shop isn't going to do well selling dog food because customers who walk in wanting to buy tees and clubs aren't likely to be looking for kibble. The mail order customer who sends in for your first product, a hummingbird feeder, probably won't buy your next offering if it's something unrelated such as neon neckties. But if your next product is a home for unwed sparrows or a bat house, then you'll have that customer hooked.

Fishing for Customers

Mail order innovator L.L. Bean targets its markets by sending out about a variety of different kinds of catalogs seasonally—pitching special product lines to those most likely to buy them, instead of trying to sell everything to everybody. Check out a few of L.L. Bean's specialty catalog offerings:

- ○ *Corporate Sales Gift Guide*
- ○ *Fly Fishing*
- ○ *Hunting*
- ○ *L.L. Bean Outdoors*
- ○ *L.L. Bean Traveler*
- ○ *L.L. Bean Women's Outdoor*
- ○ *L.L. Home Casual Furnishings*
- ○ *L.L. Kids, Back to School*

Selling a Service

In this book, we're generally going to discuss mail order products in terms of merchandise, but keep in mind that what you sell can just as easily be a service instead of a product. According to the Direct Marketing Association, services account for almost 40 percent of mail order revenue. While financial services make up the biggest sector of direct-marketed services, there are scads of other options, including photo processing, travel packages, consulting, genealogical research, and real estate.

The only major difference between selling a service and selling a product through mail order will come in terms of inventory. If you're selling tours to Costa Rica, for instance, you're not going to have a stack of tours sitting on shelves in your back room; but if you're selling shirts made in Costa Rica, you probably will have boxes full of shirts waiting to be sold and shipped.

The other thing to consider with service-based mail order is the matter of accessibility. You can sell those Costa Rica tours because they can be handled long-distance. You don't need to be close to your customers to perform the service. Some services, however, like lawn care, require you to be conveniently located. So unless you've got a clever take on how to circumvent geography, you can't market this type of program to those outside of your immediate area.

So Many Choices

So, what should you sell? This is the big question that you need to answer before you move forward in this industry and one that is not often answered quickly.

While you should sell a product area with which you are familiar and have an interest (and some expertise in), you might start getting ideas by taking a look at some of the top selling products.

Industry experts agree that computers and their peripherals top the list. Other than that, the answers may surprise you.

While almost anything can be sold by mail order (just look at websites) here are some of the other popular categories along with computer products:

- Art, drafting, and printing supplies
- Athletic equipment
- Books
- Business equipment
- Children's clothing
- Educational materials

▲

- Fishing equipment
- Health and fitness products
- Home medical supplies and equipment
- Industrial maintenance and materials handling
- Library and school products
- Men's clothing
- Prescription medication
- Specialty products and gifts
- Vitamins
- Women's apparel, especially big-and-tall apparel

Of course, you can also focus on something that is a popular selling item, but perhaps not a mail order leader. For example, John Schulte of the NMOA suggests wine as an excellent choice, noting that some states that have prohibited wine sales are seeing new legislation making it possible to sell wine via mail order in those states. Additionally, Schulte points out that it's the type of product that has a devoted following. Plus real connoisseurs enjoy trying new brands, meaning you can continue to market new products, and it is also not a product widely marketed by mail order.

Schulte also suggests gourmet foods and perhaps security items (since people have become more security conscious). Since computer items remain the leading mail

---

It's News to You

Many mail order mavens have found success by publishing newsletters. If you're an expert on finances, recipes, decorating, health, or any other subject you think there's a market for, you might want to consider making a newsletter your product. You'll have to have good writing skills and think your subject through carefully. You can publish monthly, bi-monthly, or quarterly. If you think you have enough material, creating and selling subscriptions to an expert newsletter may be an option for you. Keep in mind, however, that you should have the credentials to back up your expertise. If you've been a computer specialist for a number of years, you can use that as your qualification for writing a software review newsletter. If you're a teacher with many years on the job and various awards, you've got an impressive background to justify your expertise as the purveyor of a newsletter about childhood education. Volunteer jobs and club memberships can also be qualifications if you've been active long enough to garner the experience and kudos needed to qualify you as an expert. You can also try an e-mail newsletter, which we'll talk about later in the marketing section.

---

order product, it is hard to tap into that business, especially when you are going up against online mail order giants like Dell or Apple. "If you are going into that market, you need to focus on some software that has a niche market," suggests Schulte, noting that today there are niches within niches and that you can specialize within a certain niche market—as long as your specialty isn't so tight that there is not a big enough market. "Take sporting goods for example, that is a niche in which you could specialize. Then within that niche are items for baseball, football, basketball, soccer, and so on. There are many niches within certain given niches," explains Schulte.

Think Niche

To be a mail order success story yourself, you must find your own niche, one that has not been heavily targeted, and one from which lots of customers will want to buy. We'll talk about how to do this in Chapter 3, but for now let's peruse the pages of current mail order successes to see what's already out there and what might spark a brilliant specialty catalog concept in your mind.

Gourmet Goodies

One way to a mail order consumer's heart is through his or her stomach. Gourmet goodies are perennial favorites, from coffees to chocolates to steaks. How about chili peppers, Australian wines, caviar, cherries, or teas? You can even order home-cooked meals to stash in the freezer.

And if that's not enough, many mail order firms offer goodie-of-the-month clubs in which they send a different type of fresh fruit, fudge, wine—or whatever—to the chosen recipient once a month for a year.

Mail order foods go over great with home consumers, but they're also a terrific draw for corporate types who always need something posh—but not too personal—to send to that special client, especially during the holiday season.

If you're thinking food, keep in mind that some treats, such as fresh meats or seafood, require refrigeration and that most foods need special packaging so they don't arrive squished, squashed, dented, or broken.

Getting Crafty

With the new American ethic of getting back to quality time and quality projects, crafting is increasingly popular. Catalogs abound for all types of craft supplies, from cross-stitch patterns to knitting needles to rubber stamps—even handmade vintage wallpapers! You might also consider selling your own finished crafts or those of your talented friends and family members.

▲

If you're thinking about selling craft supplies, it's wise to take the specialty catalog idea one step further and specialize in one theme, say, stained glass or ceramics, instead of trying to be all things to all crafters.

Natural Duds

Apparel is always a popular product category. But just because the biggies like Spiegel, J. Crew, and their ilk dominate the roll call, don't think there isn't room for entrepreneurs. All you have to do is get creative. Think full-figured outfits, maternity wear, natural-fiber duds, sports team apparel, uniforms for a profession (or several), easy-dress attire for the disabled, or baby layettes. The key is (still!) to come up with a special take on clothing, one for which an ample market exists, and go with it.

Setting Up Camp

The secret to sports and camping catalogs is also specialization. Target your market. Trying to sell paraphernalia for every sport under the sun doesn't work, but catalogs tailored to specific recreational pursuits, such as canoeing, fishing, bicycling, equestrian events, golf, or tennis can be mail order winners. Companies like Campmor and Wiley Outdoor Sports have discovered that people who like to sleep under the stars are terrific targets for mail order camping gear.

For More Information

One of the most marketable—and easily attainable—mail order products in the world is knowledge. We're talking about information, including plans, recipes, formulas, tips, and tricks. If you can build a cabinet, repair a watch, prepare a tax form, or cook a knockout tuna casserole, then you have information you can sell.

What are the advantages to selling your secrets? For starters, information is easy to package… it's also profitable. You can print a small book or pamphlet for a dollar or less and sell it for several dollars, which gives you a markup of 400 percent to 600 percent over your cost. (We'll talk about mark-ups in Chapter 5.). Remember that any material you consign to print is yours, and once you've copyrighted it, no one can legally reproduce it without your permission. Of course, you can't liberate somebody else's information either, so make sure that chocolate chip cookie recipe you're so famous for isn't the one that came off the back of the Nestlé Toll House Morsels package—remember the episode of "Friends" with Phoebe's grandmother's cookie recipe?

Take It Personally

Except, of course, on those envelopes from the IRS, we all like to see our names in print. Personalized gifts—everything from stationery and monogrammed shirts to baseball caps with your Little (or would-be Big) Leaguer's name inscribed on the bill and children's stories featuring a specific tyke—are perennial mail order favorites.

Just about anything can be personalized with ink, embroidery, engraving or computer technology, and it's not a service you can easily find at retail stores like Wal-Mart. So when you think mail order gifts, think personalized.

> **Fun Fact**
>
> The perennial *Hammacher Schlemmer* catalog was first issued in 1881, six years earlier than the first Sears catalog. A far cry from its initial print run of 500 copies, the company now prints 12 editions a year and mails catalogs to customers on every continent.

You Are What You Eat

If you're thinking wealth, why not think health? People who haven't got the time or the energy to visit the health food store, perk up at a mail order source of vitamins, minerals, herbs, and other health supplements. These customers can also gobble up natural food products like nuts, grains, and gourmet vegetarian goodies.

When you think health, however, think regulations. You'll need to check in with the Food and Drug Administration to make sure the products you're offering meet with government approval.

Bookworm Central

Along with computer peripherals, books are at the top of the mail order hit parade. Catalogs for by-mail bookworms encompass everything from New Age and self-help to mysteries and books on tape. There are book catalogs for the do-it-yourself woodworker, the do-it-yourself attorney, and the do-it-yourself gardener. When you think books, think—as always!—specialization, especially when going up against Amazon.com.

The Envelope, Please

Every business needs paper, envelopes, pens, staples, and all the other accoutrements of office life—and most businesspeople are so busy that they are drop-to-their-knees grateful for anybody who will deliver to their door.

As a general rule, mail order office products firms do best targeting companies with 50 or more employees, but you might shine as a purveyor to homebased entrepreneurs or the small business owner who may not be in the market for 1,000 staplers and 3,000 calculators, but may need 50 of each at a reasonable cost. Whatever route you take, keep in mind that people who order office supplies usually need them now, so you'll have to be able to offer a very fast turnaround time.

Pampered Pets

People are more enamored with their pets than ever before and pet products provide big business opportunities. From fancy foods to toys to collars to glow in the dark booties, pet supplies can be a big mail order favorite. Make sure your catalog or website has plenty of photos of our furry friends and see if you can come up with some unique but practical items that will generate attention. You can also provide pet personalization. There's a world of possibilities.

Mail Order Catalogs

Along with deciding upon a product (which we will return to), you need to consider how you will reach your market.

Today, the savvy mail order maven can choose from a wondrous variety of vehicles through which to market his or her products or services. The internet continues gaining by leaps and bounds as the vehicle of choice, but television, radio, and classified ads also shine as good sources of revenue. Of course, the tried-and-true catalog sent streaming through the mail is still as popular as ever, especially now that it can be used in conjunction with the internet. People see items in catalogs, then buy them online. Therefore, before focusing on websites and other means of reaching your audience, let's take a brief look at the old standard: the catalog.

No Nos!

Although the mail order industry is open to just about any product or service you can dream up, there are some things better left unsold. Why? Because they're illegal. They include:

- ○ Chain or pyramid schemes
- ○ Firearms
- ○ Any type of explosives
- ○ Illegal narcotics or prescription drugs sold without a prescription
- ○ Lottery tickets
- ○ Master keys to motor vehicles (no car-theft supplies or accessories)
- ○ Materials inciting criminal activity (no books on bank robbery made easy)

Mail Order Dinosaur

Traditional catalogs fall into two main categories, *general* and *specialty*. The general catalog, like the old-fashioned general store, sells just about everything—from shoes for your feet to tires for your car—in one big package of pages. With a few exceptions, as noted earlier,

Stat Fact

According to the American Mail Marketing Association, more than 10,000 mail order catalogs are produced every year.

the giant "everything" catalogs have gone by the wayside. Colossal increases in the costs of paper and postage have made it a mail order dinosaur, too big and too cumbersome to support itself.

Specialty Catalogs

Think *Victoria's Secret*, *Sharper Image*, or *Smith & Hawken*, and you're thinking specialty catalogs. By selling—respectively—slinky lingerie, high-tech toys, and gardening products, these companies have fine-tuned their product lines. Instead of trying to be all things to all customers, they've gone the boutique route, carving out a niche amidst the avalanche of available products.

Good Catalogs

Of course, we will be talking about catalogs throughout the book, but it's always worthwhile to start off with some of the basic tricks of the trade. So, with that in mind, the following list should give you some ideas of what makes up a good catalog.

1. Plan the entire catalog first, rather than making it up as you go along. This way, you don't get stuck cramming items in, running out of space, or adding pages that will increase your cost.

2. Separate items into groups or categories such as brand new products, limited editions, staples in your industry, seasonal items, etc.

3. Look at the types of products you are offering and consider your target audience for each group. What makes each group important to your buyers? What are the highlights? List these, since you will want to feature them in your copy.

4. Depending on the size of the catalog and the size of each page, determine how much—photos and copy—you can effectively put on a page without crowding. Then layout pages accordingly with dummy copy and boxes where photos will go.

5. If you are working on a second or third version of the catalog, review the previous best sellers and poorly selling items—this will help you place them in the catalog. Put your poorer sellers in the back and try coming up with a new sales pitch.

6. Write and re-write copy many times until you feel that it best describes the product and what is appealing to your target audience.

7. Make sure to highlight what is unique about a product, such as a limited offer, or if you are doing a second or third catalog, a new entry to the catalog. Highlight new items.

8. Add additional tidbits of information such as a very brief history of a product, how it works, how it was made, or what makes it unique.

9. Maintain a consistent look, image, and even theme throughout your catalog.

10. Make sure to have all contact information on every page.

11. Make sure photographs clearly illustrate the product. If possible, show the products in action with models wearing them, someone using a tool, etc.

12. Direct readers to shipping information and make sure it is very clear. Have a phone number for customer service shipping questions prominently featured—and be ready to field calls about shipping.

13. Have a customer service phone number on every page.

14. Promote your website where you can feature new products that come out in-between printed versions of your catalog.

15. Make sure all ordering instructions are painfully clear. Ask friends, neighbors or anyone nearby to review them and see if they would have any problem ordering.

16. While you will probably put your lesser selling, or least interesting products toward the back of the catalog, save some room in the back to promote your next catalog, your website, and even a couple of photos of products featured earlier. People remember the first and last things they see, so if they browse the entire catalog, the last pages will be remembered.

17. Vary your pricing. You don't have to have your most expensive items up front. Instead you want the pricing to match your target customers. If your customers are expecting $25 items and you have $40, $25 and $10 items, have some of the best, most enticing $25 products up front.

18. Have an extra order form in case the customer messes up the first one or goes back to the catalog and decides to order something else. Also make it clear that they can order by phone or online.

19. Let customers know what methods of payment are available and which methods are not. List the credit cards you offer and if you do not take personal checks, say so.

20. Include very clear return policies.

21. Use special incentives for buying certain items throughout the catalog, such as a discount, free shipping for a certain time period, or a free gift.

22. Offer gift cards and to have the catalog mailed to a friend, so they can use it as a present.

We'll mention some of these again throughout the book, along with other catalog pointers, but this should give you some basics on which to focus as you ponder your catalog(s).

Direct Mail

Direct mail is really just another name for mail order, but it usually refers to anything that is not in a catalog. This includes sales letters (like Publishers Clearing House), brochures, fliers, postcards, and any other sort of printed materials you can send through the U.S. post to elicit a mailed, telephoned, faxed, or e-mailed customer response. In reality, anything that comes via delivery falls into the category. With that in mind, let's look at some of the other means of getting your products to the public so that they can order. Remember that we are now living in a world of specialization and more so than ever people are gravitating to their favorite media outlet based on their interests, hobbies, and careers. No longer are you looking to place advertisements in major general interest publications or on the big television networks (which are unaffordable for most new entrepreneurs). Today, you are looking for the magazine that fits your niche market or the television station, website, or radio station that caters to your target audience.

Therefore, if you're selling gardening supplies, for example, you are looking at HG TV or one of several specific gardening magazines and websites.

Smart Tip

Yet another term for mail order or direct marketing is *direct response*, because your customers (ideally) respond directly to your catalog, radio, or TV spot, or other vehicle.

Instant Access

The internet is the most exciting mail order vehicle since the invention of the catalog. It's one of the simplest and fastest ways to reach a national or global audience. Having your own website today is a must for any business. Your site will provide instant access to your online catalog. What's even better is that with your own site, you're on equal footing with the big guys. A great looking website can be created by a Fortune 500 company or by two people working from their dining room table. It's all a matter of building a professional looking site that can handle the necessary volume. By doing so, you can easily compete with larger, more established businesses—and even look like one yourself—without spending a fortune. When your site is accessed through the same medium and has the same (or better) graphics, who's to know that your office is in the garage?

Mail order entrepreneurs with hard copy catalogs at the ready are also utilizing the internet as a supplement to their catalogs as a means of cross marketing. As men-

Stat Fact

According to the National Mail Order Association, internet sales recently topped $4 billion in annual mail order dollars. The hottest sellers? Computer products, books, gifts, clothing, and general merchandise.

tioned by John Schulte of the NMOA, some entrepreneurs will put their best ten or fifteen products in a small catalog and promote their website, which will have the full line of 30 or 40 products. It's cheaper to mail the smaller catalog and a marvelous way of getting people to your website.

Potential customers have come to expect companies to have a web presence, especially for any computer-related product or service. Everything from gift baskets to insurance to concrete—even airplanes—can be purchased online, and people who are internet-savvy use the web the way they once used the Yellow Pages.

While we will discuss your own website in greater detail later, it is also worth noting that you can advertise on other websites to draw people to your site. Look for a similar target audience. For example, a gourmet food site that doesn't sell wine may be a great place to advertise your wine selling business. Likewise, a site with parenting articles might be a great place to advertise your children's furniture. Spend time surfing the internet and look for other sites from which to draw people to yours.

Don't forget eBay and other established sites where you can also hawk your merchandise. There are numbers dealers selling all sorts of mail order goods from eBay, cashing in on the name recognition of the eBay phenomenon. Follow the instructions carefully for becoming an eBay seller and you can build a tremendous online business without having to do as much promotion, since, after all, eBay already draws millions of visitors to their site.

Real TV

Another form of mail order is the TV commercial: the one that advertises knives that slice through concrete or the greatest recording hits of your parents' generation and provides the ordering information on-screen. Television advertising can be less expensive than you might guess. The price of TV time depends on various factors, including the size of the market, the length of your ad, the time of day or night your ad airs, the program rating, and how much advertising you buy.

Prices also vary according to whether you're advertising on a local independent station, a network affiliate, a cable channel, or public access television.

One problem will be the cost of putting together a professional looking commercial. A commercial that looks like it was made in your garage may not actually get people to fork over money. Spend a lot of time preparing good copy, find someone who can read it professionally, and plan exactly how you want the commercial to appear before spending money in a TV studio (which can be costly). Home video equipment is great for doing plenty of rehearsals. However, you will probably need the professional stuff to make an impact.

Also, hone in on what your target market is watching. You'll waste a lot of time selling sports items on soap operas or food products on "America's Grossest Videos." Placing one ad also won't work; rather than spending your life savings (and mortgaging your home) to buy that Super Bowl ad, you could run 50 ads on a late night cable channel for a fraction of the cost and get more bang for your buck. Hint: If you're asking people to call in, have enough operators at the ready. If you're asking people to send $19.95, make sure the address is clear and that you are prepared to fill the orders immediately. Too many well-intentioned sellers jump the gun and air commercials before they are adequately prepared to handle the responses.

Give It a Shot

The one-shot is a perennial mail order vehicle, so called because you market just one item instead of an entire line, and you therefore have one shot in which to sell it. You might sell, for example, a pair of sunglasses with removable shade lenses and a flashlight attachment so the wearer can see as well at night as during the day. A keen concept, perhaps, but not one that's likely to garner a lot of repeat customers. Once a customer buys one pair, he's unlikely to buy more—he's off your list.

One-shots are typically advertised through sales letters, classified ads, radio ads, and television commercials. You can also find them in the colorful supplements that fall out of your Sunday paper, in magazine ads, and in direct-mail ads.

The advantage to one-shots is that you know immediately whether your ad and product are successful. You don't have to spend a lot of time fine-tuning a whole catalog full of products and then another chunk of time waiting to see if your creative labors are successful. And if your one-shot works, you get a quick turnaround on your investment.

The one-shot method has a serious downside, however, which is that you can't build a mail order business solely on one-shot products. Since each one-shot is liable to vary radically from its predecessors, you have no opportunity to build a solid base of repeat customers, which is where most entrepreneurs make their money.

Beware!

Don't undersell yourself—or your competitors. It's illegal to price a product at less than your cost if your intent is to injure your business rivals by luring away customers.

Radio Face

Let's face it. Radio commercials also constitute mail order. Advertising on big stations in major markets can be cost-prohibitive for mail order newbies, but you can buy effective and affordable ad time from more intimate local stations for less money than you might think. These smaller stations make up the majority of commercial radio stations in the United States. Their lower-power signals limit their geographic reach, but this isn't necessarily a minus. Since the programs on local stations are specifically designed to appeal to their own regional audiences, your advertising can be more closely targeted. Look for stations and programs that fit your audience, such as placing your sports apparel on an all-sports talk radio station. Also, keep in mind that a block of commercials makes your business stand out in people's minds. Buy in bulk, save money per commercial and again, remember to make it sound professional. Since people can't see what's going on (but they can hit the buttons in the car to change channels) keep your radio spots relatively simple. Also, make sure to repeat the phone number twice.

Strictly Classified

For some mail order entrepreneurs, a classified ad in the newspaper—that tiny inch or so of black newsprint—is a highly effective vehicle. Classified ads usually run from three to ten lines in length, are one column wide, and excel at minimalism: They have no line art, no photos, no graphics of any kind, and the wording is as brief and concise as a Vermont farmer's idea of chitchat. So what makes them valuable? For starters, they're very inexpensive yet cover a relatively wide audience. Also, because they're so inexpensive, they're a terrific way to test new products and markets.

On Display

The display ad is a vehicle of a different sort. Because it's larger and usually incorporates photos or some other type of artwork, it's more expensive, but it can be extremely effective if you're advertising a high-end product. You'd use a classified ad if, for example, you were advertising Aunt Polly's famous Macaroni Surprise recipe but a display ad to market a Recipe-a-Month Club that comes with not only the recipe but all also the ingredients for a complete dinner.

Follow the Rules

Once you've test driven every mail order vehicle, you're ready to roll. But as with operating a motor vehicle, there are rules you must follow. Like the road rules for cars, trucks, motorbikes, and buses, mail order's rules are logical and easy to understand. And like the rules for motor vehicles, you can land yourself in a world of trouble if you fail to heed the proper regulations. So here's the scoop.

No Cheating

The Federal Trade Commission (FTC) regulates all companies that conduct business across states lines, which of course includes mail order businesses, and the FTC has very strict rules. As a mail order maven, you cannot engage in any sort of false advertising. This means:

- *No taking money under false pretenses.* If you do, you can be convicted of fraud.
- *No fooling.* Your direct-marketing materials are considered illegal if they are designed to fool consumers.
- *No misleading product claims.* You can't advertise that keen gasoline additive guaranteed to give any car 100 miles to the gallon unless that's what it will actually do. The majority of mail order mavens, of course, being honest types, wouldn't dream of out-and-out lying about a product. But some people tend to get carried away with enthusiasm and end up making claims that aren't quite realistic. Make sure this isn't you.
- *No false medical claims.* When advertising medical or health products, you must have scientific proof that the product will do what you claim. Don't use words

A Little Freebie

Don't mail people anything they haven't asked for. It's illegal for you as a mail order maven to send unsolicited or unordered products to potential customers and then ask them to pay for them. A consumer who receives such a product—whether you sent it inadvertently or on purpose—is under no obligation to return it or pay for it and can consider it a nice little freebie.

The exception to this rule is for charitable organizations that are soliciting donations. They alone can send samples or gifts, so long as they clearly spell out that the recipient can keep the product with no strings attached.

like "cure," "banish," or "remedy" unless you can prove through clinical studies that this really is the case.

- *Don't pretend to do something that you don't.* Don't use titles like "laboratory" or "manufacturer" or any other description in your company's name unless you actually perform the function you claim.

- *No false pricing claims.* You can't say things like "formerly priced at $5" unless the product really was priced at $5 and you actually did sell a substantial number of units at that price.

- *No fabricated testimonials.* If your ad includes words of glowing praise from satisfied customers, make sure they're real words from real customers, not testimonials you invented yourself.

- *Sell what you claim to sell.* If you say you sell chicken, don't send a tofu chicken substitute.

- *Make sure you send out the products that people order.* Collecting money for items and not sending them is mail fraud, which equals big trouble with the federal authorities.

The Ticking Clock

In 1975, the FTC instituted what was then called the Mail Order Merchandise Rule to regulate direct-marketing businesses. The name of the law was later changed to the Mail or Telephone Order Merchandise Rule, and it now also applies to orders placed via fax, e-mail, and the internet. You can find yourself flailing in rough seas if you ignore the Rule's guidelines, but not to panic! Unlike a lot of government legalese, the guidelines actually make sense and are easy to follow:

- You must send ordered merchandise within the time period specified in your ad or, if you don't specify a shipping time, within 30 days. The clock starts ticking on this time requirement when you receive the completed order. An order is complete when you receive your customer's cash, check, or money order or have charged the person's credit card account, and have all the information you need to process and ship the order. If the customer doesn't specify essential information, such as size or color preferences, the order is considered incomplete.

- If you don't specify a shipping time and your customer is applying for credit to pay for the purchase, you have 50 days to ship after receiving the order. This is the one exception to the 30-day shipping rule.

- If you can't meet the shipping deadline, you must notify your customer and offer an alternative option: The customer can either receive a prompt refund or agree to a delay. Your notice must include a new shipping date, instructions on how to cancel the order, and a postage-paid way to reply.

- If your customer agrees to a new shipping date and you can't meet it again, you must send a second notice as soon as possible. Unless the customer signs and returns this second postage-paid notice, you must automatically cancel the order and refund the person's money.
- If you can't ship the merchandise on time and you don't notify your customer as required, you must count the order as canceled and send a refund.
- If your customer cancels an order, you must refund his or her money. If the order was paid for by cash, check, or money order, you must return the money within seven business days. If the order was paid for by credit card, you must credit the customer's credit card account within one billing cycle.

The Mail or Telephone Order Merchandise Rule applies to almost everything ordered through direct-marketing sources. The exceptions are: photo-finishing services, magazine subscriptions (after the first issue), c.o.d. orders, seeds, and plants.

The Postal Police

The FTC is not the only government entity keeping an eye on mail order activities. If you're part of the vast majority of good-egg direct marketers, you've got nothing to worry about. But if you should decide to get a little too creative with what's legal and what's not, you're liable to stumble over:

- *The U.S. Postal Service (USPS).* The USPS employs postal inspectors who can arrest you if you engage in illegal mail order activities. These postal police can have you sign a statement that lets them stamp "Refused Out of Business" on your packages. If you're convicted of mail order fraud, you can be fined and/or thrown in the slammer, or you can simply be put out of business.

- *The Food and Drug Administration (FDA).* The FDA does not look kindly on people who make false claims on drug, cosmetics, or food labels, and it, too, is empowered to take action against you.

- *State fraud commissions.* These organizations act as watchdogs on the state mail order front.

- *The Better Business Bureau (BBB).* It's not a government agency, but the BBB has developed an advertising code and responds to complaints about unethical business practices.

> **Tip...**
>
> **Smart Tip**
>
> To get a complete copy of the Mail or Telephone Order Merchandise Rule from the FTC, call (877) FTC-HELP. You can also visit the FTC online at www.ftc.gov/bcp/conline/pubs/buspubs/mailorder/index.htm and check out *A Business Guide to the Federal Trade Commission's Mail or Telephone Order Merchandise Rule*, which explains how to comply with the rule and gives answers to important questions.

▲

You've now mastered Mail Order 101. You know the different types of mail order vehicles, where to go as far as targeting a specialty audience and where not to go as far as illegal activities are concerned. Now let's get on with the fun stuff in the next chapter: Products, Customers, and Market Research.

Products, Customers, and Market Research

Every business needs consumers for its products and products (or services) for its customers. In this chapter, we look at both ends of this equation, finding a product or service to sell and determining to whom you will sell it. Both take plenty of research and go hand in hand. After all, since business is about supply and demand, you need to find something to sell that people want... hence there is a demand. Then, your job is to supply that product or service.

Finding Your Place

To be successful in any business, you must define your own special market, one where a genuine need or desire for your products or services exists and one where the competition isn't overwhelming. To do so, you will want to conduct your own due diligence—or do your homework so to speak, to determine how full the market is and where you can make a dent. You want to carve a niche, but not one that is so small that your family is your only buying market.

To determine your product choice, you need to combine your personal interests and knowledge along with a commercial sense of what others will find as fascinating... and actually purchase.

Start by thinking about what you enjoy and know about, along with what your potential customers need or want. Then match your ideas up against these three guidelines:

1. *Is your interest something that many people share?* Are there clubs, organizations, and numerous websites and magazines about this area of interest? This is a way of determining the popularity of your area of interest. This will also help you determine if you have a large customer base from which to draw, or not. For example, you might know everything there is to know about fireflies, you may find them fascinating and have a huge collection under glass, and that's swell. But you're not going to find many people who will want to order firefly merchandise. If, on the other hand, you're into fly fishing, you'll have a huge number of enthusiasts all over the world from which to draw.

2. *Do you have a well-defined specialty?* You may have a reputation as a shop-'til-you-dropper, and your friends and family may turn to you as the gift chooser of choice, but it's unlikely you'll succeed with a broad catalog of gift items or preppy clothing. There are already too many major big companies out there doing the same thing, and they're too huge to compete against. But if you choose gifts or clothing for a specialized market—say, children, seniors, cat lovers, or gardeners—you're moving in the right direction.

3. *How easy is it to order, ship, and stock your product of choice?* You may love elephants, but no, you're not going to be able to send them by mail. Pianos may be hard to handle as well. Obviously, you will want to consider products that can be shipped without costing either you or your customers a fortune, can be stored in your garage if you plan to have an inventory on hand and do your own shipping, and have a fairly good markup. For this, you will need to begin looking up vendors and

wholesalers to get an idea of how much such items cost. Remember, buying in bulk reduces costs, but other factors can add up—shipping, handling, and packaging are the major ones—plus insurance, particularly on breakable items. Factor all of the above into your equation when determining what to sell.

Generating Some Product Ideas

Now, if you just can't come up with a line of products or services that's unique but widely embraced, don't panic! There are ways to generate ideas:

- *Get creative at gift shows and clothing marts.* Once you've got your fictitious business name (which we will cover in Chapter 4), you're official. You are allowed to enter the hallowed halls of these huge trade shows, which are held periodically at convention centers across the country. Displays by manufacturers, suppliers, and wholesalers line aisles crammed with the latest in giftware and fashion apparel. Roam around. Try to get a feel for what's hot, what's not, and how you might put together a line of items that are related in some way—say, dolls for every season or high-fashion clothes for chubby kids.

- *Get crafty at craft fairs and art shows.* Local artists often have terrific wares just waiting to be sold. Use the same strategy described above to sketch out ideas for potential products. How about a line of handcrafted jewelry or a line of art representing the region you live in? Bear in mind, however, that arts and crafts are not mass-produced, which can be a drawback in a business in which sales numbers are your bottom line. Therefore, if you go with handmade items, make sure your artists will be able to keep up with the potential demand, or have a large stable of artists and craftspeople. Of course, you could have lines of mass produced products as well as specially handcrafted alternatives, thus allowing you to keep sales numbers high while also drawing from a market audience looking for diverse items.

- *Drop in at boat shows, home shows, garden shows, and auto shows.* Use your wander-and-wonder strategy to get ideas from all the products displayed.

- *Ask people!* Ask your family, friends, and neighbors what mail order merchandise they buy and what they would like to buy that's not available through mail order. You might hear something that strikes a chord.

- *Surf the internet* and see what people are talking about in chat rooms and on discussion boards.

> ## Bright Idea
> Business-to-business sales—terrific mail order markets—can encompass more types of products and services than you might think. Take a common product and give it a new twist. Instead of selling fine art prints to consumers, for instance, how about art for the office?

Evaluating Your Choice

You've chosen a specialty, you've got a line of products or services, and you've decided that there are plenty of other people out there interested in the same thing. Good! But your work's not done. Now you need to ask yourself some important questions:

- *Is it fashion or fad?* Unless you're going the one-shot route, it's unwise to pin your product line on a fad. If the major rave this year is, for example, happy faces, and your entire merchandise line is happy-faced, it's only a matter of time until the fad fades and your smiles are turned upside down. Make sure your specialty has staying power.

- *Is it Christmas in July?* Stay away from products that are popular in only one season. If you're selling just Christmas ornaments, for example, your sales will shrivel in April and May. Instead, broaden your horizons (and sales potential) by selling festive decorations for holidays throughout the year—New Year's, St. Patrick's Day, Independence Day, Halloween, and Thanksgiving. This way your cash flow is steady, and so are your nerves. Even the chain retail store called "The Christmas Store" follows this approach, selling various items for various holidays.

- *Is it reasonably priced?* Go with merchandise you can offer your customers at a price they can afford. If you're planning to sell designer diapers at $50 each to people on the Neiman-Marcus mailing list, you might do all right. But if your target market consists of middle-of-the-road young families, you're pricing yourself out of the market and into the proverbial diaper pail.

- *Is there room to grow?* Choose a specialty with room for expansion.

Using the Worksheet

The "Merchandise Planning Guide" that follows will help you choose that perfect specialty for your mail order business. But first, some thoughts to ponder before you start filling in the blanks.

1. *Product or service.* Go back over the first part of this chapter. Then do some brainstorming and choose a product or service that fits the criteria we've outlined.

2. *Complementary products or services.* If you can't think of anything else to go with your initial idea, give it an instant "F" grade and choose another product. As we've

Merchandise Planning Guide

Use this worksheet as a planning guide for each of your merchandise ideas. (Make copies so you have one sheet for each idea.) Answer each question carefully.

1. Product or service: _____

   _____

2. What other products or services will complement it? _____

   _____

3. Can you put a name to this target line (e.g., classic car parts and accessories, or backpackers' clothing and gear)? _____

4. Are you knowledgeable about this product or service? _____

5. Do you enjoy working in this area? _____

   _____

explained, unless you plan to leapfrog from one-shot item to one-shot item, you must choose a product or service you can develop into a full line of complementary merchandise or services. This keeps your customers coming back for more.

3. *Name that target.* In the movie biz, when an idea or concept can be expressed in a short, simple phrase, it's called a "high concept." If you can't give your line a high-concept title, chances are, no one else will be able to, either. What that means is your concept is too broad, too vague, or too obscure.

4. *Special knowledge.* Remember, you need some level of expertise regarding your choice of products (unless you plan to hire or team up with an expert). Do you know enough about this specialty to fully develop a line around it and also answer the questions and fill the needs of your customers?

5. *Enjoyment.* Do you like this specialty? If you plan to offer word processing services because you've been a secretary for 20 years but you hate typing, your interest will fizzle before your business gets fired up.

▲

Exploring Your Target Market

In conjunction with deciding on a product, you also need to determine an audience for that product. The two go hand in hand—as we've alluded to, you want to sell something in which you have some expertise. However, you also need to make sure there is a market for the product.

The two things you need to determine are:

1. *Who is your target market?* What is the demographic group who will buy your product line?

2. *Is there a large enough target audience to make your line profitable?*

To answer these questions, you will need to do some demographic research. You can utilize the following sources.

- *The internet.* You can find all sorts of demographics without leaving your home. For starters, check in with the U.S. Census Bureau at www.census.gov (yes, it collects all that data for a reason—here's your chance to take advantage of it). The Census Bureau is part of the Department of Commerce, which has other divisions that may have useful information about your target market. You can visit the Department of Commerce at www.doc.gov. Another of the many possibilities is www.emarketer.com, a subscription site that pulls together resources from over 2,500 sources. Of course, the more you search, the more demographic sources you can find. Hint: Make sure you look at the dates of the research and only utilize the most recent data.

- *The public library.* Reference librarians can be extremely helpful with this sort of thing. All you have to do is call and tell the librarian that you need to know how many medical professionals—or fly fisherman, or disabled children under age 14—there are in the United States. A good reference librarian will look up the information and call you back with the answer. Or you can go into the library and dig through whole books of demographic statistics yourself, unearthing tons of facts and figures.

- *Organizations and associations.* What better places to go for information on your specific market? If you're targeting senior citizens, for example, you could contact the American Association of Retired Persons (AARP) for data on their members. For a count of primary school teachers, you'd talk to the folks at state and regional teachers' associations.

> ### Bright Idea
> One of the largest markets is the senior set. While many merchandisers knock themselves out catering to Generation Xers, the hale and hearty 60-plusers are often underserved.

Once you have determined how large a potential market is out there, you should start looking around to see if there are numerous players already in the field. If you are selling camping gear and find 200 catalogs selling camping gear, you will need to figure out:

1. If you can find a niche within the market.

2. If you can find a unique spin on that which is out there, by selling a variation of a popular camping product that is not so widely available or by having a unique means of marketing your products.

3. If the field is over saturated.

For the clever entrepreneur, there is usually room to find a niche and proceed forward. In some cases, however, you are up against bigger players who have the market very well covered, such as in selling computers by going up against Dell and Apple.

Finding Your Niche

Almost every possible product or service has a niche market. The question for you is: How does one find their niche?

First, ask yourself what you can offer. This is a major factor in developing your niche. Think long and hard about what will make your products different from those of your competition. If you're selling books, for instance, what will make your company shine above mail order booksellers like Amazon.com, Barnes & Noble, Doubleday, and Harlequin? If you specialize in children's books, reference volumes, or books on tape, you've got a niche. If you can't come up with anything new, you're thumbing through the wrong tome and you probably won't succeed. "If you try to saturate a market that's very broad, you're just dooming yourself to failure," warns Beth, the gluten-free foods purveyor in Connecticut.

Kate, the college football fan's entrepreneur, founded her entire product line on a very special niche—one she takes care to explain to her customers. Each catalog features a personal letter, and Kate used that letter in her first catalog to describe how she started the company as an exclusive mail order service for fans of her alma mater. "I don't mix schools," the former bookkeeper explains, "because everybody likes to know they're a little bit special. The more exclusive or item-specific (or in this case, school-specific) the merchandise is, [the better]. People want their own little niche."

Once Kate had chosen her niche market, she narrowed her sights even more, aiming at a highly segmented target audience. "I think part of the reason we've done so well is that we knew our market—because we are it," says the university sports memorabilia entrepreneur. "We knew we were marketing to people who are professionals, who have moved away, been gone for maybe ten-plus years, and are older. I'm 40, so

---

Creating a Customer Portrait

Knowing your customers, and being able to create a customer profile is important. If you could draw a portrait of the quintessential mail order shopper, this is what she (yes, she's a female) would look like:

- ○ Female (This gender does 58 percent of all mail order shopping.)
- ○ Age 35 to 44
- ○ Earns upwards of $40,000 per year
- ○ College educated
- ○ Professional/managerial career
- ○ Homeowner

I kind of take myself as an average consumer and ask, 'What do I like? What would I buy my husband?' That's a large part of how we select our products."

Part of your niche market may be based on location. After all, people in different parts of the country (and the world for that matter) have different needs and different buying habits. Kate W., for example, based her entire line on her awareness of her alma mater's many alumni football fans living out of-state who still want team logo goodies. If her research had turned up only a handful of out-of-staters, she would have had to revise her game plan.

If you can be the first to reach an underserved area with your product line, you are can hit a potential goldmine. As mentioned earlier, much of the initial premise for mail order was centered on the fact that certain parts of the country did not have access to the same goods that railroads brought to other areas of the country.

You'll also want to investigate where potential customers are currently getting their products. This is a major consideration. If your potential customers are already purchasing the same sorts of products from other mail order sources—or from shops they're madly in love with—you may want to scratch this line and start over with something else. If, on the other hand, you discover that the products you'll be offering are typically hard to find or will be replacing those of inferior quality, then you'll have a definite head start on building a solid customer base. You can also come up with a competitive edge, whether it's pricing, faster deliveries or possibly personalized attention.

In Connecticut, Beth H. has also developed a highly segmented niche market, based on an entirely different set of parameters—foods for people who are allergic to the wheat glutens found in store-bought cakes, breads, and bakery products. While her only intention initially was to provide mixes to people in gluten-free support groups, she soon found herself the recipient of national publicity.

"We were reaching people in all these little places all over the country," Beth recalls, "the Ozarks and West Virginia and places where they thought they were the only celiac in the world and didn't have access to a natural food store.

"Also at that time, in 1993," the former food writer explains, "the natural food industry was made up of a lot of little independently owned stores. They were organic—they didn't want sugar and they didn't want salt. Mine was a separate mission: to make mixes that were good for people who were gluten-free, things that tasted like the products they had to give up when they went on this diet. My mission didn't meet the natural food stores'. But the only place people knew to look for gluten-free products was the natural food stores, which didn't want to carry my products. I knew the end users wanted them. So I started a mail order business."

Smart Tip

Tip...

One of the factors that makes Beth H.'s gluten free foods business a winner is that she's providing products her customers need to order regularly. You don't make one loaf of bread stretch over an entire year. Staple foods, particularly for special diets, are things that need to be purchased again and again.

Armed with her intimate knowledge of what people on gluten-free diets wanted, and of how to provide those products, Beth began selling her mixes to this very specific niche market, using a simple flier as her direct-mail piece. Soon her business grew. "I began to add other things," the Connecticut mom explains, "because I realized that these people in the Ozark Mountains and West Virginia really desperately needed things they couldn't get. I was, in effect, the lifeline for these people. I started adding more things, like pastas, cereals, and then some soups, and then bread machines—just a whole bunch of products that would make life easier for people."

In forming your niche, you need to be specific about your target customer base.

You must also be able to identify your potential customers in a way that's specific and high-concept. For example, if you're planning to sell clothing, "people who wear clothes" is way too broad a market. "Medical professionals who want fashionable work wear" is a great answer. It targets a specific market with a specific need.

Customers: Finding You or Joining Clubs

Patty, who also served the gift market, responded to her customer's inquiries about where to get the paper folders/frames for photos. She was getting a steadily growing number of inquiries and, in the spirit of supply and demand, she saw that there was a demand for the products. Thus, she sought out a means of supplying them. "I did a lot of digging and searched the internet for suppliers. I finally found a vendor who would drop ship, so I put it on my website so people could order and they would drop ship them," explains Patty, who, as an expert in the broader party planning field narrowed her niche to the fun photo frames that are very popular today. In keeping with the ever-changing market, she later added the 4 x 6 digital photo frames, which have grown rapidly in popularity.

While you're brainstorming what your niche will be, why not think about starting a club? It can pay to structure your company as an exclusive membership organization rather than an anybody-can-buy retail one. That's what Caryn, the fabric merchandiser in Georgia, did.

"Because we charge wholesale prices and we really work on a low profit," Caryn says, "we felt we needed to sell to people who were truly looking for our product. By having people join our club, either by placing an order or paying a small membership fee, we rule out people who will just keep requesting [catalogs and samples] because they're free. You get people who are serious about your product and want to do business with you, and you have a better opportunity to do business with them. That's why we came up with the idea of having people join. That's worked very well for us.

"Being a mail order company, if you're spending a fortune on mail going out and printing costs, along with so many other costs, and you don't have it coming back to you, you can't stay in business."

How exactly does the club work? Caryn has set up several plans, based on customer desires. "There's no membership fee if somebody places an order," she explains. "That automatically makes them a member. If somebody wants to become a member [without placing an order], we have two different memberships. We have one that is all apparel fabrics, and that is $10 a year. And then we have one that's for people who are only interested in 100 percent cotton fabrics, people like quilters; that's $5 per year. It doesn't cover postage and it doesn't offset much. But if a person's willing to pay a small fee, it does let us know they're serious about our product."

There is a downside to a fee for membership club. Since so many websites and catalogs are free, you will have to really stand out, offer something special, and work that much harder at marketing and customer service to get people to join.

Researching Your Market

Along with determining your special niche in the mail order world, you'll want to go directly to your potential customers to find out how they really feel about the products you plan to offer. Would they buy them? How much would they pay?

Up Close and Personal

One way to research your market is to get up close and personal with a focus group. This is an informal gathering between you and a medley of potential customers, usually about five to twelve people. Once you have gotten them assembled and you've distributed some sort of refreshment (always a nice touch), you have a captive audience to respond to your most pressing marketing concerns.

Typically, you can hold such a focus group in a local meeting spot, such as a hotel meeting room or in a school, church, or temple. You want to make sure you are inviting people who are in your target market demographic groups—and are not biased (meaning don't invite your best friend who will likely agree with whatever you say).

One of the most common problems of focus group planning is that people do not plan beyond finding the room, ordering the food, finding the people, and asking a few questions. Therefore, in the end, the focus group is not very helpful. However, if you plan well, you can benefit greatly from running a focus group.

The effort put into advanced planning for a group always pays off in terms of the overall quality of the output from the process. This includes determining the manner in which participants are recruited, the questions they will be asked, the follow-up questions for various responses, the product photos or videos (plus other external stimuli), and having a means of recording the responses. In fact, it even means determining who will be asking the questions and what they should be wearing. While it may be sexist, the reality is that a sexy woman in a low cut dress asking a roomful of straight men whether or not they like a specific product will typically illicit positive answers no matter what the product is. Therefore, the moderator plays an important role in running a focus group. Someone who is condescending will elicit far more negative responses just by his or her manner.

In short, you can never do enough planning for an effective focus group.

The moderator of the group also has to know how to communicate effectively in such a forum. It's not as easy as it looks. First, you want to allow everyone to participate, without putting people on the spot. You also need to keep people on track and avoid tangential discussions. Additionally, you need to have a knack for making everyone feel good about voicing an opinion. As soon as someone feels that they are being embarrassed, or they are told that their opinion is wrong, you will silence many of the other participants and your focus group will suffer.

In the end, you also need to evaluate responses fairly and not look for the answers

> ## Smart Tip
> An effective moderator should be able to draw people out in a group environment, listen well, maintain an objective position, and interpret the results of the focus group discussion sessions.

No Couch Potatoes

Make sure your focus group consists of people who represent the specific audience you want to reach. If you're targeting physical fitness buffs, don't invite couch potatoes. In this instance, you could cull your group from members of your local gym or fitness center, local college athletes, or members of a nearby running club.

Some market researchers entice participants—frequently lured to a conference room while shopping at a mall or roaming a college campus—with a small payment, maybe $30. If you feel on more intimate terms with your target market—for instance, you're specializing in merchandise for junior equestrians and your own kids are involved in every dressage meet in the county, you might invite those very equestrians and their parents to be your focus group for an evening. In this case, you needn't offer payment because you know these people and you can make it a semi-social occasion. Just make sure you remember the point of the get-together and get your group really brainstorming on your behalf.

that you wanted to hear—likewise the phrasing of the questions should not be designed to justify your current conclusions. Finally, you must not show any prejudice or discrimination. The worst dressed person in the room, or the individual without a high level of education, may have the most significant input.

You'll probably want to conduct a few of these focus groups, in comfortable environments.

Delve into the sample "Focus Group Questionnaire" for an idea of how to formulate your own question-and-answer sessions. Obviously, your questions will relate to your own target market. Instead of chocolates, you might be asking about auto parts, craft supplies, or cat grooming products. Keep your questions focused on your objective: finding out which products people find the most appealing and coming up with a pricing structure for your products.

Ask as many questions as you feel your group can comfortably handle in about 90 minutes maximum (don't try keeping people captive until three in the morning). Hand out the questionnaires, have plenty of pens and pencils on tap, and encourage discussion. You'll learn more than you would have imagined!

Always Flattering

Telephone surveys are another market research tool, although not quite as up close and personal. Some folks are delighted to answer questions—after all, it's always

Focus Group Questionnaire

Sample questions for a fine chocolate mail order business.

1. How many times a year do you purchase fine chocolates for yourself? _____

2. How many times a year do you purchase fine chocolates as gifts:
   - for your spouse or significant other? _____
   - for your children? _____
   - for other relatives? What are their relationships? _____
   - for clients or co-workers? _____

3. Do you prefer dark chocolate or milk chocolate? _____

4. Do you prefer to choose your own selection (say, nuts, chews, creams, etc.) or would you rather purchase a pre-boxed assortment? _____

5. How much do you usually spend for a one-pound box of chocolates? _____

6. Would you pay more for a box specially wrapped for a gift occasion? _____

7. For which special occasions do you purchase chocolates? _____

8. How much would you expect to pay for this half-pound box of gold-foil-wrapped chocolate stars? *[Here you show the product to your group.]* _____

9. How much would you expect to pay for an 8-ounce solid chocolate Elvis Presley? *[Here you show the product to your group.]* _____

10. Would you buy an 8-ounce solid chocolate Elvis Presley? _____

11. How many times in the past year have you purchased something by mail order? _____

12. Were you pleased with your purchase? _____

13. If so, why? _____

14. If not, why not? _____

15. Would you feel comfortable about the freshness of chocolates you received through the mail? _____

16. What would you expect to pay for shipping and handling? _____

17. Please comment on the name Chocoholic Central (love, like, dislike, or hate, and why). _____

18. Please comment on the name For Chocolate Lovers Only (love, like, dislike, or hate, and why). _____

> ### Bright Idea
>
> Be sure to collect the names and addresses of all focus group participants. They will be the seeds of your in-house mailing list!

flattering to have somebody seek your opinion. Others in this era of Caller ID are wary of all unsolicited calls and refuse to squander valuable time on telephone strangers. Unless you've got a thick skin, it can be a little difficult to make cold calls to people you don't know and pick their brains. But if you can home in on people in a specific audience and explain why you're calling, you'll have a much better shot at getting relaxed responses.

Where do you get the phone numbers for a telephone survey? If you belong to an association or an organization that just happens to be affiliated with your target market, you've got it made. You may already have a directory packed with names and phone numbers. If not, you may be able to beg, borrow, or buy a directory from the organization's main office. If your specialty is something more common, like chocolates (who doesn't love chocolate?), you might still start off with the members of your club or group. Your membership will act as the proverbial foot in the door.

You can also set up a booth at a good location where you can gain names and numbers by providing a free chocolate sample or some such goody. Also, get their e-mail address if possible and permission to e-mail them.

Getting Feedback via the Internet and Mailings

First, you can gather plenty of information on your website by using survey questions or even simply asking for user feedback. If you provide a free download or some other small incentive, perhaps entering participants in a contest, you can get plenty of responses. A simple, short answer online survey can be very effective. If you have a permission-based e-mail list, you can also use that to reach your target market. Keep the questions short and to the point. Also, in any survey, do not ask people personal identifying information and do not ask for their social security number or any other such information. In a world where identity theft is on the rise, you do not want to give anyone the impression that you are seeking such identifiable information.

Direct mail is also a terrific market research tool. You can use the same lists or directories you'd use in your telephone surveys (but don't attack the same people with both phone and mail questionnaires—choose one form or the other).

Keep in mind that people are unlikely to return a mail survey unless you can offer them an incentive. Extend an invitation to be put on your mailing list. Make respondents "charter members" of your club, if that's how you're structuring your company. Give them a coupon for 10 percent off your first mailing or catalog.

Take a look at our sample direct-mail questionnaire on page 54. It's been designed as a two-page spread, with a survey page the respondent can tear off and mail back. The reverse side is a stamped and addressed self-mailer. Let's explore the text on the first page:

- It draws in respondents—who are also potential customers—by asking questions that inspire them to read on.

- It enhances customer recognition of the company's name by putting it in a typeface that stands out from the rest of the text and repeating it frequently.

- It asks customers' assistance by stating that the company is being tailored to their needs and desires.

- In bold, italic type that can't be missed, it promises enrollment as a charter member just for filling out the questionnaire. Everybody wants to get something for nothing—or almost nothing—and this does the trick. Plus, being invited to become a "charter member" has a certain cachet; it sounds exclusive.

- It offers a discount certificate for returning the survey. This accomplishes two things: It keeps potential customers anticipating that first mailing and anxious to open it when they receive it, and it motivates people to order something so they can take advantage of the certificate.

- It displays the company's address, phone number, and e-mail address on the certificate, which the customer will retain. Always make sure you've got this information somewhere on each mailing piece you send out. You want your customers to be able to reach you!

Why does the letter read as if the company is already up and running? You've got more credibility as an existing company with a name and a game plan.

Now let's look at the questionnaire side of the sample mailer. The questions have been designed to help the mail order entrepreneur determine her customers' decorating likes and dislikes so that she will know what products and services to offer.

Making Your Mailings Count: Key Points to Include

- *Return address.* This is how you, as an entrepreneur, will gather the names of people who have responded to your mailing. These names are very important for two reasons: 1) out of all the names on the initial list, they are the ones with the most purchasing potential, and 2) if you used a mailing center to send the questionnaire out to a purchased list, they may not have any names except the ones who respond.

Smart Tip *Tip...*

You've learned how to conduct a focus group survey with people you know, but how can you get feedback from the general public? A tabletop testing station in a mall or outside a supermarket can be a good way to get responses from the person on the street. Make sure you get the mall or store manager's approval before you set up. Ask participants for answers on the spot. If you give out questionnaires to be mailed back, chances are you'll never see them again.

Netting Names

Some people collect stamps. Others collect coins. Mail order mavens collect names. Here's a list of potential freebie sources to get you started collecting names for your first mailing:

- ○ Athletic associations or organizations
- ○ Client lists
- ○ Colleagues and co-workers (Large companies often have employee directories.)
- ○ Condo, neighborhood, apartment, or time-share associations
- ○ Fraternal organizations (Elks Lodge, Soroptimists, Jaycees)
- ○ Hobby groups, clubs, and other organizations
- ○ Networking groups (That's why they exist!)
- ○ Professional associations and organizations
- ○ School or university groups (Don't forget alumni associations!)
- ○ Scouting groups (Boy and Girl Scouts, Campfire Girls, etc.)
- ○ Sororities and fraternities
- ○ Your own address book (You've probably amassed more names than you realize.)

You can probably add your own list sources to the ones we've gathered here. Keep in mind, however, that you're wasting your pennies if you send mailings to people on just any old list. You've got to tailor the list to your product.

Also, make sure that you are using a list that you have permission to use. For example, if an organization sends their membership list to all members (and you are a member) then you have permission to have the list. However, if the membership forbids anyone to use the list of marketing purposes, you can find yourself in hot water (or kicked out and bad mouthed) if you disregard the warning—not to mention other members may not see your marketing efforts in a very positive light. If, however, there is no such warning or doctrine, you can usually use the list.

Today, in a security-conscious world, you have to be extra careful about putting together a mailing list—people will go out of their way to make your life difficult if you are obtaining their names and addresses, phone numbers or web addresses illegally.

Even if nobody challenges you, the public is so saturated with junk mail, SPAM, and annoying telemarketers, that you can give yourself a very poor reputation by reaching out to people whom you should not be contacting. Therefore, be careful, creative, and stay within ethical and legal boundaries when assembling a mailing list.

- *Self-addressed, stamped envelope.* Potential customers are unlikely to stick their own stamp on a piece of mail like a survey or questionnaire. Likewise, they are extremely unlikely to take the time to address their own envelope. But if you print the address on the envelope for them and supply the stamp, the only thing they'll have to do after they fill out the questionnaire is mail it.
- *"Dept. 1A" after the street address.* Here's a fundamental mail order secret: There is no Department 1A. This is what's known as a key code, and it's used to clue you in to which segment of your list replied to your mailing or ad. For example, you may have complied a list from different sources; this will let you know which source served your needs. Use Dept. 1A on one list and Dept. 1B on another. You can do the same with advertising to see which ads and promotions are more effective.

Shopping the Competition

No matter how specific and specialized your niche is, you're going to face competition from some avenue. This is okay—a little competition is healthy. If you do your homework properly and structure your niche wisely, your company will shine regardless of your rivals.

The market research phase is the time to scrutinize those rivals. What are they doing that is absolutely perfect? What can you successfully emulate? What are they doing that you can do better? What can you offer that will draw customers away from them and to you? This is known as developing a competitive edge and is a key to success in all areas of business. You can learn a lot by performing the following research tasks:

- *Go ahead, shop the competition!* Send for all the catalogs you can. Study them. What works? What doesn't? Why? Buy something, see how long it takes to reach your home–is it what you ordered? Was the description accurate? What is the return policy? What is the customer service like? Call and find out.
- *Surf those internet sites.* Again, study what your rivals are doing and explore what works and what doesn't.
- Dissect those direct-mail pieces in magazines and your own mailbox.
- Find out exactly who your competition is. Beth's competition, although indirect, is natural food stores. Kate's is mall-based sports memorabilia shops. What might yours be?

Once you've conducted your market research, you can use the "Catalog Concept Evaluation Worksheet" provided by John Schulte of the NMOA (see page 57) to give your catalog idea a final check.

53

Your Own Personal Interior Decorator
OnCall for Pennies!

How would you like to have your very own interior decorator available any time you need her—to redecorate a single room or your entire home, or just to answer all those "little" questions, like what color to repaint the kitchen or how to make the kids' rooms more organized?

Sound wonderful but too expensive? Not so! With *OnCall Designer*, you can get professional interior design services for as little as $50 per room. And we'd like to offer you a charter membership!

But first, we need your help. In order to tailor our service to your needs and desires, we're asking you to fill out the attached questionnaire and send it back. It's a self-mailer, so it's easy! And to show our appreciation for your help, we'll **enroll you as a charter member** of *OnCall Designer*. This entitles you to:

○ *Monthly newsletters packed with design tips and ideas*

○ *Fantastic discounts on designer books, kits, and products*

○ *10% off your first decorator request*

Sound exciting? It is! When you receive your first mailing, you'll be thrilled with the quality of our products and services—everything you need to give your home that exclusive designer look. Your friends will want to know how you did it!

Ready to get started? It's as easy as 1, 2, 3:

1. Fill out the attached questionnaire.
2. Fold it and send it back in its own mailer to *OnCall Designer.*
3. Keep the certificate! When you receive your first mailing, you can use the coupon for your 10% discount on the product or service of your choice.

OnCall Designer

This Certificate entitles_____,
a charter member of *OnCall Designer*, to a full 10% off
any product or service offered in Mailing No. 1.

Enjoy!

123 Décor Drive, Dept. 1A, Art Deco, FL 30000   (305) 555-9800   www.oncalldesigner.com

OnCall Designer
Charter Member's Questionnaire

1. What is your favorite decorating style (country, contemporary, traditional, etc.)?
   _____
   _____

2. How often do you redecorate?

   Every year _____

   Every two years _____

   Every time you can stretch your budget _____

3. When was the last time you redecorated? _____

4. Which room or rooms did you do and why? _____
   _____

5. About how much did you spend on this project? _____

6. What are your biggest decorating problems or concerns? (Go ahead—tell us everything!) _____
   _____
   _____

7. How many people make up your household? _____

8. If you have kids at home, what are their ages? _____

9. What is the approximate square footage of your home? _____

10. Is it a house, condo, or apartment? _____

11. How many bedrooms? _____

12. How many baths? _____

13. Do you have a separate family room, office, or den? (Please circle all that apply.)

14. Do you have a patio or deck? _____

15. Would you be interested in tips, tricks, and products for outdoor entertaining?

16. What is your annual household income? _____

17. Do you have a computer with Internet access? _____

18. Do you own and use a digital camera? _____

We appreciate your answers and comments. They'll help us make

OnCall Designer perfect for you. Watch for our first mailing—coming soon!

Direct Mail Questionnaire, Page 3

From:

_____

_____

_____

↑ Important! Be sure to fill this out.

To: *OnCall Designer*
123 Décor Drive, Dept. 1A
Art Deco, FL 30000

- -

Fold Here

OnCall Designer

Your Own Personal Interior Designer!

Tape Together Here

Catalog Concept Evaluation Worksheet

Planning a catalog? The chairman of the National Mail Order Association, John Schulte, has kindly provided this worksheet to help you gauge the potential of your catalog idea.

○ *Availability.* Will your customers feel the products you're offering are more readily available from you than elsewhere? _____

○ *Authority.* Why should people buy from you instead of their present source? What gives you the right to say what you're saying and expect to be believed?

_____

○ *Value.* Can you price your merchandise to fit the value considerations of your audience? _____

○ *Satisfaction.* Can you assure customers there will be no hassles when they buy from you sight unseen? _____

○ *Mailing lists.* Do you have lists of known catalog buyers who would be interested in buying the kinds of products you plan to sell at the price points at which they will be offered? _____

○ *Facilities.* Do you have access to facilities suited for a mail order catalog operation? _____

○ *Staff.* Do you have personnel with catalog experience? _____

○ *Money.* Do you have sufficient financial backing to carry a catalog through its unprofitable development period (typically three to five years)? _____

○ *Desire.* Do you really want to be in the catalog business? Enough to stick with it during the whole developmental period? _____

○ *Bright idea.* Have you come up with something that will give your catalog a unique position in the highly competitive catalog marketplace? _____

_____

_____

Packaging Your Business:

Choosing a Name and a Structure

You've done your market research. You've decided what you'll sell and how you'll sell it. In fact, you've even explored your target market. Terrific! Now you'll need to design a tight, sturdy package for your new company, a structure that will keep it not only looking good, but solid enough to weather anything life might dish out. In this chapter, we guide you through that packaging—the features that form the basics of the business—from a company name and legal structure to licenses, insurance, and beyond.

Name That Business

Every business, like every child, has to have a name. You should devote almost as much thought to choosing an appellation for your company as you would for your human offspring. After all, you plan to have your business baby around for a long time. You want a name you can be proud of, one that identifies it—and, by extension, you—as worthy of your customers' confidence.

Customers usually form an idea of the type of business they are dealing with from the store's exterior. It's a large warehouse-style building, or an intimate boutique, or a high-tech studio blazing with neon. As soon as they walk through the door, their impressions are strengthened—it's a self-serve emporium stacked to the rafters with office supplies, or a ritzy clothier layered in silks and fine leather, or a trendy gallery pulsing with abstract art. Since your customers' first impression of your store comes from the front page of your catalog, your website, or direct-mail piece, you'll have to make sure your name gives the proper first impression. Additionally, since your mail order business will be different from everybody else's (because you've developed that special niche), you want to convey your uniqueness to your customers as well.

Biz Whiz

Your business name can reflect your products or services, or even your niche customers—for example, Biz Auto Whiz for a company that insures business automobiles or Perfectly Kids for a catalog that caters to the tiny tot set. Just make sure your company's name doesn't limit you. If the business insurance company decides to branch out to residential insurance a few years down the road, its name will no longer accurately reflect its services.

Sourdough Bread

Companies often go with a name that reflects their geographic location—San Francisco Clothiers or Des Moines Demographics, for example. This is not the best decision for mail order entrepreneurs. By definition, mail order is non-geographic; your products or services can go anywhere. So unless your name is a direct reflection of your products—something your customers will recognize and want because of its regionalism, like San Francisco Sourdough Bread or Louisiana Spices—you'll do better to leave your city, state, or region on the map instead of in your company's name.

What's So Special?

A catch phrase or slogan can be as important as your business name in creating a mail order identity. A well-turned phrase can capture your customers' attention and imagination, as well as clarify your mission and market position. Like the name itself, the right slogan gives prospective customers the color, scent, and flavor of what you're offering and helps them remember what's special about you.

Take a look at these terrific examples:

- ○ "Affordable software solutions direct to you"—*Parsons Technology*
- ○ "America's authority in home fashions"—*Domestications*
- ○ "Where value and selection come home"—*Home Decorators Collection*
- ○ "Offering the Best, the Only, and the Unexpected since 1848"—*Hammacher Schlemmer*

Listening Comprehension

Whatever name you go with, remember that you—or your order processors—will be repeating your name every time you answer the phone. Sound out that moniker before you settle on it. Some names look great in print but are difficult, if not impossible, to understand over the phone. M&A Gifts, for instance, may sound like a great name for partners Marty and Andrea, but when spoken it sounds like "MNA" or "Emenay."

Most callers rate about a C-minus in listening comprehension. No matter how clearly you enunciate, they're not going to understand M&A. So save yourself hours of frustration and choose something crystal clear. In a web-savvy world, you also want something that is easy to spell for your website.

Searching to make sure a name is available is especially important for a mail order business because you are going national—and even international. Sure there can be a Ray's Pizza in each of a dozen different cities because they do not compete with one another. You, however, are competing with companies far and wide. No, there may not be another Perfectly Kids in your town, county, or even state; but can you be sure there's not another company with the same name somewhere else in the country? Can you picture a worst-case scenario of printing up 10,000 catalogs only to discover that another Perfectly Kids is suing you for using its name? Or finding out that some other company—that is shabbier and sloppier than yours—is using the same name you have chosen and confusing customers, who think your firm is the shabby and sloppy one?

For some top-notch name ideas, check out the mail order companies listed as resources in the Appendix. You'll want to choose a name that's as individual as you are, but looking at the names of existing companies can start those creative gears turning.

Making Your Business Name Official

Once you've decided on a name, you'll need to register it. Even though you are doing business on a national and international level, you still need to be a registered business somewhere—the IRS likes to know where to find you. For this reason, you will need to register your business locally. Make sure to do a business name search before registering. You do this for three reasons:

1. It ensures that no one else in your local area is using the name and gives you dibs on it.

2. It makes your local authorities happy. Most cities or counties require that you have a fictitious business name or dba (doing business as); this way, they can keep tabs on you for tax or other licensing purposes. And you go on public record so anyone who wants or needs to can look up the name of your company and find out whom it belongs to.

3. Most banks won't allow you to open a business checking account—one with your company name, which gives you credibility among suppliers and others—unless you can show them proof that you've registered a fictitious business name.

Obtaining a dba is quick and easy, and you can absolutely do it on your own. The process varies a bit in different states and regions of the country, but the local licensing bureau will fill you in on what you need—call them to get the details, or go to their website, before making the trip to the licensing bureau.

If you are going to be using the web, as most businesses do, also make sure the domain name is available for a website, which should be the same as your business name to avoid confusion. You will need to register your domain name. Since so many domains are already being used, you should think up several versions of the name you want in case one or more have already been taken.

Of course, you will need to do a domain name search prior to registering a domain name. One way to do this is by going to www.networksolutions.com and checking to see if your name choices are available. Following the easy directions, check to see if the domain name you've chosen has already been taken. If it has, choose another. When you find a permutation that's available, register it online. You may also register some similar names if they are also available, such as both the .com and .net suffixes of the name, or common misspelling. For example, if, while trying to go to

Business Name Brainstorming

List three ideas based on the products or services you plan to provide (e.g., children's clothing, custom menu design, aromatherapy products):

1. _____

_____

2. _____

_____

3. _____

_____

List three ideas based on your special niche (e.g., affordable children's special-occasion clothes, exclusive designs for the small restauranteur, aromatherapy for the office environment):

1. _____

_____

2. _____

_____

3. _____

_____

List three ideas combining a favorite theme with your special niche: (e.g., Tea Party children's party clothes, Table For Two menu designs, The Tranquil Desk aromatic office products):

1. _____

_____

2. _____

_____

3. _____

_____

After you've decided which name you like best, ask yourself these important questions:

- ○ Is it easy to say out loud? (Has it passed muster with your family? Have you had a friend call to see how it sounds over the phone?)
- ○ Have you checked your local Yellow Pages to make sure the same or a similar name is not already listed?
- ○ Have you checked with your local business authority to make sure the name is available?
- ○ Have you tried it on the internet to see if there's a similar business with the same domain name?
- ○ Have you started your trademark search?

Google.com, you type www.gogle.com, www.gooogle.com or www.googel.com, you will still get www.google.com!

Of course, in thinking of a name today, it not only has to look and sound right, but it needs to be easy to spell and to remember. Also, for the sake of typing in a web address, don't make it too long. Nobody wants to type in the website address www.anniesmailorderflowerbusinessinc.com; instead, use www.anniesflowers.com.

Once you've checked that the name is available and the domain name is available, it's also a good idea to get your name registered as a trademark—which takes some time. You can find out information and do a trademark search through the U.S. Trademark and Patent Office at www.uspto.gov. You can also hire an attorney or a trademark search firm to handle the job for you (for a fee, of course).

Laying Your Foundation

There's more to laying the foundation of your business than choosing a name. You'll need to decide on a legal structure, check into zoning regulations and insurance coverage, and line up an attorney and an accountant—all the nitty-gritty stuff that will give your company a solid base on which to build.

On Your Own

To appease those picky IRS people, your business must have a structure. You can operate as a sole proprietorship, a partnership, or a corporation. Many mail order newbies go with the simplest version, the sole proprietorship. If you'll be starting out on your own, you may choose the same option. It's the least complicated and the least expensive. You can always switch to another format later on if you take on partners and/or employees.

Business Structures

Sole proprietorship, is, by all accounts, the easiest structure under which to run a business. You get a business license and file the necessary business forms applicable within your state and you are in business. There is very little paperwork and few formalities, other than paying taxes. Your income is reported on your personal or jointly filed tax return. The drawback, however is that if your business gets sued, so do you—personally. In other words, you are held liable and it can put a serious dent in your personal finances. In a litigious society, it's often more comforting when dealing with such a broad-based business as mail order to take greater precautions.

Incorporating is a popular choice for vending entrepreneurs. When you're incorporated, the corporation carries the liability instead of you personally. You can also use such incorporation more effectively when negotiating with banks by reminding them the corporation guarantees the note. Even though the bank will probably still ask you for a personal guarantee, you can use your corporate status during such negotiations.

The biggest plus for incorporating, however, is that the business stands as a separate entity, meaning that you are typically not personally held liable if your product injures someone. However, with incorporation comes a lot of paperwork and various requirements that you must fulfill as set forth by the state in which you incorporate. There is also the possibility of double taxation when you form a corporation, meaning you pay corporate taxes and then when you take money out of the corporation, you pay taxes again on your personal income. You need to sit down with a business attorney or your accountant and weigh the plusses and minuses of incorporating as well as how to avoid such double taxation.

A Limited Liability Corporation (LLC) is another, newer, option that is somewhat of a hybrid between incorporating and going solo. The advantages of forming an LLC are that the members are afforded limited liability and have pass-through taxes similar to a partnership. By forming an LLC, rather than a corporation, you receive nearly all of the benefits of a corporation but avoid some of the drawbacks, such as double taxation, some requirements, and excessive paperwork. LLCs are not offered in all states, so you will need to inquire in your state.

As for partnerships, proceed with caution. Make sure you have a partnership agreement spelled out detailing who is responsible for which tasks and functions. Also make sure you determine in advance whether one of you is a silent partner or a limited partner. You will need to have an attorney draw up such an agreement. There also need to be very clear guidelines about how the partnership can be dissolved.

Zoning Regulations

Such local regulations typically try to separate business and commercial areas within a town or city. They include regulations regarding garbage removal, parking, signage and types of businesses that can be run in a particular area. All businesses should know the local laws of the land—especially homebased businesses that are typically operating in residential neighborhoods.

If you plan to work from home, you need to check into zoning regulations. Since your shop will be virtual, you won't need signs pinpointing your location. Also, since you'll rarely have customers knocking at your door, you won't need to worry about parking restrictions. But unless you ship from an outside location, you will have UPS

> **Tip...**
>
> **Smart Tip**
> Always get a name, department and phone extension when you call someone in government officialdom. This can save you hours of re-explanation if you need to call again. Plus, you'll make a buddy who can probably help with other matters later down the line.

or other delivery trucks pulling up to your front stoop every day. It's unlikely, but possible, that a pesky neighbor could take this as a reason to report you to the local authorities. So it's a good idea to play it safe. Find out from your local government whether any permits are necessary, and if so, file them. If zoning regulations prohibit operating a business in your neighborhood, you can apply for a zoning variance, a special permit granting you the legal right to run your business at home.

Attorneys and Accountants

Attorneys are like plumbers—you don't think about hiring one until you have an urgent problem. But as a business owner, you should have a good attorney on call, one who knows small business, and preferably one well versed in the mail order business. You will want your attorney to check over any contracts you enter into with manufacturers, suppliers, and other vendors and to advise you on the fine points of mail order law. You won't need to call your attorney every week or even every month. But there's no point in waiting until you've got a problem to try to establish a relationship with an attorney and get help.

Along with that on-call attorney, you'll want to look into hiring an accountant. Unless you go with a full-service fulfillment company, you'll handle the day-to-day data entry yourself—tracking customers' orders and payments, generating returns and tracking ad responses. (We'll get into this in Chapter 10.) But you will probably want an accountant to advise you of any special ways you can save money with your business structure, to oversee your operations, and to fill out those tax returns.

Also, don't forget your insurance agent! Insurance agents can be invaluable sources of information and expertise. If you're going to be homebased, you'll need to find out if your homeowner's package covers your business assets, inventory, and equipment or if you need additional coverage. If you're based outside the home, you need coverage for these same items, as well as your physical location. If you plan to hire employees, you may also need workers' compensation insurance.

Look Before You Leap

We've given you a peek at some important business basics. Remember, however, that other licenses and fees can crop up, depending on what your special niche is and what products or services you'll be selling. Do your homework. Make sure you understand what's necessary in each situation. In other words, look before you leap into that mailbox! Consult with an attorney and an accountant early in the process.

5

Into the Money Bag: Figuring Your Finances

That old refrain, "The best things in life are free," doesn't quite apply when you're starting a business. This chapter, therefore, dips into the murky waters of startup costs, operating expenses, financing, and budgeting—and, like chlorine, clears them up.

▲

Startup Costs

One of the many nifty things about launching a mail order business is that startup costs are comparatively low. You've got the option to be homebased, which cuts office lease expenses down to nothing. If you're working with a supplier who will drop-ship, you've got no inventory. Even if you do have inventory, you won't need fancy display cabinets or kicky décor. Your major financial outlay will go toward office equipment, advertising, your website, your catalog, and/or other direct-mail pieces. If you're like many, you've already got the most expensive piece of office equipment: a computer system.

But let's take it from the top. The following is a breakdown of everything you will need to get up and running:

- Computer system with modem and printer
- Internet access
- Website design and promotion
- Software
- Electronic credit card processing
- Bulk mail permit
- Market research
- Phone
- Voice mail or answering machine
- Call center
- Stationery and office supplies
- Shipping and packaging materials
- Postage
- Initial inventory
- Business license and any other necessary requirements for doing business, such as a zoning variance if necessary.

Of course, you can add goodies to this list. For example, a copier is a plus. It's also nice to have bona fide office furniture: a tweedy upholstered chair with lumbar support that swivels and rolls, gleaming file cabinets that really lock, real oak bookshelves. We'll cover office equipment in depth in Chapter 8, which features a sort of shopping bonanza.

But let's consider that you're starting from absolute scratch. You can always set up your computer on your kitchen table. You can stash files in cardboard boxes. It's not glamorous, but it will suffice until you get your own business steaming ahead.

You may wonder why we don't have an allocation for mailing lists and advertising. Good question! The answer is that in mail order, these items—rather than being considered startup expenses in and of themselves—are calculated into the cost per order, which is used to determine your product prices. Take a look at the "Figuring Profits" section in this chapter and the "Advanced Break-Even Worksheet" in Chapter 12 to find out exactly how this works.

Computer Candidate

A computer system heads the list of startup expenses. Actually, however, for the majority of people today, it is not on the list because you already have a home computer. It is estimated that computers are in some 80 percent of American homes and that may be a conservative number. You may need to upgrade or add a faster means of internet services (going from dial-up to broadband) but it is likely that you already have the basics in place: hard drive, monitor, mouse, modem, and printer. If not, or if you choose to buy a new computer dedicated solely for your business, you should allocate about $2,500. We'll go over the various permutations in Chapter 8, but this will give you a figure to pencil in for starters.

Fax Facts

When fax machines first appeared on the scene, everyone needed one. Today, just a few years later, thanks to scanners, most faxes have been replaced by e-mail. This isn't to say a fax machine is a negative—it can certainly be beneficial as it gives you greater accessibility to customers and vendors. However, you can use a fax software program in your computer as an option to buying a fax machine.

If, however, you choose to buy a stand-alone fax machine, you can get one for under $300 that should meet your needs. Hint: If you're working from home, do not give the number out to everyone. The more you give out your fax number, the more likely you will receive junk faxes—sometimes at 2 A.M! Trust me, I remember those late night phone calls. Unlike junk e-mail that you delete, junk faxes cost you money in paper and toner. Look for a fax machine with a good track record. Read up on the best selling brands (typically Brother, HP, Canon, Panasonic, Sharp and Xerox) and make sure you get one with easily accessible tech support and a good warranty.

Go to www.shopping.com/xPP-Fax_Machines to compare various models and consider the features you need most.

The Internet

Good internet and e-mail service is a must for the mail order maven. The first step is to find affordable, fast, and reliable internet service through an Internet Service Provider (ISP). Most internet service providers, or ISPs, charge about $20 to $25 per month and give you unlimited access and e-mail. You will want a broadband, or cable, hookup rather than a dial-up service, which is way too slow for today's business transactions. If you will be using broadband, you will need a network interface card (NIC). Typically,

▲

this is an Ethernet connection that is already installed when you buy a modern computer. If you have an old computer, an Ethernet card can be purchased and installed with software to guide you. Your choice of broadband internet service providers (ISPs) are typically limited by what is available in your area. However, since broadband access uses the same cable wiring as cable television, it is available nearly everywhere by some provider. In fact, combination deals with your television cable provider may be offered. Be forewarned that such combo deals do not ensure that a good cable television provider will also offer quality internet cable access.

When deciding between ISPs, it pays to shop around. Since company service reps will answer positively to any question regarding their service—after all this is their job—you should get opinions from other users in your area. Ask friends, neighbors, and colleagues about their internet experiences. Seek out other home-officers like yourself and get their opinions on productivity using a specific ISP. Personal references bode well, especially when asking about customer service and problems that others have had with their ISP.

The next step is to call the ISPs and make sure they offer the following services:

- *Local access phone numbers if you use their dial-up service.* You don't want to pay long distance charges every time you go online.

- *Internet access 24/7.* While service may typically be down on any ISP once in a while, you want reliability. A good ISP should be up and running smoothly 99 percent of the time. You should be able to get online all the time, unless there is a power failure or a problem on your end—such as your dog chewing through the cable wire.

- *A customer service desk that is open 24/7.* Find out what the average length of time is to get repairs done.

- *Ease of installation.* Most ISPs make installation relatively painless, featuring home installation kits—or they will send someone who will install it for you, depending on the plan you choose and your comfort with technical tasks. How user-friendly the service is will depend in part on the service and on your computer competence.

- *Cost.* Since this is a highly competitive business, many ISPs will be similar in what they provide. Remember, the lowest price isn't always the best buy. Compare costs including installation and additional fees. Find out if they offer monthly billing plans regardless of how many hours you use or offer a set number of hours for a specific rate.

- *Speed.* As you can imagine, faster is better. Ask about connection speed. Ideally, you will want to have a connection that allows you to download files at no less than 384Kbps and upload files at no slower than 128Kbps.

Among the most familiar big name ISPs, you'll find Adelphi, AT&T, Bell South, Cablevision, Comcast, Cox, EarthLink, MCI, SBC (which features Yahoo), Time

Warner (which includes AOL), and Verizon. For a solid review of ISPs you might look at Home Office Reports (www.homeofficereports.com) and see their ratings and rankings of the various service providers. When reading the descriptions and pricing, you'll find that some ISPs are clearly designed for larger scale business use than the needs of a typical home office, while others are more compatible with your needs. Another place you may want to look is at the ISP Buying Guide, or www.ispbuyingguide.com. If you'd like to check on the fastest ISP connection speeds and look up other comparable categories of service providers you can go to www.CNET.com where they will break it down by cable, DSL, and dial up.

Dollar Stretcher

Website design and hosting fees may be higher in large urban areas. Shop around. It doesn't matter if you're in Atlanta, Chicago, or Los Angeles. You can hire a webmaster in Pipsqueak, South Dakota, and work with the person as easily as if he or she were next door.

Your Own Website

Along with being online for research, e-mails, and so forth, you will need your own website. Like just about everything else in direct marketing, the cost of setting up and maintaining a company website can vary considerably. The entrepreneurs we interviewed all got their sites going in penny-wise fashion by keeping it all in the family. There are various websites and software packages that offer easy means of building a site. However, in time, you will want to progress to a more professional-looking site. "I started my own website five years ago," says Patty, the party planning expert who runs www.instantphotoframes.com. "I've done well but probably could have done even better with a more professional-looking site," adds Patty, who has since hired a pro to improve on the look of the site and the functionality.

Mary's son set up her site and keeps it running. Beth's husband does hers and Caryn has mastered the fine art of website construction and maintenance herself. "It took me four months," the Roswell direct-marketer recalls, "and it was truly one of the biggest accomplishments that I've ever done on my own. I was outside screaming at my husband, who was doing some gardening, and he didn't know what had happened.

"You can be successful, but you've got to work at it," Caryn advises. "You've got to commit to spending the time to figure it out."

If you plan to go the website route and you're lucky enough to have a computer brain in the family, or if you take the time to become your own computer expert, you can pencil in a zero under website design costs.

What can you expect to pay if you outsource your site construction? Prices depend on the complexity of your project and how much you're willing do to help the

▲

Dollar Stretcher

Use your e-mail service to contact suppliers abroad. Why place a pricey international call when you can send an e-mail message virtually for free?

designer. An online catalog with 20 to 30 products and five to 10 variations on each could run from $2,000 to $7,000 depending on how fancy you want it to look and what features you include. You can trim costs by supplying your own text files—giving the designer your product descriptions and other written material electronically—so that he does not need to charge you for typing all that stuff in. Typically, the price estimate is based on designing a site that features "shopping cart" technology. A web shopping cart is the online equivalent to an actual shopping cart that you would find in a brick-and-mortar store. Customers load their virtual carts with purchases, then check out when they're finished shopping. The system then calculates their total purchases and processes their credit card payments.

A savvy web designer may also be able to advise and assist you with promoting your site on the internet. Web optimization is a whole new field onto itself, which we will discuss in more detail later. Remember, having an advertising strategy for your website is a wise move because there's no point in having a site if no one knows about it. We'll explore this topic and how to build an effective website in Chapter 11, but for now, you can pencil in about $2,500 for help designing your website. And while it depends on the firm, you may be able to negotiate free domain-name registration and free registration with search engines, the sites that direct shoppers to you—and your competitors—when they type in "gourmet chocolates," or whatever it is you're selling.

The Software Skinny

As you know, your computer needs software to give it brains. Software prices vary dramatically, depending on which programs you buy and from whom. The jury is still out on whether or not you need special mail order software. Kate, who with the help of her trusty computer runs a one-woman office, uses a good general accounting software program. Beth started with a general accounting package but now—with her company's bank of seven computers—relies on a program tailored to the mail order industry. For special mail order software starter packages, you can expect to pay in the range of $300 to $1,600.

To find a list of industry specific software programs you can go to the National Mail Order Association's website at NMOA.org. They list some 40 different options for mail order software. Three of the leaders among these are:

- AnyOrder, www.ronwatters.com/RonSoft4.htm (PC/Windows based)
- iCODE: www.icode.com/index.asp (PC/Windows based)
- In Order www.morsedata.com (PC/Windows based)

Whether you go with industry-specific software or not, you'll also need a good word processing program, a desktop publishing program, and an accounting program. Again, this is a subject we'll discuss in depth in Chapter 8. For startup purposes, let's say you'll want to allocate about $500. Of course, if you are buying a new computer for the business, it is very likely you can get such a program bundled into the package (which simply means included).

That's Bulk!

To take advantage of bulk mail rates, which are less costly than consumer ones, you'll need to purchase a bulk mail permit from the U.S. Postal Service. Pencil in a one-time $100 fee for your permit number and then an additional $100 for the annual fee to retain your permit. (You must use your bulk mail permit at least once every two years or you lose your privileges.) To take advantage of the cost savings for bulk mail, you'll have to sort each piece according to postal regulations.

Rates for Standard Class bulk mail vary according to the many different factors. In any particular bulk mailing, you may find that different pieces will qualify for different postage rates, even though the pieces may be appear to be physically identical.

One exception, however, is for mailings consisting of barcoded flats. These flats are prepared in "bundles" of a small number of pieces rubber-banded together. They are then placed into sacks. For barcoded flats, the postage rate for any piece is determined by which bundle it is in rather than by which sack it is in. Note that this exception does not apply to flats that are not barcoded.

For mailing identical pieces, standard class is inexpensive, although it is a slower means of travel. Standard Class mail is processed after First Class, and typically arrives within a few days (for local mail) to a few weeks (for mail traveling cross-country).

Each mailing at Standard Class rates must consist of at least 200 pieces. (Exception: If each piece weighs more than 4 ounces, the mailing will meet the minimum if the total mailing weighs at least 50 pounds.)

You'll find more on mailing in "Fun with Mail Sorting" (Chapter 7).

Charge It!

In the modern world of sales, credit card processing is a must, especially to survive online. This means you can ship the merchandise immediately, which makes for happy customers, and you can have the money deposited in your bank account immediately, which makes for a happy you.

Before you can accept credit cards, however, you need to set up a merchant account. Many banks balk at setting up merchant accounts for SOHO (small office/home office) and mail order businesses because they fear a heavy credit risk. But if you shop around, you can locate companies who welcome SOHO and mail order entre-preneurs.

What can you expect to pay for an electronic terminal? Fees depend on which company you go with and, in some cases, the type of business you're building and you personally.

"Every client is different," says Dennis Varvarigos of Electronic Card Systems in Los Angeles, California. His company scrutinizes:

- The product or service you're selling. It will be happier, for instance, if you're marketing cookbooks than if you are selling one-year club memberships. Why? Because it considers the membership, with its finite term, a liability. And this means it'll probably require you to put up a 5 percent reserve.
- The volume of business you expect to do. The bank will adjust your rate according to your sales volume.
- Your own credit history. You'll get a better rate if you've got a flawless credit record than if you've had credit problems.

So what's the bottom line? Varvarigos quotes the following: Assuming you've got a gold star for credit worthiness, you can expect to pay about 30 cents per transaction, a 2.65 percent discount rate (this is the percent you're charged per transaction), and a $10 monthly statement fee. You'll also be charged $25 to $30 per month to lease the processing terminal. Then, too, there's the $195 application fee and any reserves you may be required to deposit.

Market Research

As we've explored, the amount you'll pay for market research is a variable. It's almost entirely dependent on your personal style and how comfortable you are with the niche you've chosen. If you're going to be selling books to horse lovers, you know every equestrian within five states, and you absolutely know they'll buy the kind of books you'll be offering, you can cut your market research expenses down to nearly nothing. If, on the other hand, you're casting for products to sell and then have to determine how salable they are, you've got a lot of research ahead of you.

So let's say you're somewhere in the middle. You're planning on a catalog featuring everything for the horsy set, from currycombs to muck rakes to t-shirts, but you're not quite sure which products will sell. You can see our sample budget on page 75; you'll need to modify to suit your own needs, but this should give you a good idea of what your market research budget might look like.

Phone Fun

It's important when running a homebased business to install a separate line (or several lines) for business calls, especially if you anticipate taking a significant number of

Market Research Expenses	
O Purchased mailing list of 3,000 names at $50 per 1,000 names	$150
O 3,000 two-color brochure/questionnaires designed on your computer with your desktop publishing program and copied and trifolded by your local print shop	$380
O Postage, 3,000 pieces at bulk rate	$840
O Two focus groups (including room rental, recruiting and refreshments)	$1,000
Total Market Research Budget	**$2,370**

phone orders. Costs, of course, depend on how many fun features you add to your telephone service and which local and long-distance carriers you go with, but for the purpose of startup budgeting, let's say you should allocate about $50 per line. You'll also need to add the phone company's installation fee, which should be in the range of $40 to $100. Check with your local phone company to determine exactly what these costs are in your area.

You should also have your cell phone handy for necessary business calls. However, you do not want to use this number for incoming orders or it can run your bill sky high, even with a high number of minutes on your cell phone plan. Again, shop around before you decide on a cell phone plan—prices vary greatly. As for the phone itself, you probably won't need a lot of features, such as watching movies or playing games—remember, this is for work. Primarily, your cell phone should be for speaking with vendors, handling special problems that arise, and checking in with your answering machine or phone service from the road.

When You Can't Get To The Phone

An answering machine, or a voice mail system, are the two primary options today. Answering machines today are usually built into basic telephones and can be purchased for anywhere from $20 to $100, which will serve you well. For a small business that is doing the vast majority of ordering over a website or through mailings, you can use an answering machine with a message that is brief and sounds professional.

Of course, voice mail has become the standard in business today. Essentially, this is an automated system (replacing operators) that manages phone messages for various businesses. The system is computer run and the business owner has a touch-tone ID of sorts to retrieve the messages for the business. Calls can be forwarded to your

▲

Tip...

Smart Tip

For those of you who are tired of listening to that Valium-ized voice on your cell phone voice-mail system telling you that you have 5-new-messages. You might opt for SpinVox, SimulScribe, or CallWave, which are voice-recognition software systems that transcribe voice-mail messages into e-mail.

cell phone if you so choose or through a directory of options to various departments—which is unlikely in the early stages of your mail order business, since you're the manager of each department. Voice mail services can be found for anywhere from $5 to $25 a month depending on features and the anticipated volume of calls.

You can also spend upwards of $1,000, or even $2,000 to purchase your own voice mail system—this guarantees maximum efficiency and dedication to your business, since it's all yours. However, it is a costly upfront expense. More on making the decision later.

Your Business Card

Business cards and company stationery are as important to your mail order image as a well-answered phone. Even though your customers may see only a catalog or website or specially designed direct-mail piece, you'll still need stationery for your dealings with suppliers, vendors, manufacturers, and bankers. To help build that solid, established identity that will make other businesses eager to work with you, you'll need professional-quality letterhead, envelopes, and business cards.

You can purchase blank stationery, including business cards, and print everything up yourself inexpensively with a desktop publishing program. Or you can have a set of stationery and business cards printed for you at a copy center such as those found in Office Depot or Staples. Either way, you should allocate about $200.

Supplies

Don't forget about basic office supplies: pens, pencils, and paper clips, plus a stapler, a letter opener, tape, and those all-important printer cartridges. You'll also need blank paper for designing ads and catalogs and for printing out invoices, receipts, and return vouchers. If you figure that you're purchasing all of this brand-new for the business (as if you didn't have scads of pens and pencils floating around the house), you can write in about $250.

Shipping and Packaging Materials

Unless you are 100 percent drop shipping, you will also need shipping and packaging supplies. This is another startup category where you'll have to get down to the nitty-gritty on your own, depending on your particular products or services. If you're selling refrigerators, for instance, the cost of shipping and packaging supplies will be considerably higher than for someone who's selling dried flowers.

Keep in mind that we're talking not only boxes or crates but also that snappy bubble wrap, shredded paper to replace those environmentally uncouth Styrofoam peanuts, mailing labels, tissue paper, and—unless you are shipping refrigerators—gift wrap and ribbon.

For businesses dealing in merchandise more manageably sized than those you need to deliver with a forklift, figure about $500 for boxes, bubble wrap, and so forth.

The Mane Event

How much initial inventory should you purchase? You can use the results of your market research as a guideline. Let's say your surveys show that 90 percent of your respondents are really interested in the horse mane conditioner. You plan on an initial catalog mailing of 5,000. Now, let's say you get a 1 percent response. That means 50 people order from your catalog. And if 90 percent of them go for what seems to be the main event—the mane conditioner—you'll need to have at least 45 bottles on hand. If your cost for the conditioner is $3.15, then you'll probably want to pencil in 45 bottles plus about 15 extra in case a few customers order more than one (and also to have a few promotional bottles always on hand). Therefore, at $3.15 x 60, you will be spending $189, which might round off to $200 with shipping.

You'll also need to consider your supplier's order cycle. If you've got a six-week window between the time you place an order and the time the order arrives, what's a reasonable amount of time? It depends on your company's strategy. If part of your sales strategy is sending out merchandise within 48 hours of the customer's order, you're going to need fresh stock from your supplier a lot faster than if you've promised your customer delivery within four to six weeks. Now, make like a banker and scrutinize each of your products this way. Then add up your total cost for initial inventory.

In the event that you have a rapid turnover on a product, you may want to have more than one supplier for the same item. This way you can stagger your orders and always have products on hand.

All That Jazz

Other expenses you'll need to plug into your startup expense chart include business licenses, business insurance, legal advice, utility deposits, and all that jazz—the costs intrinsic to any company's beginning. You can use the worksheet to list your own startup costs. If you copy a couple of extra sheets, you can work up several options, compare them all, and decide which will be the best for you.

Sample Startup Costs

The following provides a range of startup costs from a home business office to renting an office environment in a commercial location.

Costs	
Rent (first two months)	$0 - 3,000
Office equipment & furniture	2,000-10,000
Mailbox rental	300
Market research	2,500
Credit card processing	150
Software	400
Licenses	150
Permits including bulk mail	250
Phones including voice mail (2 month's bills, includes installation and cell phone)	400
Utility deposits (includes increase in home bill)	150
Legal services	400-800
Accounting	200-500
Internet service	20
Website design & promotion (depending on whether or not you set up the site yourself)	500–4,000
Office supplies	250
Insurance	500-1,000
Shipping materials (depending on drop shipping)	150–500
Initial advertising and promotion (about 15% of your budget)	$ 1,450–4,380
Miscellaneous expenses	$500
Total Startup Costs	**$10,270–$29,250**

Add to this the cost of your initial inventory, which ranges dramatically depending upon what you are selling and the size and scope of your initial mailing. An initial inventory of $10,000 means you can anticipate spending roughly $20,000 to $40,000 depending on whether you are homebased or working from a commercial office.

Startup Costs Worksheet

Costs	
Rent	$
Office equipment & furniture	
Market research	
Credit card processing	
Software	
Licenses	
Permits including bulk mail	
Phones including voice mail (includes installation and cell phone)	
Utility deposits	
Legal services	
Accounting	
Internet service	
Website design & promotion (depending on whether or not you set up the site yourself)	
Office supplies	
Insurance	
Shipping materials	
Initial advertising and promotion (15% of your budget)	
Miscellaneous expenses	
Total Startup Costs	$

Figuring Profits

Now that we've determined how much it's going to cost you to get your business up and running, let's turn to the fun part—figuring out how much you can expect to make. Actually, you will want to start determining this when you select a product and start researching the cost of buying from vendors and determining the sales price to consumers—hence your markup. For example, if, in your research, you determine that the cost of a product from vendors, even in bulk, will only allow a small markup, you might stop before starting with that particular product. Markup, by the way, is the price you can charge above and beyond the price at which you bought the items. More on this in a moment. Keep in mind that in the beginning, your startup costs will eat away any potential profit. Most businesses typically operate in the red at the beginning. The key is to determine your ongoing costs, after starting up and then see how much profit you will make in time. Remember, it takes most businesses anywhere from two to five years to start making money. Since your startup costs, if you are homebased, should not be that high, you can recoup and start making money sooner than later.

Add In the Ad

Before you can actually begin to calculate your profits, you have to set up a pricing structure based on what is competitive in the market. You then have to factor in your means of reaching your audience (advertising and/or marketing). One of the constants in mail order is advertising. Unlike a startup cost that is a one-time item, such as buying that fancy desk for your home office, this will follow you with each item you sell.

Therefore, when you figure out your cost per order, you want to factor in advertising. Let's say you're selling gift boxes made of pure, decadent chocolate, and you've decided to place a small display ad in the regional issue of a national magazine. After haggling hot and heavy with the magazine's salesperson, you negotiate a cost of $1,100 and place your ad. It's a success! Five hundred chocolate lovers call and e-mail in frantic requests for your product. Now you can figure that your cost per order is $2.20.

Dollar Stretcher

Manufacturers or suppliers will typically give you a much better per-unit price when you order a larger amount of product. For example, you might pay $3.15 per bottle for up to 50 bottles of mane conditioner but only $2 per bottle if you purchase 100. On any fast-moving product, use this to your advantage unless the product will be out of date or "spoil" quickly (which may explain why there are few mail order milk companies out there).

Here's the formula you use:

Ad cost ÷ Orders received = Cost per order

Now plug in the numbers:

$1,100 ÷ 500 = $2.20

This is valuable information, but you still don't know how much to charge for those sinful chocolates. So let's go one step further—or back. Through terrific negotiating earlier in the game, you've convinced the manufacturer to give you the high-end chocolate boxes for $5 each. So we tack that cost onto your cost per order, using this formula:

Cost per order + Cost per item = Product cost

Now, lets plug in the numbers:

$2.20 + $5.00 = $7.20

Gee, now that box is more expensive. Not to worry! You now know exactly how much your product will cost you, and you can start playing with how much you'll charge your customers. If you apply a 400 percent markup (meaning you multiply your cost by 400 percent), you'll price each box at $28.80.

We'll bump that up to $28.95 because people feel more comfortable with retail prices at "something and 95 cents" than at an oddball number like 80 cents.

Now, if you sell one box to each of your 500 ad respondents, you'll gross $14,475, which we determined with this formula:

Product cost x Orders received = Gross profit

Using the numbers from our example:

$28.95 x 500 = $14,475

Doesn't sound gross at all, does it? But keep in mind that in accounting, "gross" means your profit before you deduct your expenses. (Remember, if you eat all the chocolate, you won't have any profit at all!)

Tweaking Figures

Where did we get the 400 percent markup? By tweaking our figures until we came up with a price that:

- Meets our customers' expectations of what a box made of gourmet chocolate should cost (too incredibly high or too implausibly low, and we lose our customers)
- Is comparable to competitors' prices for the same or similar goods (this is very important—if you out price your competitors, they will likely outsell you, therefore know competitive prices!)
- Adequately covers our expenses and provides a healthy profit

The norm in the mail order industry is a mark-up of 300 to 400 percent on each product to cover the cost of advertising, shipping, and product manufacture or purchase. This is an excellent rule of thumb, but keep in mind what we said in the previous paragraph. You have got to take a variety of factors into consideration before coming up with your final price. You can have customers pay for shipping, which takes that out of the equation. But again, look at competitors pricing—if they pay for shipping and it makes your product above competitive market prices, you'll be stuck with a lot of chocolate.

Also, keep in mind that if you are advertising a number of different items, you need to calculate what percent of the ad goes to each item. Therefore, if you are advertising chocolates in the same ad as gummy bears for the kids, and half of the ad is devoted to each product, you can divide the advertising cost in half. Then, you need to watch very carefully how each product does. The chocolates may be a hit, while the gummy bears fall flat. This way you will see which items are successful and which are not.

Catalogs, Too

If your advertising consists of printing catalogs with your merchandise, you need to factor that into your costs. Therefore, if you've spent $20,000 on 20,000 catalogs ($1.00 per catalog) plus a mailing cost of $400, which results in 2 percent sales, since this is a very targeted mailing, you would have 400 sales. You need to factor that in as well. That would be $6 per sale per item ($2,400 divided by 400 boxes) This is what separates the success stories from the also-rans. Can you print a 4-color catalog and make a profit? Can you print a two-color catalog and make a profit? These are decisions you will need to make. For the example in this section, we're using an ad, a website, and a brochure. Catalogs can bring in higher rates of return and are often held onto longer than advertisements or direct mail pieces. However, they can be costly, so you need to do the math carefully to determine how much profit you can make from a printed catalog and if it is worthwhile. Some mail order entrepreneurs still swear by the catalog; ask the folks at Victoria Secret. Others, especially newcomers, are more likely to go with the web version, which is much less expensive. They then place ads and have brochures at the ready for the fan of printed material and to draw potential buyers to the website.

Dollar Stretcher

Shoulder as many direct-mail campaign tasks as possible on your own. Delegate as many more as you can to knowledgeable (and willing) family members. The less you outsource, the more money you save! However, outsourcing can save you time, which is valuable, and provide expertise if someone is more capable at a specific task (such as bookkeeping) than you.

Incredible Discipline

You may have other expenses to figure into your cost per order. Let's say you've exercised incredible self-discipline and not eaten your way through your inventory. Then you decided to place a classified ad instead of a display ad. And you've decided to make it a two-step ad. (Remember, this means the customer calls or writes for your catalog or brochure.) Now you've got to calculate not only the cost of your ad but also the cost of printing your catalog or brochure and the cost of mailing that printed material.

Take a look at "How to Price a Chocolate Box" on page 84. Here we've taken 400 orders (which is not the same as the number of inquiries—you may have gotten 450 people to request a brochure, but only 400 of those have actually ordered). We've spent $200 on printing up an inexpensive brochure, and we've spent $166.50 on sending our material out first-class mail (37 cents each) to the 450 people who requested brochures. (You must have a minimum of 200 pieces of mail to take advantage of a bulk mail permit, and we've opted to send out brochures as fast as inquiries come in instead of waiting until we've got 200 saved up.)

Once again, we've arrived at an oddball final product cost of $19.56, so we've bumped up our price to $19.95. Our customers will perceive this as $19, and we'll perceive it as an extra $216 in profits.

You'll also have other expenses to account for (pardon the pun!). We'll discuss fixed and variable expenses in the next section, "Operating Expenses." These include costs like telephone bills, inventory, and supplies.

Blip in the Time Line

Now, you may have noticed a blip in the time line here. We're figuring how to price your product based on orders you haven't yet received. Heck, you haven't even placed your ad!

But you have done your market research (right?), and you've carefully calculated that you can expect at least the number of orders we've plugged into our computations. If you get more orders than your 400 minimum, your cost per ad goes down and your net profit goes up. (Conversely, of course, if you get less than 400 orders, your net profit goes down.)

Check out the Product Pricing Worksheet on page 85. Make copies so you can experiment with advertising costs, expected numbers of orders, and product prices.

Remember, be very conservative in your estimate of how many orders you will receive from an ad or a mailing. If, for example, you advertise in a magazine that reaches 10,000 (circulation) people with an interest in your product, such as *Chocolate Lovers Magazine*, estimate about 1 percent response, or 100 orders. If you've also done a mailing to another 10,000 people, whom you have targeted from market

How to Price a Chocolate Box

1. Figure your cost per order:

Add:	Cost of ad	$ 240.00
	Cost of printing	200.00
	Cost of mailing	166.50
Divide by:	Number of expected orders	400
Equals:	Cost per order	$ 1.52

2. Figure your total product cost:

Add:	Cost per order	$ 1.52
	Cost per Item	5.00
Equals:	Total product cost	$ 6.52

3. Figure your markup price:

Multiply:	Total product cost	$ 6.52
	Markup	300%
Equals:	Markup price	$ 19.56

4. Arrive at your final product cost:

You can use the last dollar amount in Step 3 above ($19.56) or round up to a more common retail price like $19.95.

5. Figure your gross profit for this advertisement:

Multiply:	Final product cost	$ 19.95
	Number of expected orders	400
Equals:	Gross profit	$ 7,980.00

Product Pricing Worksheet

1. Figure your cost per order:

Add:	Cost of ad	$_____
	Cost of printing	$_____
	Cost of mailing	$_____
Divide by:	Number of expected orders	_____
Equals:	Cost per order	$_____

2. Figure your total product cost:

Add:	Cost per order	$_____
	Cost per item	$_____
Equals:	Total product cost	$_____

3. Figure your markup price:

Multiply:	Product cost	$_____
	Markup (usually 300 to 400%)	_____
Equals:	Markup price	$_____

4. Arrive at your final product cost:

You can use the last dollar amount in Step 3 above ($_____) or round up to a more common retail price like $_____.

5. Figure your gross profit for this advertisement:

Multiply:	Final product cost	$_____
	Number of expected orders	
Equals:	Gross profit	$_____

▲

A Toll Order

Another of the many startup decisions you'll need to make is whether or not to provide customers with a toll-free number for ordering. Shoppers often expect to reach catalog sales companies through toll-free numbers, so if you choose not to offer this service, you could be cutting yourself off from potential sales. If you expect that most of your sales will be through standard mail or the internet, you might want to stick with your own area code, at least until you build up some working capital.

Look into various plans and pricing packages from companies offering toll free service and compare the rate per minute plus all fees that you will be billed before making your decision.

research including surveys, you can again add on 1 percent or another 100 people. While you may get a 2 percent response, and you should have a little more than the 1 percent of products available at your drop shippers or in your homebased inventory, you should always use very conservative numbers when making estimates. Over estimating, not only in mail order but also in retail stores, has led to disastrous results for many businesses.

Operating Expenses

We've gone over your startup expenses, your product costs, and your product pricing. Now we need to talk about operating expense, those other expenditures that make up the backbone of every mail order operation. These are the ongoing expenses you will include on a regular basis that, once subtracted from your projected gross profits, will tell the true tale of how much you'll be making.

We're going to assume once again that you'll be homebased, so we won't worry about expenses for office rent or utilities. We do, however, need to consider the following:

- Telephones
- Mailbox rental
- Voice mail (unless you use an answering machine)
- Postage (not for shipping your materials or merchandise but for paying bills and corresponding with manufacturers, suppliers, and customers)
- Web hosting

- Shipping and packaging materials
- Stationery and office supplies
- ISP (internet service provider)
- Loan repayment

Dial Toll-Free

As we discussed in the startup section of this chapter, high-quality phone service is a must in the mail order business. Most of the entrepreneurs we interviewed for this book offer customers a toll-free number.

If you anticipate a high volume of phone orders, you may opt for two or three phone lines. Between an 800 number, another phone line for your other business calls, your cell phone, and voice mail, you can pencil in at least $400 for monthly telephone expenses.

Mailbox Rental

If you're going to be homebased, you'll probably want to rent a box from a mail center like Mail Boxes Etc. so your company has the benefit of a street address but your customers, should they be in the neighborhood, don't pop in on you uninvited. Expect to pay $10 to $20 per month for this service.

Bloomin' Postage

Since you're adding your shipping charges to the cost of each order, you might think you can scribble out the "postage" line on your operating expenses worksheet. However, as with phone expenses, you'll have all the routine mailing costs every other business has—mailing payments to manufacturers, suppliers, advertising venues, and other creditors, as well as sending correspondence to customers and vendors. This correspondence include information dealing with returns, complaints, compliments, and other customer service issues, as well as the catalog requests you'll send to suppliers. (After all, they're dealing in mail order, too.)

As your company grows, your postage expenses will bloom, too, but for your first year of operation, you should be able to keep it to a minimum. If you figure on an average of two pieces of mail per day at the first-class rate of 41 cents per piece, you can pencil in about $20 to $30 per month.

Web Host

For your website, you'll need a web hosting service. While you can manipulate your site from your home/office computer, it takes a much, much larger server to handle

Smart Tip

Tip...

For information about mailing and shipping rates, visit the U.S. Postal Service online at www.usps.gov, or go directly to the "U.S. Postal Service Rate Calculators" page at www.usps.gov/business/calcs.htm.

the complexities of web traffic, and that's why you need a host. Some site designers provide hosting and updating services, Roy Fletcher of Fletcher Consulting explains, for about $150 to $600 per month—again depending on exactly what your needs are. If you feature specials on your website that change every other day, your costs will be in the higher range, but if you make only a couple of merchandise or price changes a month, you can expect to pay lower fees.

If you want strictly hosting, and you'll make any changes and additions (or deletions) yourself, you can expect to pay in the range of $10 to $75 per month for a hosting service.

Keep on Shippin'

As we explained in our startup costs section, your costs for shipping and packaging supplies will depend on your product line. Do your homework! Once you've determined your line, you can get estimates from companies that supply shipping and packaging materials.

Bagging Evidence

Once you've made your initial outlay for office supplies and stationery, your fixed expenses in this category should be fairly low. Staplers last a long time, you can reuse paper clips, and unless you're planning some violent activity with your letter opener and scissors for which the police will bag them as evidence, you shouldn't have to buy another set.

Your main expense will be paper: paper for your printer and fax machine, fine-quality paper for stationery, and envelopes. Be economically and environmentally smart: Reuse your printer paper. Instead of practicing hoop shots into the trash with all those versions of letters, price sheets, and other printed materials that you decided you didn't like, set the pages aside. When you've compiled a tidy stack, load them back into your printer and print on the blank side. Save your "good" paper for the final draft that goes out in the mail. You can expect to pay $4 to $6 per ream for multipurpose paper.

Paying the Piper

We've set aside a fixed expense called loan repayment. If you don't borrow money to start your business, you won't need to bother with this one. If, however, you finance your startup costs in any fashion, you'll need to repay the piper. Here's where you pencil in whatever your monthly fee is.

Putting It All Together

You may have many more expenses than the ones discussed here, such as: travel to trade shows or crafts fairs and hotel and meal expenses; employees and the worker's compensation and payroll costs that go with them; auto expenses; subscription fees for professional publications, and so on. We've put rent, utilities, and employee payroll costs on our worksheet because they're a common feature of financial projections and you should be familiar with them. If they won't apply to your business, of course, you won't need to worry about them.

Once you've added up your projected monthly operating expenses, you can subtract them from your projected gross monthly earnings and—voilà—you've got a projected net monthly income total.

Romancing the Bank

Now that you've done all the math, you can determine just how much you'll need to get your business up and running. And as a bonus, you can present all these beautifully executed figures to your potential lender to show that your business is a good risk and that you'll be able to repay the loan without difficulty. To make the best possible impression on your banker, assemble your startup materials in a professional-looking folder along with your desktop-published brochure or price list. You should also put together a business plan, which is detailed at the end of this chapter. The more businesslike your company looks, the better chance you have of not only getting startup funding, but getting loans as you need them in the future and attracting quality employees should you expand from a one person, or family, operation. A business plan is a blueprint of your business now and in the future.

You might want to consider financing through your bank or credit union. There are also private investors (sometimes called "Angels") who may be looking for a company in which to invest. They can be an excellent source of knowledge and offer better rates than a bank or credit union if they believe in you and your business plan. However, it is important to determine in advance how much the investor wants to be involved in the business—some want to simply provide financing and perhaps some advice, while others want to be more hands on. In any case, your projected startup cost and income figures are extremely important. Any lender will want to see all of this, neatly prepared and calculated. You'll also want to present all the statistics you can gather about the bright future of the mail order industry.

Projected Income and Operating Cost Worksheet

Projected Monthly Income	$
Projected Monthly Operating Expenses	
Rent	
Utilities	
Mailbox rental	
Phone service (including toll-free number)	
Voice mail	
Credit card processing (electronic terminal)	
Employee payroll	
Miscellaneous postage	
Insurance	
Web hosting	
Miscellaneous expenses (stationery/office supplies)	
Shipping & packing materials	
Loan repayment	
Internet service provider	
Total Operating Expenses	$
Projected Net Monthly Income	$

The Business Plan

There are books, articles, websites, and software packages designed to guide you through the steps of putting together a business plan, complete with templates to follow so you need not reinvent the wheel. The inclusion of some business plan basics here is designed to start you thinking about possibilities. Whether you are opening a small part-time mail order business or launching into a major full-time operation, a business plan is worthwhile for several reasons.

First, a business plan is a way of organizing, on paper, all of the pieces of the puzzle, from your equipment needs to your weekly schedule of ordering from vendors. It provides you with a "blueprint" so that no stone is left unturned. A business plan is also a way of showing other people, from friends and family to investors (who may also be friends and family) that you have crossed all the "t's" and dotted all the "i's" in the process of conceiving your mail order business. A well thought out business plan tells the story of your business and details your vision in such a way that it can help you generate the necessary funding. Finally, it is a living, breathing document that can not only serve as a benchmark, but also can be altered and expanded as your business grows and changes over the years.

Included in a typical business plan, will be the following:

1. *Executive Summary.* This is a short, broad, yet enticing summary of the business. What is the business all about and why are you excited about it? Although it usually appears first, this part is often written last, after you've put all the pieces in place.

2. *Products and/or Services.* Here you can include specific items that you will sell or services you will offer. Include products and services you expect to offer down the road. Explain their value and why they will be sought out by your customers.

3. *Industry analysis.* Here you will paint a picture of the overall mail order industry in which your business will be a player. From your research, talk about the "big picture." By learning about and writing a short report on the mail order business, you will learn more about the industry in which you are about to embark.

4. *Competitive analysis.* This is a biggie. Do your research carefully and know who you are up against. Be realistic and list the strengths and weaknesses of the most direct competitors. Then, see if you can provide something—a product, a service, faster shipping, better customer service—that your competitors do not provide. This can be your competitive edge.

5. *Marketing and Sales.* Now that you have plenty of details regarding what you will be selling, you need to explain how you will let the world know that you are in business. In this section, you discuss your plans for marketing and promoting your mail order business as well as how you will sell your products and services. Are you selling strictly over the internet? If so, how will people find your site? Where do you plan to advertise and why did you select such options? Are you printing and mailing out catalogs? This is where to define your plan of attack. If you are seeking funding, this is a very important section.

6. *Management.* Another important section is management, where you will let readers know who is running the business. Potential financial backers will be particularly interested in this information, since they want to know to whom they are lending their money. Include all of the key people involved in making this business happen. If this is a solo venture, use a bio that features applicable experiences in your career or personal life that applies to this venture.

7. *Operations.* From how often you will send catalogs, to how your drop shipping works, describe the overall operation of the business. Start with whom your vendors are and how much time you will need to allow for their orders to arrive, then go on to whether you are maintaining the inventory in your garage or a warehouse, then on to what you will post on your website, and so on. Talk, or in this case write, your way through a few days in the life of your mail order business. While writing this, you may find that you've left out some areas of importance, such as when do you order and re-order your shipping materials?

8. *Financial Pages, or Forms.* The goal here is, with help from your accountant or financial planner, to make realistic projections based on researching similar businesses. Here is where you show the math problems we demonstrated earlier and then project on a year's worth of profits and/or losses. Then show how long it will take to start showing a profit. Also include a cash and balance sheet for a year to show a cash flow. Hint: Be conservative in your financial estimates.

9. *Financial Requirement.* It is very important, if you are seeking funding, to include the amount of financing needed, based on the previous sections, to reach your goals. Again, be realistic; research costs carefully and also indicate how much money you anticipate putting into the business venture yourself. Hint: You stand a much greater chance of getting investors interested, or bankers to approve a loan, if you have invested your own money into a business.

Add to this supporting documentation, which will include various financial reports and you will have a business plan. Do not try to dazzle prospective readers with hype, but provide the real story of the business so that it is clear on paper how it will operate and when you anticipate making money.

Of course, this is just a very basic outline. Before you sit down and start writing, you will need to do research and look at other business plans in books or online to see the phrasing and style of such a business plan. If nothing else, thinking about each aspect of the plan will force you to start thinking about all of the many details that go into starting up a business. That's when it gets exciting, and a little scary, as you see all of the pieces come together.

Remember, just as we have mentioned that a realistic expectation on a mass mailing is 1 or 2 percent, you need to maintain that type of realistic approach all the way through a business plan. Investors can see through exaggerations, plus you don't want to fool yourself into thinking you will be making more money than is practical for a new business.

Signed, Sealed, Delivered:
Daily Operations

By this time, you're probably wondering what exactly a mail order maven does all day. Slit open envelopes full of checks, take a spin down to the bank, and then sit back and sip piña coladas? Spend all day with an ear pressed to the phone, scribbling down orders? Or sit on the floor surrounded by cardboard boxes and packing peanuts?

The answer is a combination of all of these—minus the piña coladas—plus a whole lot more. In this chapter, we'll take a peek into the mailbag of a direct marketer's daily life and explore the ins and outs of mail order operations.

The Juggler

One of the great joys of running a mail order business is that you can arrange your workload around any schedule you choose. Some mail order entrepreneurs work best in the early morning; others pace themselves throughout the day. The hours they spend and the time frames within which they structure those hours are as individual as each entrepreneur.

"Most of the time, I liken myself to a juggler with six balls in the air," says Beth H., the Connecticut gluten-free foods seller. "If I have more than six, I'm liable to drop one; if I have less than six, it's kind of boring."

A typical day for Beth includes meeting with the printer to go over the latest version of her catalog (for which she does all the graphics, copywriting, and layouts), rushing home to care for her puppies, and then spending an afternoon stint in her office. But that's not all. "I'll probably be here until about 3:50 P.M.," says the entrepreneurial mom, "then I have to pick up my son from school and get him back to my office for an hour for a snack and homework so he can go to swim team [practice].

"After that, we'll go home and have dinner. And I'll probably work a little tonight after I help with his homework. So that's the way my day goes. I start at home, usually spending an hour on the internet answering e-mail and working on projects I really have to concentrate on. Then at night, I'll test recipes... it's pretty wild."

Kate W., the on-the-go team logo merchandiser, runs her mail order business from her home in Kansas. "I start working early, and I work pretty late at night," the former bookkeeper says, "but I do like to be around for my family. We warehouse our inventory. I get around during the day to make sure the inventory is there, but I do my actual work from home.

"Most of the business we do is via an 800 number," Kate explains. "We have a service that handles all our calls. For cost reasons, I couldn't hire somebody to answer [the phone] 24 hours a day, seven days a week—which I believe you have to do in mail order. They take most of the calls, but I try and take the bulk when I can. They handle all of the incoming calls, and then everything is faxed to my office."

A typical day starts with Kate checking the fax machine to see what orders the call center has taken and forwarded to her. She enters everything into her computer, which generates sales invoices. Then she processes credit cards. Next, she fills the orders and gets them ready for shipping.

"After that," Kate says, "we'll go and pick up the mail. If there's something I really want to get out, we make a late-night run and go straight to the UPS distribution center. We'll run packages up there until 8 P.M. One of our policies is to turn orders around within 48 hours. Generally, unless it's really busy, we'll do it in 24.

"So first I do all the paperwork. As soon as it's done, I go fill all the orders and ship everything. Then I come back and start again. It's a long day sometimes.

"Last year for the holidays, we were shipping 25 to 30 packages a day. Again, that's just me, processing them in the morning and shipping them in the afternoon."

Don't worry, as we've said before, you can organize your day in whatever way suits you, your family, your lifestyle, and your energy level.

Kate admits that she doesn't actually have any days off but says there are ways to compensate. "If I know I need to be gone the next day, I'll get it all done the night before," she explains. "It's a whole lot more flexible when it's just you."

> **Tip...**
>
> ## Smart Tip
>
> To find knowledgeable advisors in the mail order business, you might check out SCORE (Service Corps of Retired Executives), billed as Counselors to America's Small Business. Some 10,500 volunteer counselors have more than 600 business skills. The SCORE volunteers are working or retired business owners, executives, and corporate leaders who share their wisdom and lessons learned in business. Visit their website at www.score.org and look for an expert in mail order in your area. It can be invaluable.

Three-Armed Skeleton

If you took an x-ray of any mail order company, you'd see three distinct arms:

- Sales and marketing
- Order processing and fulfillment
- General management and administration

In most startup companies, however, these three arms are all attached to one body—the owner's. As a mail order entrepreneur, you'll have days where you're not only using (or wishing you could use) a third arm but also wearing a dozen different hats: product development director, advertising campaign director, graphic designer, copywriter, and marketing manager. You'll also be in charge of (and sole employee in) the order processing, customer service, and fulfillment departments. This is all in addition, of course, to your administrative tasks as bookkeeper, accountant, file, and mailing list manager, and supplier liaison. As is the case with many successful entrepreneurs, you can hire someone to do those tasks that are cutting into too much of your day. If you're lucky a family member may help out, working for a good barter deal.

Most mail order mavens enjoy the bulk of the workload—and some of the above mentioned areas are not daily occurrences, such as designing the catalog. Important as it is, it is something you do when planning for the next catalog to be printed. Remember, if you've done your homework and chosen a specialty and a target market that you relish, then everything else is—if not always a snap—enjoyable. "I love what I do," says Patty from Minnesota, who enjoys the mail order business she launched from her years of party planning.

Mailing Lists

One of the mail order maven's key tasks is to get that catalog or other vehicle to its ultimate destination—the customer. Classified or display ads will reach their targets through whichever newspapers or magazines you place them in. Radio and TV spots will hone in on prospective customers through the broadcast venues in which they're placed. You do want to follow up and make sure the ads ran as specified. Get CDs from the tv/radio stations and tear sheets from the print ads.

But what about catalogs and direct-mail pieces? How do you get a catalog or direct-mail piece aimed at dog lovers in the mailboxes of puppy-philes and not those of cat fanciers, tropical fish fanatics, or professed pet haters?

You know the answer: through mailing lists, those Santa-sized rosters of names, addresses, and phone numbers. List brokers provide a means of finding mailing lists so that you need not compile your own. The savvy mail order maven not only knows this but also takes advantage of these lists to whisk catalogs straight into the hands of target customers.

List Seekers' Secrets

A good list broker has hundreds of lists of qualified buyers and can pull out just about any criteria or selects you're interested in: for instance, people who own dogs, earn over $50,000 per year, have high-school-aged children, and have purchased something by mail order within the past six months.

So if your catalog is aimed at dog lovers, the list broker can provide you with a mailing list compiled from dog magazine subscribers, kennel club members, and purchasers of other pet-related merchandise. And if your direct-mail piece is targeting ladies who would like church-themed children's clothing patterns, the list broker might pull your list from parochial-school parent associations, quilting club rosters, and church groups.

List brokers get their lists from virtually every wellspring you might imagine—magazine

> ### Smart Tip
> **Tip...**
> A *qualified buyer* is somebody with a reputation for having bought by mail order already, for demonstrating an interest in the area you've targeted, and for having the income to pay for your merchandise.

subscription lists, the customer lists of mail order businesses, club and organization membership rosters, professional and political association membership lists, financial ratings lists, school directories, and more. They're always on the lookout for new lists.

Mailing lists are big business in the direct-marketing world. Their costs can vary tremendously, depending on what sort of list you're renting and how many selects, or variables, you want. First, you'll need to decide whether you want a compiled list, made up, for example, of people who by age and income might be Hawaiian cruise prospects, or a response list, made up of people who have actually purchased Hawaiian cruises already—those qualified buyers we have mentioned.

> **Tip...**
>
> **Smart Tip**
>
> You can request an nth name selection for your list, which means you get every nth name, say every seventh or 10th, instead of every name from "A" through "D." This way, you get more of a cross section of names.

Because the compiled list is not as specific, it is cheaper. You can expect to pay an average of $50 per 1,000 names, according to Daren Cicchillo of Lighthouse List Company in Fort Lauderdale, Florida. The response list, on the other hand, may cost as much as $120 per 1,000 names, plus $5 to $10 extra for each select you choose (age, income, geographic region, etc.).

Business-to-business names can be even more expensive, Cicchillo says. Fewer people offer them, so they're harder to come by. Expect to pay $75 to $200 per 1,000 names for this type of list.

Most brokers will insist that you rent a minimum of 3,000 to 5,000 names. Why do we say "rent" instead of "buy"? Because the list broker who provides you the names can charge you each time you request another use. You're only allowed to use the names once—and brokers have ways of making sure you comply with this rule. That's the bonus on the broker's side. The plus on your side is that because the broker keeps the list, he or she is responsible for its care and maintenance. The list broker is the one who goes through and weeds out all the nixies (the return-to-sender names of people who've moved and left no forwarding address). The broker is also the one who compiles and recompiles the lists based on any criteria you specify.

Of course, where there is an easy solution (a list broker) there is always a catch. Many businesses end up with lists that are outdated, meaning many names and addresses are incorrect or phones have been disconnected. Others sell e-mail addresses obtained without the permit of the individuals, which means if you're sending e-mails, you are spamming, which is not only illegal but are automatically deleted by spam filters.

Therefore, you need to get some references for a list broker from satisfied clients who have used the list and gotten positive results. Remember, anyone can make up a list and rent it out. You want a list that is actually geared to the criteria you are seeking and a list that is current.

▲

Additional Profit Center

Of course, while you're renting lists from someone else, you can start compiling your own lists based on the customers you've already mailed to, breaking them down into those who have ordered, those who are still potentials, those who have ordered a certain dollar amount or are living in a particular region, or whatever suits your needs.

Then—and this is really key—you can rent your list to other direct marketers. The money you make from renting your list is a sort of gravy on top of the "real" earnings from your mail order sales and is referred to as an additional profit center. Of course you're a fool if you are renting it to direct competitors. Yes, you want to make money, but you don't want your closest competitors acing you out of business.

You can use the list broker as an intermediary, just as you would a real estate broker to rent or sell property. You can rent your list directly to other mail order companies without going through a broker, or you can swap lists with other mail order mavens.

A list broker usually charges about 20 percent of whatever you earn from renting your list. So if you charge $50 per 1,000 names and you rent 10,000 names to another company, you've made $500. You give the broker $100 and count the other $400 as profit.

How do you know the broker isn't going to give your hard-earned names to a company that's in direct competition with you? The industry has built in some fail-safes. One is that the broker isn't going to get very far with a reputation for selling out his customers. Another is that a good broker will ask the list renter for a sample of his or her mailing piece. If it's too competitive with yours, the prospective renter doesn't get the list.

You protect yourself from someone else stealing your list or using it for more than the one-time rental by salting, or seeding, it. You mix a few fictitious names and

Beverly Hills 90210

If you're selling products geared toward a specific socioeconomic group, you might identify a target ZIP code and make that one of your list criteria rather than just indicating the city. This way, you can be assured that those catalogs touting caviar in mother-of-pearl saucers, for instance, go to upper-crust neighborhoods. This is a good strategy in large metropolitan areas like Los Angeles and Atlanta, where Beverly Hills and Buckhead have their own high-falutin ZIP codes. In small towns with one zip, this tactic doesn't work.

addresses in with all the legitimate ones—addresses you know will come straight to you. How do you accomplish this? Rent a few post office boxes to use as your addresses. (Commercial mail centers like Mail Boxes Etc. will give you a post office box with a street address so it looks more like a residence, for added plausibility.) Or you can salt the list with the names and addresses of people who will be certain to report any received mail to you. (How about your mom? Moms love to help out with this kind of thing.) If you or one of your seeded addresses gets mail from a company that isn't supposed to be using the list, you can sue the business for damages. Since all of this is often more effort than it is worth, most mail order businesses do not rent out their lists except, perhaps, to other business owners they know and trust.

When you swap lists, you choose a buddy mail order firm, one whose interests are compatible with yours but not the same, say a company that sells dog food while you're selling dog health insurance. This way, they're not treading on your turf or vice versa, yet you can both feel fairly confident that the dog owners on both lists will be interested in both companies' products. Then you exchange lists, either as a one-use deal or as a permanent trade, and you—and your swap partner—get free names! And since list rental makes up about one-third of your mailing expenses (the other two-thirds are printing and postage), you've suddenly "found" money you can put to other uses.

Close Encounters

Your personal, exclusive mailing list, which you can rent to other companies, is one additional profit center. But there are more. And they, too, can add to your earnings without increasing your fixed overhead (like rent and utilities) or at least pay you enough to defer your mailing and postage costs. Give these profit centers a spin:

- *Piggyback products.* There are other mail order entrepreneurs out there who will gladly pay you to have their advertising materials or samples tucked in with your merchandise. This will save you a bundle in postage by bundling product offers together.

- *Add the advertising.* If you're mailing a newsletter, book, or other published information, other mail order mavens will pay to advertise within your printed copy. Likewise, sell advertising space on your website to companies hawking similar, but not competitive products. Just don't oversell or your site will lose the look and feel of your business. Exchanging links is another way of getting yourself on other sites.

Your best bet for both of these profit potentials is to find businesses compatible with your own target market. If you sell gifts and apparel for UFO enthusiasts, for example, your customers would probably love a brochure from a mail order bookstore specializing in books about close encounters of the alien kind. If your catalog caters to home brewers, you might include promotional material from a gourmet pretzel and popcorn company.

Keep in mind that these piggybacked products will reflect on your own company. Even though they have somebody else's name on them, your customers will associate the products with you and may even want to hold you accountable if they don't like what they get. You'll want to be sure your piggybacked products:

- Match the type of merchandise you're selling
- Meet your own high quality standards
- Increase your customers' enthusiasm for your products

Thanks for Calling!

You've placed your ads or media spots or purchased your mailing list and sent out your catalog or other materials. Now it goes without saying that a significant part of your day will be taken up with order processing. This is good! It means your customers have found you and you're making money. But it also means that you—and your order takers—need to put your brightest face forward at all times, especially when you're taking orders over the telephone. Since your customers' visits are all virtual, their first—and lasting—impression of your company will be the one made by that voice on the other end.

Some mail order entrepreneurs like to field all calls in-house so they have seat-of-the-pants control of their order processing. Others delegate the ordering process to an outside service. Unless you like being awakened by 3 A.M. phone calls or you plan never to sleep again, using an outside service is probably your best bet, especially if you're starting out as a one-person operation and you want to offer 24-hour availability. This is also a good option if you're going to start out part-time. The service can take orders while you're at your day job, and then you can fill them when you get home.

Bright Idea

When you take your customers' orders, ask for their birth dates and keep track of them. Then, as each customer's birthday rolls around, send a birthday card and a small freebie. It's a great way to help customers remember you!

Whether you answer your phones yourself or have someone do it for you, what you or your customer representatives say and how you, or they, say it can make the difference between a sale and a changed-mind, and between a ho-hum one time customer and a customer for life. A lackluster, uninformed or hurried response can spell see-ya-later to a sale. Make sure that everybody who answers you phones is familiar with your products or services and has enthusiasm for them and understands the importance of being professional and polite.

Scenario for Success

You'll want to carefully think through the way your order phone line is answered, basing your responses on your merchandise or service and your company's philosophy. To get you started, you can use the following "script" as a scenario for phone order success.

1. *Greetings!* Even if you've spent a sleepless night cleaning up after a sick child or pet (or both), you should always answer the phone in a cheerful, friendly tone. Be sure to give your company's name. Aim for something like: "Books by Jove. This is Maria. How can I help you today?"

2. *The key code, please.* If the caller wants to place an order, ask for the key code or source code, if you have one, from the catalog or order card. This code, which is printed somewhere on your sales material, tells you what ad, sales letter, or catalog the customer is responding to. A key code like MWC02, for instance, might indicate that the catalog was your Christmas 2006 version mailed to customers in the Midwest.

3. *Product verification.* Verify what your customer is ordering. When the customer gives you the item number for the product, you can say something like, "That's the set of six holiday bookmarks." Make sure your customer agrees, so you know you're both talking about the same item.

4. *Quantity, size, and color.* Find out how many of the product the customer wants. Then ask for size and color preferences—assuming, of course, that these questions apply to the product. Repeat this information back and let the customer confirm it.

5. *Ad identification.* Ask how the customer learned about your company. If it was through an advertisement, ask where the person saw it. Take notes. This will help you in future marketing efforts.

Checking It Twice

Always make accurate order entry a priority. Double-check names, addresses, and phone numbers with your customers and take the time to enter them properly. All it takes is one wrong digit to land that order several states away from its intended recipient.

Such an error can cost you hundreds of dollars in terms of customer dissatisfaction, merchandise replacement, and reshipping fees.

6. *Is there anything else you are interested in purchasing today?* Don't assume the order is over. Also, don't forget to cross-sell and up-sell a hot new product—but don't over sell or you can turn customers off by being pushy.

7. *Customer ID.* Ask for your customer's name, address, and phone number. Read it back to make sure you've got it correct—be very careful about spelling since names can be spelled in various ways, such as Green or Greene. If you're shipping by UPS or FedEx, you'll need to make sure customers provide a physical street address like 123 Main Street. Most shipping services can't deliver to a post office box.

   Remember, too, that people like to order products as gifts and have the merchandise shipped directly to the gift recipient. Be sure to ask if the shipping address differs from the billing address. You might also ask if the giver would like a gift card enclosed—a terrific personalized touch!

8. *Payment.* Phone orders are typically paid for by credit card. Find out whether your customer is paying by Visa, MasterCard, American Express, or Discover (or whichever cards you plan to accept). Then take the account number and the expiration date. Read it back to make sure it was taken down correctly.

9. *Shipping.* Let your customer know if there are any shipping costs before completing the transaction, then let them know when the order will be shipped and about how long it will take to arrive.

10. *One more time.* Repeat everything back to your customer one more time, so you're both sure it's accurate.

11. *Thank you!* Be sure to thank your customer for ordering from you and invite him or her to call back any time you can be of assistance in the future. Wish the person a pleasant day. You want your customer to feel good about having called your company and look forward to placing another order. Remember, the repeat customer is where you earn your money!

The Captive Audience

There's more to taking an order by phone than meets the ear. Once your customer has displayed interest by taking the initiative to call you, you've got a semi-captive audience. Now is an excellent time to increase your sales.

- *Up-sell.* Offer your customer a special on two or more products of the same type. For example, if the person is ordering one box of Decadence Chocolates, offer a second box for 10 percent off (or whatever works for you). If a holiday's in the offing, suggest that a box of Decadence Chocolates makes a memorable gift. (Or if customers tell you the first box is being purchased as a gift, tell them they owe themselves a box, too!)

- *Cross-sell.* Offer customers a product related to the one they have just ordered. For customers who order the Decadence Chocolates, suggest a canister of

Amaretto Almond Dream Coffee to go with it. You can say something like (assuming, of course, that it's true), "We get a lot of orders for the coffee because it goes so well with the chocolates," or, "All of us here in our shop go nuts over the Decadence and Amaretto Almond Dream combo; it's our favorite coffee break treat."

The idea here is to help your customer on to an increased order. It's the same concept as the salesperson in the exclusive clothing store who suggests that snazzy tie or scarf or belt to go with the suit you're trying on. Your customer will appreciate it. After all, who doesn't like a little personalized service?

Talking Football

Answering the telephone can be more than just a method of taking orders. It can become a valuable marketing tool.

"We listen to our customers a lot," Kate W. says. "I handle the phones often. This is good and bad, because when I take the phones, first [my customers and I] talk about their [team] room—because almost everybody has one—and they tell you everything that's in there. Then you have to talk about football and what happened in the last game. And then you get to the order.

"So it costs me more to take the calls, but it is fun and I keep that one-on-one communication with the customers. They tell me all the time what they want. If we don't have it, we try to find it. This year it helped us a lot. We selected some of the products based on what they told us. They'll tell us, 'We couldn't find this anywhere,' and that's how we know what to buy.

"If I wasn't handling the calls at all, I wouldn't have a clue what they're telling my order representatives. But because I need to know that right now, and I want them to know there is a Kate out there who wrote the letter in the front of the catalog, I try to take as many calls as I can."

The Game Plan

The mail order maven's day consists of more than answering the phone. There's also processing the mail and opening all those fascinating envelopes full of customers' orders and payments. This may sound like a no-brainer operation, but, like taking phone orders, it requires organization and attention to detail. And, like taking phone orders, it's something for which you should have a game plan mapped out.

Why? Because turnaround is everything. Today's customers, used to life in the fast lane, expect speedy service. So the faster you process their orders and get the merchandise delivered, the happier your customers will be.

▲

Smart Tip

Tip...

If you are someone who does not stick with diets or other such plans and doubt that you will back up your own data on a regular basis, then do a search on Google, Yahoo, or your favorite search engine for Data Recovery. There are numerous places that can store data electronically for you. You probably don't need anything elaborate, as long as your data is backed up off site.

There are some really excellent mail order software packages on the market (see our Appendix for software information), and we strongly suggest you purchase one. For the price of a newbie-level program (as little as $299), you get far more than your money's worth. These programs can track your customers and your advertising by key codes, advertising venues, and dollars garnered (which means they do some of the testing calculations for you). They can process credit cards and keep track of shipping, inventory, and sales taxes—all the things that can get really messy and take hours of time when you do them by hand, time you could be spending on other tasks.

E-mails

Much of your business today will be via e-mail or online order forms. The key here is to once again process the order smoothly and in a timely fashion. Make sure your order form is easy to use and contains the pertinent information and little else. While it's nice to get additional information about your customers, don't make it required or they will stop somewhere along the endless list of questions. It is also important that your order form does not trick consumers in any manner—do not add in anything that must be deleted for them NOT to receive it. That is illegal and will destroy a good reputation. In your haste to sell more, don't end up losing the customer by trickery.

If e-mails come in requesting catalogs or other information, respond within 24-hours or you'll lose the possible sale. Let customers know that you have received their e-mail or their order form with a confirmation that includes the pertinent information, including when the items will be shipped.

Once orders are actually shipped, the customer should get an e-mail letting them know that the item or items were shipped. If there will be a delay, let them know this, too. If it is a lengthy delay, offer them 10 percent off their next purchase or some such discount. Keep in mind there are legal parameters if a delay will be extensively long. If all goes well, as it should most of the time, you can send a follow-up a week after the item should have arrived, asking if they were satisfied with their purchase and offering them an opportunity to receive your newsletter or e-mail blasts when new products come out. Also, thank them for doing business with you—being polite is a marvelous way to maintain steady customers. You can also promote piggyback items such as accessories to that which they have purchased.

Into the Bank

Take a look at the following scenario, which is based on the fact that you've taken our advice and purchased mail order software. Again, you may want to do a lot of this the hard way, with ledgers and spreadsheets, and if you do, that's OK—at least until your business grows to the point where it's no longer feasible.

Your mail- and order-handling strategies will differ slightly from this scenario, depending on your lifestyle. (That's one of the perks of running your own business!) But the following guidelines will get you going:

- *Open and sort your mail.* You're going to get a lot of it! Yes, you'll have customer orders, but you will also have bills, inquiries, returns, solicitations, and trade

The Master List

While you're tallying orders, you should put your customer information into your computerized database. This will give you instant access to your customers' names, addresses, telephone numbers, and order information. If they've filled out any demographic information on the product reply card you've cleverly incorporated—such as age, income, and interests—you can add it in. Remember, all this stuff, including the all-important clue of how your customer found you (display ad, direct-mail piece, etc.), is vital. You absolutely, positively must have a master list of all your customers. Each time someone new places an order, his or her name and information goes on the list. This is how you build your own mailing list, the one you'll use over and over again. Also, it is very important—make that imperative—that you back up this mailing list. There are companies that back up your data for you and keep it on their servers in the event you need to recover data. However, if you can make it a hard and fast rule to download the database to a CD every Friday and take that CD to a safety deposit box, you'll be potentially saving your business from ruin. Computers act up now and then and you do not want to risk losing everything because of a computer meltdown. Another reason to find a secure (off-site) location for your important customer data is in case your home or business office is hit by fire or any type of natural disaster. This way your business won't disappear. For victims of Hurricane Katrina, backup data helped some businesses get back on their feet and continue in the months after the disaster, while other businesses were completely destroyed because their data was lost forever. Don't underestimate the need for backing up your data and being able to recover it at a later date... it's crucial in the modern high-tech world.

publications—not necessarily in that order. You should have a designated place for each mail breed: a box or file or drawer. Just make sure you don't stash things where they'll never see the light of day again, or you will forget they ever existed.

- *Sort again.* Now you'll want to sort your customer orders by payment type, separating the credit cards from the checks from the money orders. Place any faxed or e-mailed orders in the proper stack.

- *Enter info into the computer.* Enter customer and order information for all credit card payments into your software program. Don't forget to enter the key code—remember, this is how you track the success of your advertising campaigns. (See "Key Code Roundup" in Chapter 10 for more details.)

- *Decide how you will handle checks.* There are two schools of thought on this. Some mail order mavens insist on waiting until checks have cleared before mailing out merchandise. Others, operating on good faith, send out the product as soon as they receive the order. Some mail order entrepreneurs have been burned by bounced checks. In one case, the buyer intentionally sent a check for $500 for a $300 software program. The business owner sent a $200 check back for the overpayment. When the $500 check bounced, not only was the business owner out the software, but he was now out $300 plus the $200 that he had sent back. It's a con game and one that can get you, if you operate too much on good faith.

You'll have to decide for yourself how to handle this issue, based on the feedback you get from others in your target industry, the cost of your merchandise, and your own faith in your fellow humans. If you decide to wait until the checks clear, put them in a pending file—again, one where you won't lose track of them. If you go ahead and ship, enter the checks on your bank deposit slip and then enter the orders in your computer. The customary waiting period for checks to clear—especially if they are out-of-state checks—is about 5-7 business days. If you haven't received a returned item slip from the bank by that time, you can assume they're OK. Let customers know the policy on checks immediately so they are not anxious when they don't get their products quickly—post it clearly wherever you list payment options.

- *Dealing with money orders.* These are easy. Since money orders are basically the same as cash, you don't need to worry about getting them authorized or cleared. Enter them on your deposit slip and then enter the orders in your computer.

- *Make deposits regularly.* Tally up your bank deposit slip, slide it along with the day's checks and money orders into that snazzy vinyl pouch the bank gives you when you open your account, and make that deposit.

- *Credit cards are easy.* Your credit card charges are automatically entered into your bank account electronically through your computer's software.

Fulfillment

Fulfillment in mail order lingo means getting orders in customers' hands—fulfilling their wishes. As we've explained, the faster you fulfill, the more dedicated your customers will be. If you're the type of person who can't be torn away from the wrapping paper and ribbons at gift-giving times, then every day for you will be Holiday Central. If you're the other type, one who'd just as soon give that gift in a brown paper bag, read up anyway because this is an important part of your daily operations.

You'll need to create an invoice, or packing slip, a receipt, and a label for each package. If you're clever, you can make an all-in-one packing slip and receipt. Each one should show:

- Billing and shipping addresses
- Date your customer placed the order
- Date you shipped the order
- Order number
- Phone number or e-mail address from which the order was placed
- Name or description of each product
- Quantity, size, and color, if applicable
- Price of each product
- Shipping cost
- Total cost, including shipping, for all products in package
- Method of payment (credit card, check, money order, etc.)
- Your thanks (This is important!)
- Your return form, which includes your return policy (This should be printed on the other side of your packing slip.)

Check out the sample packing slip/receipt and return form on pages 108 and 109. You will, of course, keep a copy of this form for your files. It will give you just about all the information you'll need if you, your customer, or your accountant has a question. The only thing you may need to refer to separately will be a credit card number, and you'll have that on your credit card receipt.

You can design and print a similar form with a desktop publishing program on your computer, have one made up at a local printer, or let your mail order software do it for you.

Smart Tip

If your merchandise can't go out to the customer right away, send a postcard indicating that you've received the order and are processing it. This builds good customer relations and keeps your customer from worrying that you never got the order.

Packing Slip/Receipt

Chocoholic Central

123 Cocoa Court
Truffle Bay, FL 30000
Toll-Free (800) 555-4000
Fax (305) 555-4242
Internet Orders: www.ChocoholicCentral.com

Bill to: Ship to:

    Charlie Coffee   Cindy Coffee
    458 Cafe Circle   17 Latte Lane
    Cookieville, IL 60000 USA   Port Indulgence, TX 70000

Your order of October 11, 2002 (order no. 101155579) from (312) 555-8214, shipped October 12, 2002

Qty.	Description	Product No.	Our Great Price	Total
1	Decadence Chocolate Assortment	12651	29.00	29.00
1	Almond Amaretto Dream Coffee, 1 Lb Canister	12656	12.00	12.00
2	Chocoholic Central Coffee Mug	11175	7.50	15.00
1	Chocoholic Central T-Shirt, Size Sml	211822	14.00	14.00
			Subtotal	70.00
			Shipping & Handling	9.90
			Order Total	79.90
			Paid via MasterCard	79.90
			Balance Due	0.00

**Thanks for shopping *Chocoholic Central.* Please call on us again soon.
And may all your dreams be sweet!**

Return Form

Chocoholic Central

Our Return Policy:

You may return any product in its original condition at any time for a full refund of the merchandise cost. We can only refund shipping costs if the return is a result of our error. Just fill out the return information on this packing slip and include it with your return. Please wrap the package securely. Send it to:

> Chocoholic Central
> Returns Department
> 123 Cocoa Court
> Truffle Bay, FL 30000 USA

For your protection, please use UPS or Insured Parcel Post.

Reason for Return:

_____

_____

_____

_____

_____

_____

_____

Questions, Suggestions, or Problems?

If you have any questions about this order or any Chocoholic Central product, please contact us by phone at (800) 555-4000, fax at (305) 555-4242 or e-mail at orders@ChocoholicCentral.com.

Thanks for shopping *Chocoholic Central.* Please call on us again soon.
And may all your dreams be sweet!

(Some programs will generate a packing slip/receipt and shipping label in one smooth move.) Or you can purchase invoice/receipt forms from an office supply store. Go for the ones that come in duplicate: One copy goes to the customer, and one copy goes into your files for inventory and accounting purposes.

How often do you wear your fulfillment cap? It all depends on your sales volume. Most mail order mavens are proud of their quick turnaround and take pains to ship packages within 24 hours of order placement. If this is you—and it should be—you'll probably be shipping every day.

Fulfillment Houses

If you love the product development and advertising aspects of mail order, but you're all thumbs when it comes to taping packages, you might consider using a fulfillment house. This is an outsource company that does everything from packing and shipping those orders to answering your phones, processing customer credit card payments, and depositing your money in the bank for you. Some fulfillment houses will also manage your mailing lists, print your materials, and mail them out.

The big plus here, of course, is that instead of wearing all those hats at once, you've got somebody else to take over a portion of the work, leaving you to concentrate on the creative genius and number crunching stuff. The big minus is that you're no longer in complete control. You can't know exactly how the fulfillment house's representatives are handling your customers at all times, and you miss all the customer feedback that can be so crucial when you're first starting out.

Still, a solid relationship with a good fulfillment house can solve a lot of headaches. You'll want to carefully screen the company, which includes screening their customer service people to make sure they are compatible with your company's philosophy.

Many mail order entrepreneurs use fulfillment houses today. It's advantageous to get references and to talk to other mail order mavens about houses that they have used and why they stuck with one of the others. A fulfillment house that does not meet your needs will damage your business and your reputation, so it is essential that you find such a house (or houses) that you can depend on. There are also restrictions that some fulfillment houses will put on you. For example, Patty, from www.instantphotoframes.com has a fulfillment house handling one of the many products on her website that will only do orders of $25 or more. Therefore, she had to make a choice whether to no longer use that fulfillment house, or to mark next to that product that orders must be for $25 or more. She chose the latter. Review the restrictions of the fulfillment house before signing any contract—also have your attorney look over any agreements.

The best thing to do is to shop around, compare prices at several fulfillment houses, and decide with which owners you feel you can establish a good rapport—

Things to Ask a Fulfillment House

Set up fees: What is the cost for setting up to acquire and stock your products?

Order Processing Fees: What is the cost per order? Is there a flat fee for x number of orders or a fee per order processed?

Order Processing Minimums: Are there minimum amounts for shipping and what are these amounts? This will likely be a greater issue if you are selling low-cost items.

Return Processing and Re-Stocking Fees: Find out what you are charged when a customer returns the merchandise and how this process will be handled. Are there re-stocking fees?

Storage Fees: This is typically a monthly fee based on your space in the warehouse. You may be charged per pallet, per cubic foot, or in some other manner—ask.

Fees to receive merchandise: Look for charges to check shipments into the facility, verify the box count, and look for visible damage.

Product Assembly: A fulfillment house can often assemble your product or kit for you, charging you on an hourly basis or a time-costed per-piece basis.

Growth Capacity: How much can the fulfillment house handle in the event your business takes off and goes from 200 orders per month to 20,000?

References: Can they give you some names of satisfied customers?

Record Keeping and Maintaining Data: How do they keep track of orders processed and how are you apprised of orders that have been shipped? This is typically handled by computer software nowadays.

Minimum Contract Period: If you decide to go with them, sign for a short term period at first in case you are not selling as much as you had hoped or are not satisfied with the fulfillment house.

remember this is a very important part of your business and an open line of communication is essential.

The Professional Look

If you're handling your own orders but outsourcing your packaging and shipping operation, you can automate fulfillment into a system where your orders go to the fulfillment house once a day, once every few days, or once a week. You tally requests for

---

Your Back End

One key to making multiple sales in mail order is developing a good back end. Yes, it sounds like some sort of hard-body weightlifting regimen, but your back end really is your list of repeat customers. Your prospects, those you've mailed material to but who have not yet bought anything, are called your front end.

So how do you develop that firm back end? By developing follow-up merchandise to sell to your first-time buyers. People who have an interest in one product will generally be just as fired up over the next one and the one after that, provided they're all in the same category.

The home handyman who buys that set of all-occasion screwdrivers, for example, will also want the holiday hammer collection, the drill bit of the month, and the wrist-saver wrench. (Not to mention the build-it-yourself books, the tool box assortment, and the carpenter's apron.)

And there's your back end!

---

particular products on a large tracking sheet and attach shipping labels preprinted with your customers' addresses. Then you affix a code number to each label, indicating which product goes to which customer. This way, the center knows not only how many of each product it needs, but also who receives what. The fulfillment house's turnaround is faster, and this makes your company look all the more professional.

Working with Suppliers

Part of your daily routine will involve working with suppliers, since most mail order businesses deal in tangible goods that have to come from somewhere. If you're selling services or information from your own mind, such as recipes, how-to guides, or newsletters, your inventory is on tap: It basically consists of the knowledge you put on paper for your customers to access. But if you're selling gifts, books, tools, or shampoo, you've got to buy them so you can resell them. This brings us to suppliers.

Shopping Around!

Depending on your inventory selection, you may need anywhere from a handful of suppliers to several dozen. Sometimes they'll contact you through their sales representatives. More often, particularly when you're in the startup phase, you'll have to locate them through trade shows, trade journals, wholesale showrooms, surfing the internet, and attending conventions, as well as some less traditional sources. You'll also find vendors by belonging to mail order associations, reading industry magazines, and becoming active in the industry. Meeting other people in the field can certainly help you network. Follow along as we take a spin through the realm of mail order suppliers:

> **Bright Idea**
>
> Craftspeople and artisans often have mailing lists of their own. When you take them on as suppliers, ask if you can use (or reasonably rent) their lists. Or how about a list exchange? Their customers will see their wares showcased in a new light—your catalog—and you'll get new names.

- *Manufacturers.* Most mail order mavens buy through manufacturers' sales reps or through independent sales reps who handle the wares of several different companies. Prices are usually lowest from these sources, unless your location makes freight shipment a problem. Larger cities like Los Angeles, Chicago, and New York have permanent gift marts that house manufacturers' showrooms. As a mail order entrepreneur, you can shop 'til you drop any time during business hours. Just make sure you have your business cards and wholesale license with you to verify your status as a retailer.

- *Distributors.* Also known as wholesalers, brokers, or jobbers, these people use quantity discounts to buy from two or more manufacturers and then warehouse the goods for sale to retailers. Although their prices are higher than the manufacturer's would be, they can supply you with smaller orders from a variety of sources. (Some manufacturers won't break case lots to fill small orders.) This is a great way to diversify.

- *Independent craftspeople.* These people will often offer exclusive distribution of one-of-a-kind creations when you attend gift fairs or trade shows. While they can supply some of your best buys, the problem is that they are typically limited in terms of quantity.

- *Import sources.* Mail order mavens often buy foreign goods from a domestic import wholesaler. Some mavens travel abroad at least once a year in search of new and exciting goods. Research the import/export business carefully (and the laws) before going this route. One positive of buying overseas products is that they can be inexpensive. The downside is that shipping can be slow. Make sure you are working with a reliable wholesaler when dealing with overseas products.

- *Trade shows.* In most industries, major suppliers display their wares at seasonal trade shows in an attempt to out-wow each other and attract retailers with new products. Although you can buy all year long from the sources we've already listed, the trade show is typically the shindig of the year, the main event in every retailer's buying cycle. Almost every major city hosts one or more trade shows that may be relevant to your mail order business. Contact your local chamber of commerce or convention bureau for the shows in your city or state. If there is a major convention center at which these events are usually held, contact them as well for a schedule. There are industry associations, such as the National Mail Order Association (www.nmoa.org), that can help you find local trade shows.

You can also check out the Tradeshow Week Data Book, which is published annually and lists important data on all trade shows in the United States. For details about this book or information on other Tradeshow Week publications and resources, visit www.tradeshowweek.com.

- *Closeout sales.* When manufacturers go out of business, they stop a production line, which results in closeout sales that savvy retailers take advantage of. You can buy closeout lots at great savings that you can pass on to your customers. You can often purchase thousands of items for a fraction of a dollar apiece—and sometimes you can purchase the dies and molds, too, so you can start your own production line if you like. This is a terrific way to obtain proprietary or ownership rights to a product. Sources for locating closeouts include newspaper classifieds, going-out-of-business sales, and government auctions. You can also buy from wholesalers, who can offer you credit. But make sure you don't pay so much for the materials or the new manufacturing that you lose your profit margin!

- *Business and trade magazines.* Make it a point to read and research magazines in your target market—this is where lots of new products are advertised. If you're specializing in giftware, for instance, look in the classified sections of giftware magazines, where suppliers, importers, and manufacturers advertise. If you're not sure which magazines cover your industry, ask your local librarian, surf the internet, or check with the National Mail Order Association (www.nmoa.org).

- *Drop-shippers.* As you know, a drop-shipper sends out its products for you when you receive an order. For instance, you run an ad in a magazine for a $10 garden spade. When you receive an order from a customer, you send $5 (or whatever percentage has been agreed on) to the drop-shipper, along with the name and address of your customer. The supplier then sends the spade to the customer. It's not all that easy to find a supplier willing to drop-ship. You'll probably pay more for the product, and you won't get the same profits as if you keep the spades in inventory at your own facility. But if you can find someone willing to make this arrangement with you, it leaves you free to put your money where it will earn you the most—in advertising and marketing, instead of tied up in inventory.

- *Catalog houses.* The catalog house is an attractive proposition. It's also an extremely risky one that you should probably pass right by. A catalog house sells you preprinted catalogs filled with items it will drop-ship to your customers, with your company name imprinted on each catalog and order form. This seems good: You forgo the heavy expenses of catalog preparation and printing, as well as the cost of maintaining inventory. You mail the catalogs to prospective buyers, and when the orders and payments come in, you send those orders—and up to 50 percent of the retail price, plus shipping—to the catalog house, which then drop-ships the merchandise to your customer. The problem here is that by the time you pay for the mailing list (which is how you get your first customers), the shipping, and half the merchandise revenue, you don't have enough left to call an income. You don't have that all-important niche in the market—you're "copying" somebody else's success. Plus you don't always know where the catalog is being mailed—or when.

While you're shopping for suppliers, remember that as a mail order entrepreneur you're only as good as your merchandise. Reliable suppliers will steer you toward hot-selling items, which—if everything works the way it should—will increase your sales. But don't let anybody pressure you into a sale. Analyze all advice before making a purchase.

When all your supplier searching pays off and you're able to offer an exclusive item, one that only you are contracted to sell, make sure your catalog or advertising copy tells your customers so. They'll get the thrill of getting a "your company" original, and they won't have to worry that they might find that item for less money somewhere else.

Zero In on Merchandise

Adding new products is a terrific way to keep your customers coming back—and buying. But how do you decide what new goodies to offer?

Kate W., the Midwest team-logo merchandiser, took a careful look at what her customers wanted and then built up her merchandise line accordingly. "We decided that, instead of going with products that are available to someone in Florida or California, we would offer the things that are not so accessible, the novelties," says Kate. "That's really what we've built our business on: the gifts, collectibles, and memorabilia. In our first year, that's all we had in the catalog.

"This year, in an effort to expand the line, and because we got so many requests, we started to add a little bit of apparel. Again, I had a niche market that I felt was not being adequately served—and that's women's apparel. You can find men's stuff everywhere. But where can you find a cute little polo for a gal?

"They're starting to make them, but over the years, women just wore solid reds or something like that because they didn't have the cute stuff men had. So we do a whole line of stuff exclusively for women, made for them and cut for them. And that's done very well this year. We always try to zero in on our market and then be very specific with it," Kate says. "We try to [come up with] exclusive things, design them ourselves and have someone make them for us."

Once you get started in the business, most mail order entrepreneurs agree that you begin to develop a keen eye for products that fit overall concept. Furthermore, as you delve deeper into researching and evaluating products—which are typically something you have an interest in already, you will be better able to differentiate between quality and crap—and determine all levels in-between. If you walk through a trade show with a mail order veteran, you'll be amazed at how much he or she can tell you about the various products. It's a great experience.

Customer Service

No matter how smoothly your company is run, you're going to get some customers who complain. It's human nature. Your job is to

- Be as perfect as possible so you get as few complaints as possible.
- Treat complainers with tact and understanding.
- Remember that the customer is always right—even if you don't agree.

Most people just want to vent. Let them tell you what they're unhappy about, and they're fine—as long as you let them know that you understand the problem and you plan to resolve it. Sooner or later, of course, you'll run into the rare crank who refuses to be mollified. This will test your patience and your nerves, but it's only a test. Don't

---

Customer Appreciation

The other side of the customer service coin is customer relations. The better relationship you have with your customers, the more likely they are to buy from you on a regular basis.

Kate W. holds an annual customer appreciation promotion, a special catalog mailed exclusively to people who have purchased from her the previous year. She puts together selected merchandise and offers it in the spring, her slow season, at great prices.

This is smart business. Kate's promotion thanks customers in a splashy manner that encourages repeat sales and customer loyalty, while bringing in revenues during an otherwise lackadaisical season.

take those harsh words to heart. Eventually, you will also run into the rare creep who's trying to test your policies by intimidating you into an unfair return or refund. Don't let yourself be railroaded. As long as your policies are clearly spelled out and meet FTC guidelines, you're in the right. But use your own judgment. Some people will be customers for life if you give in on something a little out of the ordinary. It's up to you.

Being polite and understanding is always the best manner of maintaining customers, in all businesses, not only mail order. Plus it doesn't cost anything to be polite.

Of course you do need to set up policies and have them in writing, even while being flexible with such policies. If, for example, a regular customer has a complaint after a year of buying from your company, you will certainly want to appease that customer. However, if a customer routinely returns items and complains, you may need to stand by your policy if he or she is looking for you to bend the rules on a regular basis. Knowing how to handle each individual situation and doing so in a reasonable amount of time are the keys to quality customer service. If you ever find yourself using the old cop-out phrase, "If we do that for you then we have to do it for everyone," go back and re-think your customer service approach. Remember, every situation is unique.

Charted Territory

What kind of customer service issues will you encounter in mail order? Well, for starters, you're going to get a certain number of returns. It's part of the charted territory of mail order and retail. The reasons for returns are as varied as human nature:

- People change their minds.
- They order the wrong size or wrong color.
- They give gifts that aren't quite right (or are entirely wrong).
- They order so late that they no longer need the product by the time it arrives.
- They receive the wrong merchandise, or it arrives in less than pristine condition.

No matter what your customer's reason is, however, you will have to deal with it—preferably in a win-win manner. You should have a return policy already in place and clearly stated in all your advertising material. If you've decided on a no-return policy, you must spell it out in your advertising and/or catalog so that, hopefully, the customer already knows this when ordering. If you've got a limited-return policy, you must clearly write this out in your advertising and ordering materials.

Stick to your policy, but remember that you want to keep your customer happy. If bending the rules a bit might make the difference between a repeat customer and one who chooses never to use your company again, you know what to do.

"Sometimes [the reason for the return] may be something you don't feel is your fault," advises Caryn O., "and you feel you shouldn't have to make it up to them, but you've got to do it anyway because it will make the customer happy. And that's what you've got to constantly remember."

Many Happy Returns

What's commonly included in a limited return policy? You might accept returns only on certain products, within a certain time period (say 30 days), with certain tags still attached, or (often in the case of CDs or software) with the product packaging unopened.

Think carefully about how you structure your return policy. More and more retail stores are allowing customers to try out products and then return them within 14 to 30 days (depending on the products). If you go for a policy like this, you could be asking for a lot of unusable, returned stock. On the other hand, you will build a reputation with customers as a friendly, here-to-please company.

And you can always offer those "test-driven" products at a discount, earning yourself happy customers of a slightly different bent. Also, check with your vendors; you may be able to send your returns back to them.

Going The Extra Mile(s)—Literally

Patty, from www.instantphotoframes.com, occasionally gets a panic phone call from someone who didn't receive (or forgot to order) something "essential" for their party. A party planner for more than 20 years, Patty can understand the sudden concern, since people planning big parties and special occasions want everything to be perfect. With that in mind, she has run to the post office on a Friday and over-nighted items to the panicky caller in time for their Saturday night shindig. Once Patty, whose products ship nationwide, and even worldwide, realized the caller wasn't very far away. "It was the only time that I actually got in my car and drove over to the woman's home to hand deliver the items she had forgotten to order until the last minute," recalls Patty. Now that's customer service!

Tried and True

Over the years, mail order mavens have adopted these tried-and-true methods of processing returns:

Beware!

Banks may charge you up to $30 each for *charge-backs,* which are refunds to customers for merchandise returns or disputes.

- Instruct customers to ship products back in the original packing materials within 30 days. This ensures that a) you won't receive returned merchandise years later, and b) you know the merchandise came from your company instead of somebody else's.

- Offer an exchange program in which the customer phones in his or her concern, and you immediately ship out a replacement product. When the customer receives the replacement, he or she puts the damaged original into the same box the replacement came in, with the same packing materials, and sends it back to you with shipping prepaid by you.

- Some companies offer an open return policy, like Lands' End. They'll take back anything for any reason any day of any year. You'll have to think carefully about whether you can financially handle a program like this—most companies cannot, especially those that are new and just starting out.

Take the time to formulate a return policy that you are comfortable with and that you can easily explain to customers. Make sure it is easy to find (and understand) on your website, in your catalog, or wherever else customers see your merchandise.

7

Inventory
and Shipping

It's difficult to be successful in the mail order business without having a good handle on inventory and shipping. After all, we're talking about two things that are absolutely essential to your business: what you sell and how you get it to your customers. In this chapter, we'll explore the ins and outs of managing your stock and discover the secrets to efficient packing and shipping.

▲

Inventory

You might think all there is to inventory control is buying merchandise. But like the groceries in your refrigerator and pantry, you have to know what to buy, when to buy it, and how much to buy. If you stock up on 40 loaves of sourdough sauerkraut-raspberry bread because it's on sale but your family won't eat it, you've effectively mangled your monthly food budget and lost your customers. On the other hand, if you come home with only two double-chocolate macadamia dream cookies and you've got a family of five, you're going to be seriously under stocked and you will, again, have lost your customers, who are down at the corner bakery ruining their dinners with somebody else's desserts.

Catch-22

Your inventory must serve two functions:

1. If you're working with a multiple-product line, it should provide your customers with a reasonable assortment of the products you offer.
2. It should cover the normal sales demands of your company.

Now we arrive at the Catch-22 of retail inventory operations. To accurately calculate basic stock, you must review actual sales during an appropriate time period, such as a full year of business. But if you are just starting up, you don't yet have previous sales and stocking figures to use as a guide. So you will have to use the information from your market research—and your intuition. Keep your ear to the ground and your eyes on your customers' buying habits. Keep good records. Stockpile all this information in your brain's own inventory for future use.

Mathematical formulas, such as those discussed earlier, are designed to help you during the ordering process. For example, if you send out 10,000 mailed pieces, a 1 percent response in the form of orders would mean that you would need 100 items ready to go. This is one way to get a feel for how much to order. The problem, however, is that on the internet, which is the favorite means of marketing products today, it's very difficult to determine how may people you are reaching when you start out. In time, you can get totals of unique visitors per month, per week or per day. At, first, however, it's up in the air. Several factors, including the price, the size, and the available warehouse space (at a drop shipper's location or in your home or garage) will all

> ## Smart Tip
> *Tip...*
> Although most mail order businesses have seasonal peaks and valleys, it pays to brainstorm ways to keep your customers buying during the lulls. Can you run a special sale or devise an off-season campaign to encourage purchases? Get creative!

factor into your initial inventory decisions—along with the longevity of the product. Obviously, you'll have to move perishables more quickly than lawn chairs. The trick to successful inventory management (and sometimes it comes about by trial and error) is not overspending on a product that sits in your warehouse while also not being in a situation where you are unable to fill orders because you keep running out of stock.

Smart Tip

Let your customers know you are recycling old boxes and newspapers. It makes you look good, and it helps your customers think environmentally, too.

Chocolate Zeppelins

Another factor you'll need to consider in calculating your basic stock is lead time—the length of time between when you reorder a product and when you receive it. OK, let's do the math. Let's say, for example, that you're selling chocolate zeppelins. You know that once you call and place your order, it takes four weeks for the vendor to deliver more zeppelins to you. This means your lead time is four weeks. So if you're selling ten zeppelins a week, you'll need to reorder before your basic inventory level falls below 40 zeppelins.

If you wait until you're out of zeppelins, you'll also be out of luck, because you'll have to put all those lovely customer requests on back-order and risk losing sales and customers. You'll also lose cash flow.

One way you can protect yourself from inventory shortfalls is by incorporating a safety margin into your basic inventory figures. You can figure safety margins by anticipating external delays or problems. For instance, you might order extra quantities of seasonal merchandise that you know sells quickly, or, if you deal with a vendor located in a winter-blizzard zone, you could order extra products before shipping delays set in.

Nightmare on Inventory Street

A word of caution: Some mail order entrepreneurs get so excited about a new product that they order entirely too many at one time. Excess inventory creates extra overhead, and that costs you money. Inventory that sits in your garage or warehouse doesn't generate sales or profits. If it's relatively "timeless" by nature, you can sell it next year. However, if it's trendy or time sensitive, you may be stuck with a loss leader. Of course you could always hold onto excess clothing orders for ten to fifteen years and they will come back in style, but that's only if the moths don't get to them first.

Newbie mail order entrepreneurs sometimes add financial insult to injury by marking overstocks at reduced prices, hoping for a quick sale. This solves the overstock problem but plays havoc with your bottom line, because that product you've written into your financial plan as selling at $100 is now pulling in only $50. It's not holding up its share of the weight. Of course, you can use this as a draw to other new products or as a buy-one-and-get-this-product-at-the-"new-low-price." Always use marketing strategies.

You may be tempted to bounce back from this nightmare on Inventory Street by getting timid with your next orders. Don't do this, either. When you reduce normal reordering, you risk creating a stock shortage, and that's not healthy for your bottom line.

We've told you everything not to do, but what makes a good inventory plan? Try the following:

- Do as much research as you can before ordering so that you can order as realistically as possible.
- Order only what you feel confident will sell.
- Establish a realistic safety margin.

The October Lull

As a mail order maven, you'll probably find that your business is seasonal. "Definitely," says Kate W., the team logo merchandiser. "The holidays—and I think this is true throughout the retail industry—is, of course, your absolute busiest season. We did [most] of our business just at the holidays. Thanksgiving through the Bowl games, which is the first of the year, we did easily 50 percent, maybe even higher. The other real big hot period is at the beginning of the football season, usually August and September.

"Then there's October. It's awfully strange, and I am glad somebody explained it to me, because last year I was really worried. In collegiate sales it's called the 'October lull,' and you slow down a little bit. After the real busy August and September, you get to sit back and catch your breath. By then, you know what's really hot and what's not, so you know what inventory you need to bring in. And you prepare yourself for the holiday rush."

Autumn rates a gold star on Greer's seasonal calendar, too. "Fall is the biggest market," the children's clothing expert says. "Back to school—definitely. We got our catalog out in early August, so we've had a great September and a great August response rate. October, November, and December should do very well for our fall catalog."

And there's more to a "good season" catalog than just higher numbers of orders. There are also price differences. "There are higher-end products for your fall catalog than for your summer catalog," Greer explains, "so you tend to make more money on your products at that time. A coat sells for something like $150, while your most expensive summer dress would be something like $100. You sell more coats and more expensive items in the fall."

In Connecticut, Beth H.'s gluten-free foods also sell seasonally. "I think probably the fall catalog is the best one for us," the former cooking teacher says, "but I'm not really sure. We don't have a particularly slow time, although we do have a couple of months that are slower than the others."

Patty, selling party photo frames from Minnesota, found that selling holiday seasonal frames was a high point of the year, as were the spring and summer months when there are plenty of parties. To enhance other seasons, Patty filled in with special holiday frames for Halloween, Easter, and other occasions. This allowed her to spread out the busy season to cover most of the year.

Slow seasons in any industry are also the best times in which to crank up the other aspects of the business. This means that you should spend the slower times designing and preparing the next catalog, revamping the website, and/or researching new means of marketing or even new vendors. Don't just cross off the slower months as time to catch up on your golf game or your reading. Utilize these times to handle the in-house work that goes into making your busy months successful.

Shipping and Handling

You've got your inventory squared away. Now you need to think about how you're going to get it to your customers. Fulfillment—speeding that package from your garage or warehouse to your customer's door—is perhaps the single most important thing you can do in your operation, aside from effective marketing. Failure to provide prompt fulfillment will result in more complaints, cancellations, refusals of c.o.d. payments, and nightmares than just about anything else in the mail order entrepreneur's world.

So exactly how will you get those packages to your customers? You've seen the TV commercials. Your main choices are the U.S. Postal Service (USPS), United Parcel Service (UPS), DHL, and Federal Express (FedEx). Most mail order mavens use UPS for packages because it's generally cheaper than FedEx, faster than the post office, and has better tracking capabilities for those nightmarish lost items than the post office. It pays to comparison shop. FedEx, UPS, and DHL offer various discounts when you set up an account, so be sure to ask—and don't forget to negotiate! They are all marvelous except for

> **Fun Fact**
> According to FedEx, its drivers—in the United States alone—cover more than 2.5 million miles per day.

on those occasions that a package gets lost—then you'll curse any one of them. It happens.

Take a look at your loss ratio when deciding whether to spend a little and ship U.S. mail or spend more and ship UPS, advises Tony Romano of All USA, an Illinois-based call center and fulfillment service. If the product you're sending costs less than $50, go ahead and ship first-class or priority mail. If it's more than $50, spend the extra dollars to send it UPS and get tracking capability.

For those packages that don't necessarily require tracking, it's smart business to offer your customers a choice of shipping services. You can tell them, for instance, that you can have their package out to them by U.S. priority mail with an expected—but not guaranteed—delivery time of three business days. Then you can offer second-day service by UPS or overnight by FedEx at an extra cost. This way people know you're working with them, in terms of both price and speed.

The most important part of shipping is making it crystal clear to your customers. Nobody wants surprises. Make sure they know shipping rates and provide some options if at all possible.

Out of Your Hands

Understanding how the relationship between your business and shipping companies affects customers will go a long way toward keeping your shipping operations on an even keel. In short, your customers will hold you responsible for any delay in receiving their merchandise, even if the delay is caused by the shipping company. So be prepared to be sympathetic to complaining customers—and stern with the USPS, UPS, and FedEx service representatives.

"One of the difficult things about a mail order business," says Caryn O. in Georgia, "is that you can work your tail off, but once you give [the merchandise] to a shipping company, it's out of your hands. For instance, we use UPS a lot. You have done everything, you take an order, you get it out, it's great, everything's fine. And then UPS loses it or takes extra time getting it there. You can have a very distraught, unhappy customer when you've done nothing wrong." This is part of the business… and almost every business relies on some outside sources. Manufacturers, for example, can build a great new toaster oven, but if the retail store leaves it languishing in the stock room for an extra week or two, then the manufacturer is in then same boat as you. Likewise, a retail store may be holding their annual 50 percent off sale on the same day that the president comes to town, closing all local roads for several hours. There are problems in all businesses over which that you do not have control. For that reason, it is always good to have alternative plans at the ready, just as Patty did by having some of her most popular, top-selling items ready in her garage, just in case someone needed some party items in a hurry and they could not be shipped from the drop-shipping house in time.

"You have to understand that the shipping company is almost a part of your company," the textiles merchandiser explains. "It's an extension, and even though you're not related, your customer doesn't see it that way. All they know is that they don't have their package. They don't care when you got it out. They want to know where it is now.

"You have to stay on top of things like that," Caryn says. "We're constantly in very close contact with UPS. If UPS causes a problem for our member, we make UPS call and apologize. We fight for our members and do everything we can to make it up to them and make them happy."

Pass the Popcorn (Packaging Pointers)

There's a method to everything, including packing and shipping. Here's a list of smart tips for shippers to help you help yourself and your customers.

- Take a tip from the shelf stockers down at the supermarket: Place heavier or larger items on the bottom of the box and lighter ones on top.

- After you've got each piece of merchandise in the box, place a piece of cardboard on the very top. This way, if your customer gets carried away with his penknife while slicing open the box, he won't slash his brand-new goodies as well.

- Use shredded newspaper or actual (unbuttered!) popcorn instead of Styrofoam peanuts. Your customers will appreciate your concern for the environment, and if you get hungry while packing, you can eat your materials!

- Indicate which end of the box should be opened first or face up. Sometimes breakable merchandise will make an entire cross-country trip in one piece, only to smash on the customer's floor because he opened it wrong side up.

- Make sure your shipping label is clearly visible to the deliverer. Some shipping companies will refuse to deliver a package if any part of the address is obscured or too small to read.

- Absolutely do not ship to a P.O. box. Most shipping firms cannot deliver to a post office box. Make sure your order takers ask for an actual street address.

- Include all invoices, receipts, thank you letters, new catalogs, and other printed

Smart Tip

If you charge your customers for "shipping," they may quibble over the price, thinking they can get it sent for less by some alternative method. But if you charge for "shipping and handling" there's no problem, because who's to say what your handling costs are?

▲

materials in one envelope with the customer's name on it, placed on top of the merchandise. This saves your customer the time and frustration of having to dig through packing materials to find these things.

- Reuse boxes. It's not only ecologically sound but also economically smart. When you reuse a box, make sure all old labels, addresses, and postage markings are covered up. Stick another label on top so the delivery person doesn't mix up whom your package is intended for.

- Design packing models so your shippers (and you) know how products fit into boxes, how merchandise is folded, stacked, or tissue-wrapped, and how packing materials are used. Weigh each packing model on a scale and make sure it doesn't go even one-eighth into the next pound. This cuts postage costs, reduces returns from damaged goods, and adds to your income by creating happy repeat customers.

- Consolidate yes, cram no. If someone orders five of the same item, and they fit into one large box, great—wrap them individually and send. However, different items should be in their own boxes, even if they are sent in one larger box. Also, make sure that items fit comfortably in the packaging with room for paper or other packing materials.

Bulk Mail

If done correctly, there should be no real "bust" when using direct mail. By testing the right type of mailing lists, and testing your offer(s) on a smaller scale there should be no real surprises when using bulk (now called Standard) Mail.

Your best use of bulk mail should be to send to current customers, (on your in-house list) not to cold (outside) lists. When you send direct mail to cold lists, this is called prospecting (i.e., you are looking to make new customers to put on your in-house list.) Gaining customers through cold direct mail is an expensive way to add new customers and many times, depending on what you are selling, and the long term residual sales that may come from a new customer, may not make it a cost effective use of direct mail to prospect for new customers.

The obvious advantage of standard mail is cost savings. Where a first-class stamp for a one-ounce letter goes for 41 cents, the postage for a typical one-ounce

Bright Idea

How about outsourcing your bulk mail sorting to a center for the disabled? Such an organization would be glad to take on the work, and you can usually negotiate a very reasonable fee. The NMOA has a National list of these types of companies available at no charge to those that ask for it.

letter (or card, tri-fold, etc.) would range from 19.4 to 25.5 cents using Standard Class. This sounds great. But—and here we get to a whole list of buts. If you're just starting out, you will have to buy a permit to send mail in bulk, which will cost $175 for the initial set up fee, plus $175 for the annual fee. Then you add up your postage: If you send 3,000 pieces and your rate comes to 22 cents each,

> ### Smart Tip
>
> Tip...
>
> Who says the post office doesn't give immediate satisfaction? There's no waiting period on bulk mail or first-class mail permits. You can use them the same day you apply.

you'll spend $660. Add your $350 permit fees, and you've got a cost of $1,010. Compare that with the first-class rate of 3,000 pieces at 41 cents each, which adds up to $1,230. The standard rate is cheaper (for the first year), but:

- You'll need to rent a postage meter and shoot each piece through the meter. Or pay your printer to imprint each piece with your permit number and postage.
- Then you have to sort. And sort. And sort again. Check out "Fun with Mail Sorting" on page 132 to learn exactly how this is done.
- Next you have to take your mail trays to an official U.S. Postal Service bulk mail center.

The more pieces you send, the more cost-effective standard mail becomes. If you're sending 6,000 letters, your cost is $1,380, compared with the first-class rate of $2,460—a $1,080 savings. There are size and weight requirements that determine what the cost per piece of mail will be. Some mail order software programs will handle the sorting for you, which makes this even more appealing. (Haven Corporation's

---

Wrap It Up

One way to lavish your customers with attention is in the way you package your merchandise. "When we send fabric," Caryn O. says, "we wrap it in tissue paper so it arrives looking neat and [attractive]. Our customers are spending a lot of money for a product they've got pictured in their heads. They don't look at it and see a piece of gray flannel—they see it as the beautiful outfit it's going to become. We want to make it presentable, so when they open the box it looks like what they expected."

Yes, attention to detail works. "We get a lot of compliments," the Georgia fabric retailer explains. "Our customers tell us, 'Thank you. I love how my fabric arrived; it shows how much you care about it.'" And how much she cares about them.

Smart Tip

Tip...

The UPS Package Lab is staffed entirely by engineers with four-year degrees in package engineering. (Bet you didn't even know there was a degree in package engineering!)

"For delivery of orders, the USPS has as service called 'Click and Ship' that allows you to print postage/delivery labels from your printer. It works with Priority Mail delivery. "We use it at the NMOA for most of our book sales," explains John Shulte, president of the NMOA.

Mail Order Wizard, for instance, offers a bulk mail supplement called Mail List Monarch, which costs an additional $495.) You can find more mail order software at the NMOA.org website. There is also technology that can sort first class mail and provide bar coding, thus bringing down your 41 cent rate as well.

Endless Permutations

Not all bulk mail fits neatly into the same one-ounce category. The U.S. Postal Service has an entire 126-page Quick Service Guide devoted to endless permutations of mail sizes, weights, and categories, each with its own rules and regulations. And although the post office seems to have made a genuine effort to make this book user-friendly, it's not. There's a major learning curve here. Of course, the folks down at your local bulk mail center are usually very friendly and will guide you through anything you need to know, but it's not as simple as licking a stamp and sticking it on your letter. (Many USPS mail centers have training sessions for preparing Standard [Bulk] Mail.)

One issue to consider is the time factor. If you're anxious to get those letters to your customers, you might not want to go bulk mail. Bulk items can take up to two weeks for delivery, while first-class letters get the first-class treatment—usually two to four days for delivery.

You should also be aware that bulk rate letters are less likely to be opened by potential customers than first-class, stamped ones because they're perceived as junk mail. This is not to say that all bulk rate items get tossed—they don't. If your presentation is clever and well-conceived (see Chapter 10 for tips and tricks), you'll probably reach your target customers anyway.

What's the bottom line? How you handle your mailings is completely up to you. You decide which are the biggest issues—cost, labor, time, or customer perception—and what benefits you're actually gaining. You need to know the average lifetime value of a customer to be able to decide if the cost of using direct mail to acquire customers is worthwhile or not.

To help you compare your options, we've provided a chart, "Standard vs. First-Class Mail," on page 133. Don't forget that you can outsource your bulk mailings to a lettershop, fulfillment center, or printing house. You won't need a permit, and you won't need to spend time sorting and resorting. Be sure to check out these alternatives before making a final decision.

Have Your Cake

If you want a discount mailing rate but you need the speed of first-class mail, you can more or less have your cake and eat it, too, by sending your pieces first-class pre-sort. Here your cost is 30.5 cents per one-ounce piece. You must presort the same as you do for bulk mail and you have to purchase a first-class permit at an annual fee of $175. And where you need only mail 200 pieces to take advantage of the standard mail rate, with first-class presort, you have to send a minimum of 500 pieces.

If you like, you can buy both a bulk mail permit and a first-class permit and have the option of using either method at any time. I believe you can still have up to 3.5 ounces per piece when using Standard Mail. First Class is limited to one ounce.

Leave the Mailing to Us

If you want to mail your materials at the bulk rate but you don't want to spend all those hours sorting by ZIP code and state, you might check into the services of a lettershop. This is a company that lets you leave the mailing to them—not only sorting and stamping or metering your pieces but also folding, inserting, and stapling.

A good lettershop can advise you on what mailing rate is best for the job you're doing, what type of label or on-the-envelope printing to use, and even what type of mailer might be best. Some lettershops specialize in big corporate jobs, while others are mom-and-pop operations geared toward entrepreneurs with small business.

The USPS business center offices in most major cities have a "Mail Piece Design Analysis" person that can tell you if your desired mailing piece fits into the USPS standards and at what rate it will mail at. It's free and everyone should use it.

Lettershops generally charge by the type of service provided, says Don Golden of Action Communications in Boca Raton, Florida. There's a minimum fee for each type of service—for instance, inkjet-printing envelopes, inserting letters into envelopes, or sorting the finished product. Expect to pay a minimum of $100 to $300 per type of service, plus postage, which you pay to the shop so it can pay the post office.

Golden, whose firm works with large mail order companies only, suggests you check with the Mail Advertising Service Association, MASA. The NMOA.org also has contacts for lettershops and mailing houses, all for free. The USPS business offices in major cities can also recommend firms. For information on reputable lettershops in your area, call those shops to find out if they're geared toward your mail level. Don't forget to check references! It is also advisable to seek out a lettershop that understands your specific needs and can act as a partner.

Fun with Mail Sorting

To take advantage of bulk mail prices, you have to presort your envelopes according to U.S. Postal Service guidelines. To get an idea of just what's involved, take a look at this nutshell explanation of how to sort standard mail, or, as the Postal Service calls it, the "packing and traying sequence." The people at the post office will provide you with rubber bands, trays, and stickers. They'll also give you help, so don't hesitate to ask for it.

	Five-Digit ZIPs	Three-Digit ZIPs	State-by-State	Leftovers
Sort	Sort all letters with identical five-digit ZIP codes.	Sort all letters with identical three-digit ZIP code prefixes.	Sort all letters going to the same state.	Sort all letters going every-where else.
Bundle	Bundle into packs of ten or more with rubber bands.	Bundle into packs of ten or more with rubber bands.	Bundle into packs of ten or more with rubber bands.	Bundle into packs with rubber bands.
Label	Affix a red label "D" to top envelope.	Affix a green label "3" to top envelope.	Affix a pink label "A" to top envelope.	Affix a tan label "MXD" to top envelope.
Tray	Put bundles in trays; no partially filled trays permitted.	Put bundles in trays; one partially filled tray per destination permitted.	Put bundles in trays; no partially filled trays permitted.	Stick all leftover bundles in this tray.

Standard vs. First-Class Mail

Issue	Standard Rate	First-Class
Permit fees	Costs $350 (one-time fee of $175 and annual fee of $175)	No permit needed.
Cost for a 1-ounce letter in a #10 (business-sized) envelope	19.5 – 25.5 cents	41 cents
Stamping or metering	Buy a rubber stamp and imprint each piece with your meter number and postage. OR Rent a postage meter and send each piece through the meter. OR Pay your printer to imprint each piece with your meter number and postage. OR Use new bar-coding software.	Apply stamp.
Sorting	Mail must be sorted by five-digit ZIP codes, by three-digit ZIP codes, by state and by mixed parcels, and then set into trays. (See chart on page 132.)	No sorting necessary.
Mail drop-off	Mail must be delivered to a U.S. Postal Service bulk mail center.	Drop mail in any corner mailbox or take it to any post office.
Delivery time	4–7 days	2–4 days
Customer appeal	May be considered "junk mail" and discarded unopened.	Looks like mail from a "real" source and has a greater chance of being opened and read.

Sorting through
Business
Equipment

Your office will be your command center, the heart of your business, and the proper equipment will contribute greatly to your success. With the right tools, your operations will run smoothly, speedily, and efficiently. Die-hard shoppers may be tempted to rush out and buy every item brand-spanking new, but this might not be necessary. Some or all of the equipment you'll need may already be sitting around in your home, just waiting to be put to use.

We've provided a handy checklist (see "The Mail Order Maven's Office Checklist" on page 156) to help you determine what you'll need, what you already have on hand, and which of those in-stock items are ready for business. After you've read this chapter, take some time to go through the checklist and evaluate your equipment situation. Is your computer mail order ready, or is it an antique that won't be able to keep up the pace? Does your answering machine take and receive clearly audible messages, or does it tend to garble crucial information? How about that printer? Can it produce professional-looking materials in short order, or does it take ages to spit out a solitary page?

Let's get started on our business equipment shopping spree. What you'll be looking for, generally, are the middle-of-the-road models. Ready? Go!

Computer Glitterati

Your computer will be the command center of your office setup, coordinating your invoicing, accounting, word processing, database, and desktop publishing activities—not to mention co-starring in all website activities and e-mail correspondence. It may be your most important startup purchase. If you already own a computer, you will want to make sure it's capable of handling the tasks you'll need it to perform.

With a good system as your silent partner, you can single-handedly perform more functions than you might believe possible. Just for starters, you can:

- Create your own catalog pages, display ads, and other direct-mail pieces
- Generate stationery, invoices, packing slips, certificates, and order forms
- Track orders
- Track inventory
- Perform accounting functions and generate financial reports
- Maintain databases of repeat and potential customers
- Access research materials and other resources online
- Sell via an online or "virtual" catalog
- Process credit card payments
- Communicate with repeat and potential customer, as well as vendors, via e-mail

What Do I Need?

Whether you are planning to buy a desktop computer or intent upon using the one you already have, you should look at for the following:

- Minimum 256 MB of RAM

Read All About It!

Make sure your brain is as well equipped as your office. One of your first steps in your new venture should be to read everything you can, not just about the specifics of mail order but about starting a small business and about marketing and sales techniques. Blitz the bookstore. Make an assault on your public library. (See the Appendix for some home office book suggestions).

- At least 120, if not 200 or more gigabytes (GB) of hard drive (the more the merrier, for storage)
- At least 1.5 or 2.0 gigahertz (GHz) processing speed (for moving your business along faster)
- At least two universal USB connections for peripherals, which will typically include your printer and perhaps a scanner
- A DVD drive
- A CD burner
- Windows XP operating system. Vista is the latest, but thus far not as "amazing" as billed—and tech staffers have claimed that they are busy trying to solve more Vista problems than those of XP. This means you can get XP for less money and interface with the many other people who are also not yet taking a chance with Vista.
- An internal modem (all newer computers have internal modems that will get you on the internet).
- 3D Graphics card which will allow you to get the latest software programs and use them to your advantage.
- 5.1 Surround Sound—not essential for your purposes, but always a plus for quality sound, such as some background music while you're in the throes of your workday.
- A firewall and anti-virus software. The firewall should be part of your purchasing deal while anti-virus programs are a must today for anyone using the internet for anything—look for PC-cillin, Norton 2007, or one of the other leading anti-virus programs.

The leading light among computers sold in today's market is the Pentium-class PC, fully loaded with Windows XP, a modem, and usually enough peripheral software to keep you on a hyperactive learning curve for weeks. You can expect to pay from $1,000

What's In a Name?

There are dozens of common PC desktop brands, although the ones you are most likely to see at the major retailers are Dell, Gateway, Hewlett-Packard, Compaq, IBM, Sony, and Toshiba. *PC Magazine* is worth browsing to see the different models and get reviews of the latest. You can buy a copy or go to www.pcmag.com. Also, visit the home page of any particular brand to find out which computer model will be the best for your needs.

If you are looking for a Mac, you can choose from a variety of options, including the all-in-one iMac or the MacPro. The Mac OSX operating system (Leopard), will run Windows as well. Check out *MacWorld* magazine (www.macworld.com) or go to the Apple website, www.apple.com, for more on the latest Macs.

to $2,500 for a name-brand computer and monitor (not including printer), with prices increasing as you add on goodies.

Mac or PC?

One of the big decisions you will have to make before buying a computer is whether you want a Mac or a PC. The Mac vs. PC discussion has evolved into many a flame war on internet chat rooms or message boards, so be forewarned when asking a computer enthusiast (a.k.a. Techie) about his or her preference.

You need not argue. Both systems will meet your basic requirements. However, the bottom line is basically this:

- Macs can be a little pricier.
- There are more computer software programs and choices for PCs, although most programs today come in both Mac and PC versions.
- The wider use of PCs means there are far more computer viruses and spyware nightmares for PCs than for Macs.
- PCs may be faster, but Macs can be easier for those less versed in computer-ease, as they come with very user-friendly programming.
- Each of their users swear by them.

Of course the end result will be which you feel comfortable using and what the people around you (in your field) are using.

If you already have a computer that you like, you can certainly seek more speed, more memory, and/or more hard drive capacity for your existing machine. It's all a matter of your budget and your needs. You want a system that can handle your current software and more, should you opt for new software programs or take on additional responsibilities that require greater speed and more memory.

Additional Computer Must Haves

Beyond the main central processing unit (CPU), which is the heart and soul of the computer, you need to purchase a monitor, keyboard, a mouse or trackball, and a printer. Some of these items will be bundled with the initial computer, although you might want to upgrade them immediately. You'll find pre-set deals both online and in stores, although you can usually work a deal of your own picking and choosing various options from a manufacturer such as Dell. Often one element in a pre-fixed deal is not up to the standards of the others, such as a smaller or "lower end" monitor or an inexpensive printer. Pay the difference to get a better or larger monitor or a faster printer if you are not happy with the one in the deal.

Monitors

For years, the typical home computer monitor has been a CRT-based display, the familiar bulky kind with the big back that looks like a television. It has that look because it works in the same manner as the televisions we've seen for years, with numerous tiny phosphor dots inside of the glass tube, each forming a line. The image is then created by all of the lines working together.

A more modern choice today in monitors, as well as in televisions, is the new flat panel screens. These liquid crystal display monitors (LCDs) utilize plasma and light emitting diodes. While LCD monitors are more technical to explain, they offer a sleeker look compared with their bulkier counterparts. Aesthetically, and from a space perspective, the flat panel monitors take up less room and are lighter if you need to move them, often weighing less than 20 pounds as compared to 35 to 45 pound CRT monitors. Here are some basic differences to make shopping for a monitor less confusing:

- LCD monitors are a little more expensive than CRTs.
- LCD monitors typically have sharper pictures but not sharper colors than CRTs.
- LCDs don't have that occasional "flicker" that you may sometimes experience on a CRT monitor.
- To see an LCD monitor clearly, you need to be in front of it; otherwise the image on screen can look distorted. A CRT monitor, however, can be seen clearly from various angles.
- LCD monitors use less electricity than their CRT counterparts.

Your primary concern is how the onscreen image looks to you. Sit in front of monitors at a nearby computer store before making a decision—even if you plan to save money by ordering it online. Some people will swear by the latest in LCDs, while others say that despite the new sleek look of the LCD, the CRT monitors are still better (although they are slowly becoming obsolete). The only one who needs to decide is you since it is your home office.

Keyboards

No, all keyboards are not all alike. You've probably seen the rectangular ones and those curvy keyboards known as "natural" keyboards. These keyboards are created in such a manner to put less pressure on the wrists and help avoid carpal tunnel syndrome. This doesn't mean that if you have the standard rectangular keyboard you will get Carpal Tunnel Syndrome. It simply means that there is an ergonomic alternative. For most people, it's a matter of preference and comfort level.

There are keyboards that include a touch pad on the keyboard itself, so you don't need to use a separate mouse. If you are limited in space at your desktop, or are familiar with using a laptop, then this is a good option. If you are comfortable with the traditional keyboard and mouse set up, the touchpad may be difficult to get used to—plus it typically costs more. You can buy a keyboard for less than $30 or spend upward of $50 on a wireless keyboard. A company called FMI makes mini- and full-sized flexible keyboards out of high quality silicon, and they sell for around $35. Not only can you roll it up like a bathmat, but you can wash it with soap and water.

Laptops and Notebooks

If you like working in different places around your office or the house—or in the backyard—there are a wide variety of highly advanced laptop and notebook computers available, many weighing less than four pounds. The lightweight models have now become very powerful and can handle the same functions as a desktop—if not more.

The biggest drawbacks and complaints of laptop and notebook computer users are the smaller screen and keyboard. While this may take getting used to while on the road, in your home office, you can use a docking station, which magically turns your laptop into a desktop. No, this has nothing to do with the Starship Enterprise. A docking station is actually a platform into which you can install your portable computer and through connectors you can use a full-size monitor, full-size keyboard, your printer and other peripheral devices.

When you are shopping for a laptop, the same rules apply to those for a desktop. The feel of the keys, the feel of the trackball, trackpoint, or touchpad, and the size of the screen will all be a matter of comfort. How does it look or feel to you? Lastly, remember that the smaller the components, the higher the prices,

> **Tip...**
>
> **Smart Tip**
> Yes, there are numerous brands of computers and printers on the market, but for the sake of getting tech help when you need it, look for the more popular, well-known brands. Also, check to see if the technical help is free. Otherwise, these costs can add up quickly!

and you can expect to pay a little more for a notebook. Popular laptops and notebooks can be found from Dell, Hewlett Packard, Compaq, Toshiba, IBM, Sony, Gateway, Fujitsu/Fuji, Acer, eMachines and, of course, Apple. You can walk away with a good quality model for around $800.

Printers

Once upon a time, there were dot matrix printers. They were painfully slow, one color, noisy, and pulled along a stream of paper that needed to be separated, unless your cat or dog

> ### Smart Tip
> Smart Shopping: Keep an eye out for what are called "bundled extras" in the computer world, while browsing and comparing prices. Intrinsically necessary items like software, ink cartridges, and various peripherals can be part of a deal that might cost several hundred dollars if purchased separately.

separated it for your. Today, printers are fast, quiet, colorful, and portable. Many can double as scanners and copiers and include plenty of ancillary features. However, when they aren't working correctly, they are a colossal pain in the butt!

Along with all the new technology have come plenty of printer glitches. Frequent paper jams, trays that feed all 25 sheets of paper into the machine at once, printers that too often require new and expensive toner cartridges, those that love to smudge, and some that have trouble reading certain software programs without installing new drivers are all common problems. The folks who provide online tech support have been known to complain that printer problems are the most frequent calls.

The basic printer choice for most home offices comes down to laser vs. inkjet. Both are sold at price points that makes them consumer friendly. Both are subject to the problems listed above. However, there are significant differences in how they work.

The Laser Printer

It is fast (sometimes printing up to 30 pages per minute), an excellent workhorse for volumes of monochrome (one color/black) work and the cartridges are easy to replace. Lasers cost more initially than inkjets, but the cartridges are less expensive than ink, making them potentially less expensive per page over time. Lasers don't smudge but they do run through cartridges quickly.

The Inkjet Printer

Inkjets are not as fast as laser printers, but can provide quality monochrome documents and are typically much better for color on documents and particularly on photographs. Inkjets are cheaper upfront than most laser printers, but the ink will cost more than the cartridges over time and you will end up spending the same or more.

Once you have zeroed in on your printer needs, try a few models at a store and ask friends and neighbors which printers they have bought. It's easy to compare prices

Equipment Shopping Details

○ **Paperwork:** Make sure all paperwork comes with the computer including operating instructions and your warranty. Save all paperwork in a safe place and remember where you put it!

○ **Features:** Don't get talked into buying a computer with additional features that you do not need. While you want the most memory you can afford, you will probably not need to upgrade the video card for your home office computer unless your work involves graphics. The more advanced video cards are usually beneficial for playing games and if nothing else, you do not want to find yourself playing games in the middle of a busy day rather than working.

○ **Good deals and bad deals:** If you don't like a deal, walk away—there will always be another, better option. A good deal is one that gets you the hardware that you want for a fair price, and even includes a few extras.

online and salespeople will tell you all the positives. However, since—as we mentioned above—printers can be a colossal pain, it's nice to know which models people like and which ones have reduced individuals to tears.

Read up on printers at *PC Magazine* and other computer websites as well as in chats and on postings, where people tell it like it is. Popular printer models include: Canon, Epson, Oki Data, Brother, Lexmark, and Hewlett Packard.

Snapshots

In producing your website or your own advertising materials (or both), you'll definitely need a digital camera. This will enable you simply snap a photo of your product and download it onto your computer to put on your site. Expect to pay $400 to $800 for a good-quality digital camera. Get a good warranty and make sure tech support exists.

Once the photo is in your computer, you can manipulate it in all sorts of interesting ways, acting as your own photo-finishing expert. You can crop it, expand it, zoom in or out on various features, blur the edges for that shot-through-gauze look, make it look like a watercolor, pastel, or oil painting, ad infinitum. This stuff is not only great for business purposes, it's a heck of a lot of fun! Many digital cameras come complete with photo-finishing software. Or you can purchase any number of programs, from Broderbund's Print Shop Deluxe, priced at about $40, to the latest version of Adobe's Photoshop, which costs about $600.

Since your product photos are very important to the success of your business, don't skimp on a good camera and a software program that lets you highlight your products.

Scanner, Anyone?

You may also want to consider buying a scanner, which you can purchase for anywhere from $50 to $500+ that imports graphics from just about any printed medium, including books, photographs, original art, advertising pieces, or postcards, into your desktop publishing program.

Remember, you can't use anything someone else holds a copyright on, whether it's graphics, art images, or text, without permission. So make sure you've obtained permission to use any copyrighted material before you scan it into your catalog or other direct-mail piece.

Canon, HP, Nikon, and Epson are among the many companies making scanners.

Equipment Expenses	
Computer system (including printer)	$2,500
Fax machine	250
Software	650
Telephones (including cell phones, voice mail service or answering machine)	400
UPS (uninterruptible power supply to keep you running when there is a power surge)	200
Calculator	25
Copier N/A	700
Printer/copier paper	50
Extra printer cartridge	80
Extra fax cartridge	80
Miscellaneous	200
Total Expenditures	**$5,125**

Just the Fax

As mentioned earlier, the fax machine has lost some of its cache with the popularity of scanners and email. Nonetheless, you should consider having one on hand or at least buying a fax software program. It's always good to be prepared for all types of communications.

A fax machine can be purchased for anywhere from under $100 to over $1,000. You'll probably end up with good one for roughly $200 tops. Keep in mind that you can also buy a combo printer, scanner, and fax machine—but be forewarned from someone who's been there—these combination scanners/printers/fax machines do break often and if one function goes, you may lose all three, giving you a combination headache and pain in the neck.

If you have some room, buy separate items and make sure the fax machine you purchase prints on plain paper. Most of the documents you receive will be keepers—correspondence, invoices, and the like—that will need to go into your permanent files.

Software That Sorts: And Much More!

The mail order entrepreneurs we interviewed for this book held mixed views on whether, as a newbie, you should spend your money on special mail order software or whether you can start off with a good general accounting program. Industry experts, however, feel you should definitely go with specialized software. Here's why:

- The biggest advantage to industry-specific software is, of course, that it's tailored to the needs of a mail order company. You don't need to spend time tweaking some other program to "force" it to do what you want, or compromise on your needs.

- Sooner or later, you're going to grow enough to really need the industry-specific stuff. Why not start off with it so there's no big switch midstream when you may not have the time to change gears?

- A starter package, which you can upgrade later, is not really that much more expensive than the nonspecific programs.

- If you use a call center to handle your order processing, and you and the call center use the same mail-order-specific software, you can get instant feedback any time you like. "Order processing information appears in your system as if you had input it," says Tony Romano, owner of All USA, a call center in Westchester, Illinois.

Mail order software prices can vary dramatically, depending on how many fancy add-ons you go for and what customer volume you anticipate. Startup entrepreneurs can expect to pay anywhere from $299 to $1,595 for a system that handles order entry, inventory, customer and list management, order fulfillment (labels, invoices, etc.), and ad tracking. How could you go wrong?

Basic-model mail order software packages often contain only a few of the functions listed on our "Mail Order Software Checklist." While you can routinely expect functions like order entry and mailing list management, other goodies—such as credit card processing and bar code printing—are usually sold as add-ons.

When you're evaluating software, eliminate packages that don't completely satisfy your needs. If you'll want to field order status inquiries over the phone, for instance, you can exclude software that can't do the job.

Smart Tip

When shopping for mail order software, ask for references from satisfied customers. When you call these happy people, find out how closely their operations resemble yours in terms of customer volume, number of products handled, and size of mailing list. Does it sound like what works for them will work for you, or are you a mail house of a different color?

In selecting your software, you'll also need to consider potential performance issues. Some programs can handle mailing lists containing literally millions of names. Others choke on 3,000 labels. The same goes for the number of orders per day. Some systems hum along with thousands, while others peak at 50 to 100. Good program vendors can tell you if their product will work for you now and in the future based on your company estimates. Make sure to know the specs of your computer and make sure you can handle the software program you select. Some require a lot of memory—you can add memory to your computer if necessary.

Item counts and item identification systems can be tricky, too. Find out how many products the program can handle and how it copes with size, color, style, and other issues unique to your operation. What happens if somebody orders more items than will fit on one invoice or packing slip? Can the program sail sunnily along, or does it glitch up and force you to create multiple orders?

Can the program generate reports that will be specific enough for your needs? If you want to see summaries of all men's sweater orders or determine your most popular boot sizes, now's the time to think about it.

More food for thought: If you will handle perishable products like foods, find out how the software will track in-and-out dates. Will it automatically warn you of pending problems?

Can the order processing software be gracefully interrupted mid-order? If the answer is yes, this feature will allow you to enter mailed or faxed-in orders during telephone lulls. What you don't want is for customers to have to wait while you finish entering a mailed-in order.

Remember that mailing lists—the manna of your business—need to be as clean as possible. With soaring printing and postage costs, you can't afford to send three or

▲

Smart Tip

Tip...

No matter how user-friendly a software package is, there will be times when you'll need hand holding. So when you shop, be sure to ask what sort of technical support comes with the software.

four identical catalogs to the same address. Make sure the software can eliminate duplicate names. Then find out if the following apply:

- Can you identify big spenders as well as inactive names? If you rent names from somebody else, can you merge them easily with your own list? This also means asking the person from whom you are renting a list what software program they use. Do this before renting.

- Can you track the use of rented names and identify their sources?

- If you decide to sell or rent your own lists, can the software export this data to a CD?

A dazzling array of software lines the shelves of most office supply stores, ready to help you perform just about every general business task. You can design and print your own checks, develop professional-quality marketing materials, make mailing lists and labels, and even act as your own accountant and attorney, all with the help of various software programs.

Your software program is probably going to be your closest partner along with your phone and computer so if you decide to use one, choose carefully. The list of software helpmates is lengthy, with a variety of capabilities and prices available from $200 to $7,000+. Among the many out there you'll find:

- **AnyOrder!**, a Windows-based software program designed specifically for small mail order businesses. The user friendly program prepares invoices, does billings, generates sales reports, handles returns, keeps track of inventory, records customer payments, tracks consigned items, and creates customer mailing lists. It's also as a shareware program, which means you can try it out for free.

- **Mail Order Manager (M.O.M.)**, from Dydacomp is a very popular program. Integration makes M.O.M. so incredibly helpful. Order importing, list management to UPS shipping, COD, eCheck, check and invoice payment options as well as credit card processing, inventory management, handling catalog requests and profit analysis are among the many ways that M.O.M. helps you with all aspects of the business. (www.dydacomp.com)

- **Mailware**, from Ohio-based Core Technologies has been going strong for ten years and features full inventory and purchasing order system, customer management, and a host of features designed to make everything run smoothly from order taking to shipping. There's a full report writer that can pre-design reports to keep you updated on all activities. A fully functional download is available from the Core Technologies website. (www.mailware.com)

Mail Order Software Checklist

Use this checklist to help determine which software program is best for you. First, make copies so you've got one for each candidate. Then go down the list and decide which items are must-haves and which ones you won't need—at least in your first year or two. Most systems let you upgrade as you grow. Check off your must-haves. Cross out the don't-needs, if you like. Then compare!

Software Candidate:_____

❏ Maintains and updates mailing lists, including address correction and merge/purge, which means combining duplicate list entries into one and purging invalid entries, such as those for people who have moved and provided no forwarding address

❏ Helps salespeople with telephone order processing and answers order status inquiries

❏ Automatically creates invoices

❏ Computes postage shipping charges

❏ Profiles customers by capturing information like past purchases and average order amount

❏ Tracks inventory and notifies you when it's time to reorder

❏ Tracks in-and-out dates of perishable products

❏ Automates credit card approvals

❏ Tracks in-house credit accounts

❏ Holds orders pending receipt of payment

❏ Creates shipping paperwork

❏ Prints labels, packing slips, price tickets, and shelf labels

❏ Creates and reads bar-code labels

❏ Tracks and fills back orders

❏ Issues FTC back-order notifications

❏ Sends personalized letters and order forms

❏ Analyzes and reports sales trends

❏ Handles discount arrangements

❏ Handles sales commissions

❏ Tracks success of ads and catalogs

❏ Uses multiple printers (to eliminate paper swaps)

- **RESPONSE** from CoLinear is another leading mail order software program that handles high volume, PC-based ordering, fulfillment, and customer service. Inventory control and management reporting are part of the full package from the Georgia based CoLinear's RESPONSE program. (www.colinear.com)

- **MACH2K** from Data Management Associates offers fully integrated programs for the Call Center, Warehouse Management, Marketing and Promotion Analysis, Complete Financials e-Commerce, and POS. The system includes Order Entry (via phone, fax, third party call center, or internet), Credit Card Processing, Picking Document Generation, Integrated Manifesting, Inventory Control, Purchasing, Receiving and Put Away, Sales Analysis, RFM Analysis and List Management, Accounts Receivable, Accounts Payable, General Ledger, Financial Reporting, and Ad-hoc database reporting tools. (www.mach2k.com).

- **Harvey Software** is the place for shipping software programs. A leading provider of shipping solutions, Harvey features the Computerized Parcel System (CPS™), for parcel shipping via UPS®, FedEx®, and the United States Postal Service®. Harvey Software, now in business nearly 25 years, also provides parcel tracking solutions such as the CPS Parcel Locator that works in conjunction with CPS SHIP eLERT® e-mail shipment notifications all from your desktop PC or other mobile device. These products and others from Harvey, in conjunction with your mail order software, can maximize your shipping efficiency, and after all, shipping is one of the key ingredients to your business and the one you have the least control over. Wal-Mart, Microsoft, American Express, Maytag, Lands End, Nike and other leading companies have all worked with Harvey. Also, if you click on Harvey's "Business Partners," you'll link to the websites for most of the software mentioned above. (www.harveysoft.com)

These are just some of the available mail order programs that are very popular.

Basic Software

Most new computers come preloaded with all the software you'll need for basic office procedures. If yours doesn't, you may want to look into the following types of programs:

- *Word processing.* You'll need a word processing program, which allows you to write correspondence, contracts, sales reports, and whatever else strikes your fancy. A good basic program such as Microsoft Word or WordPerfect will cost $100 to $400, depending on which version you purchase—look at the difference in features.

- *Accounting/Bookkeeping.* You may also want an accounting program such as QuickBooks (which is recommended by many mail order mavens who prefer not to start with the industry-specific stuff) or Microsoft Money to track your business finances. These are a sort of checkbook on a CD and make record-keeping a breeze. You assign categories such as office supplies and business travel to the checks you write, and (at tax time) you print out a report showing how much you spent for what. Your accountant not only thanks you but also gives you a discount for not having to wade through all your receipts. You can expect to pay $59 to $299 for your computer accounting and/or bookkeeping software.

> **Smart Tip**
>
> For numerous office functions all in one place, look to purchase office suite software, such as Office Professional 2007 from Microsoft, which sells for around $500.

- *Desktop publishing.* For those polished marketing materials, you'll want a desktop publishing program, such as Microsoft Publisher, QuarkXPress, or Adobe InDesign. Desktop publishing programs are not typically included when buying a computer, so you can try to have it bundled into your purchase—which means they'll work it into the overall deal. If you are purchasing such a program for a computer you already own, expect to spend in the $350 to $600 range.

Communications: The Power Touch

If you're going to be a one-person order-processing department, with one ear to stick to the phone, one voice to answer with, and two hands to take orders, you've got a problem. If your advertising methods have been effective, you'll discover early on that you can't handle the call volume. Impatient potential customers often hang up if placed on hold for too long, causing you to miss sales. If this is happening, seek outside assistance quickly.

As that one-person department, your options for handling multiple calls boil down to the following:

- Contract with a call center.
- Purchase a two- or three-line phone, and put callers on hold.
- Purchase a phone with "power touch" capability and "memory call" service.

With power touch, you get the junior version of the big companies' on-hold messages. For example, if you are taking one customer's order and another customer calls in, a red light will blink on your phone. You push a button and your second customer hears the familiar litany: "Your call is important to us. All of our customer representatives are busy. Please hold for the next available representative." (Or words to that effect.)

This is great—except that if a third customer calls in, he gets diverted to voice mail (via memory call service) and is asked to leave a message. However, many people don't want to leave a message or they leave before you can get back to them.

Still, this option may work for you if you will have a limited or spread out call volume, or if you will have close-knit customers who will leave a message. If you think power touch might be your ticket, expect to pay about $240 for the phone itself and an extra $7 per month for the memory call service.

Call Center

Another solution to the problem of making sure all your calls are answered is to contract with a call center. The call center lets you handle any call volume. It gives your customers the ability to place orders 24 hours a day, seven days a week. Additionally, it gives your startup, one-person company the ambience of a major mail order operation.

Once you establish your toll-free number with a long-distance carrier, you can arrange for the call center to handle calls using one of several options:

- *Answer your call overflow with alternate-destination routing.* The call center takes over if your phone goes unanswered after a set number of rings or if your line is busy.

- *Answer after hours with time-of-day re-routing.* The call center takes over at a preset time each evening and then releases calls back to you at a preset time each morning.

Line of Defense

A good call center will work with you at every step along the way. "We're your first line of defense," says call-center owner Tony Romano. "And we are a partnership."

When you contract with a call center, you'll provide order processors with a list of questions your customers may ask and what the answers should be. Then, as the call center works with your customers and products, it will likely provide you with a list of questions to answer—things that will help the order processors better serve your customers. The call center will also share hints, tips, and tricks of the trade to help you develop the best product codes and the best catalog copy.

Take advantage!

Not Everyone Is a Fan of Call Centers

Choose your call center environment carefully and be fore-warned about occasional backlash. Critics of call centers will point out poor treatment of workers in some of the facilities. If you go the international call center route—hiring cheap labor in other countries—you will hear complaints from people who are either concerned about the treatment of these workers or those who would prefer that you staff Americans who are in need of work before farming work out to other countries.

- *Answer all the time.* The call center handles all your calls, leaving you free for other tasks. According to Tony Romano of All USA, most startup mail order mavens choose this option, requesting that only customer service calls be routed to them.

What's the bottom line? Try negotiating for these options:

- *Price per minute.* A typical order, Romano explains, takes about 3 to 3 1/2 minutes to process and is billed at 70 cents to $1 per minute, based on the complexity of your orders. If your catalog is very specific, for instance, and your customer can easily say, "I want size small in red" and be done with it, you'll be charged less per order than if the order processor has to guide the customer through each step and explain things along the way. Price-per-minute is the standard call center billing method.

- *Price based on call type.* You might set up a program with the call center where you pay different fixed amounts based on whether the incoming call is for an order, a catalog request, or some miscellaneous objective—to make life easier, look for a one-fee situation for all incoming calls, with any clearly spelled out exceptions.

As is always the case, before outsourcing any aspect of your business, shop around carefully and ask for references from current or existing clients. Pick up the phone and dial to spot check that the call center is handling your business in a professional manner—they should be answering with your business name and be polite to everyone who calls. Remember, they are an extension of your business, so if they screw up, people blame you. As is always the case, make sure to have an agreement in writing so that there are no hidden costs. Some centers charge

Bright Idea

If you decide to start out answering your own phone, interview call centers anyway. Find one you like, then ask how long it takes to get set up and what you'll need to provide so that when you're ready to outsource, everything will be in place.

▲

Weird Hours

What's the prime shopping time for catalog purchasers? Later than you might think. "Most of our evening calls come from moms whose kids are finally asleep and they've found a moment to shop," says Caryn O., the fabric merchandiser. "Those kinds of people shop anywhere from 9 P.M. to midnight."

That's why Caryn's phones are answered by order processors from six in the morning until the witching hour. For those wee hours in between, when her company receives the least number of calls, she relies on an answering machine.

In Overland Park, Kansas, Kate W.'s phone is answered 24 hours a day, either by an answering service or by Kate herself. "As a catalog shopper myself," the former bookkeeper explains, "I shop at weird hours, after everybody's gone to bed. Eleven or twelve o'clock at night is when I sit down and go through my catalogs. So having 24-hour service was the first thing we decided on."

Of course with so much of the mail order business having moved over to the internet, you can get orders even while sleeping and simply start your day off with the fun of getting a slew of e-mail orders from late-nighters or people in other time zones.

extra for orders that exceed a certain number of items, so you need to know this ahead of time.

Call Center Fees

Fees you can expect to pay include:

- An initial deposit of $200 to $400
- A monthly minimum of $75 to $100, or the actual per-minute amount, whichever is higher
- A setup fee of $250 or more if you choose to have the call center enter all your products into the software, assign product codes, and perform any other functions needed to get your operation computer ready. If you choose to set up your own program, the setup fee will be waived.
- Additional services will cost more depending on your needs and what the call center offers.

Phones

You will probably want a two-line phone so you can put one on hold while you're answering the other. If you have a dedicated fax line, you could opt for a third phone line—otherwise you can have one phone line that doubles for faxes—remember, e-mail has reduced the number of faxes sent. Your other phone is your cell phone and that should be primarily for outgoing business calls from you to suppliers, your drop shippers, or other such business and not for incoming orders.

A speaker is also a nice feature, especially for all those on-hold-forever calls to your banker, attorney, insurance company, and the like. Your hands are free to work on financial data or your latest advertising materials, your shoulder remains un-hunched, and you're free to move about the cabin while you listen to Muzak and wait your turn.

You can expect to pay about $70 to $80 for a two-line speakerphone with auto redial, memory dial, a mute button, and other assorted goodies.

Beware!

If you decide on an answering machine rather than a voice mail service, don't "enhance" your answering machine message with background music or a cutesy script. It's not professional. Keep it short and simple. Give your company's name—spoken clearly and carefully—and ask the callers to leave a short message and a phone number. Thank them for calling and assure them that someone from your office will return their call as soon as possible.

Power Surges and You

You should invest in a UPS, or uninterruptible power supply (not to be confused with UPS, the shipping service), for your computer system, especially if you are living in an area where lightning or power surges are frequent. Remember, even a flicker of power loss can shut down your computer or cause you to lose unsaved data. With a UPS in your arsenal, you won't lose power to your system when the power in your home flickers or fails. Instead, the unit flashes red and sounds a warning, giving you ample time to save your data, log off, and safely shut down your computer.

Cool and Calculating

What do calculators and telephones have in common? A numbered keypad and an important place on your desk. Even though your computer probably has an onboard calculator program, it helps to have the real thing close at hand. You can do quick calculations and then check your work with the paper tape. Expect to pay under $15 for a battery-operated model and $25 to $50 for a plug-in job.

▲

Stress Buster

Unless you plan to walk or bicycle to the post office every day as a form of exercise and stress relief, getting a postage meter is a good idea. Depending on the model you choose, you can not only stamp your mail but also fold, staple, insert, seal, label, weigh, sort, stack, and wrap it. Phew! The fancier and faster the machine, the more expensive it will be to rent or lease (and you can't purchase them; they are owned by the U.S. Postal Service). It used to be that you'd have to lug your postage meter down to the post office and stand in line to get it reset. Not anymore! Now you reset your meter by phone or computer. What's the cost for all this technology? It depends on what you get, but as a ballpark figure, you can expect to rent a postage meter/electronic scale combo for anywhere from $24 to $117 per month.

If you're really into automation, you can also purchase letter-folding and letter-opening machines, which can process up to 4,000 sheets per hour and 600 envelopes per minute, respectively. You probably won't need this type of speed immediately (and if you go with a lettershop, you won't need it at all), but you should know that these gizmos are available.

Paper Cloning

A copier is an optional item, probably the least important on the list, but as you grow, you may find it a worthwhile convenience. Keep in mind that you should never send a piece of paper out of your office unless you've kept a copy. You can always print two copies of every document you generate on your computer, keeping one as a file copy. Often, printers can be used for copying purposes as well. If, however, you feel you will have a lot of copy needs (more than the occasional trip to Staples or the local copy shop), then you can buy a copier, which usually will run you from $300 to $700 and up.

Office Furniture

Office furniture is optional. It is important that your work environment is comfortable and ergonomic, but if you're homebased, it's perfectly acceptable to start off at your dining room or kitchen table. When you are ready to make the move toward real office furniture for that oh-so-professional look, you've got a stunning array of options to choose from.

We shopped the big office supply stores and found midrange desks from $200 to $300, a computer work center for $200, printer stands from $50 to $75, two-drawer letter-size file cabinets (which can double as your printer stand) from $25 to $100, and a four-shelf bookcase for $70.

Chairs are a very personal matter, and one that is important. While you can skimp on an old desk or a work table that is strong enough for your computer, and you can use cartons or handmade shelves for files, the right chair can significantly decrease your chiropractor bills.

Look for a comfortable computer chair that can be adjusted for height and are ergonomically designed. Chairs will run you from $100 to $600 or more depending on whether you like arms, leather, or any special features. Don't skimp by using a folding chair that is the wrong height for your computer. Back pain, wrist pain, and an aching neck will take the fun out of any business day.

Lighting is the other essential on the list that you need to take seriously. Poor lighting will result in eyestrain and headaches. Make sure your work area is amply lit. Aim lights away from your computer screen, but if you are still getting a glare, consider a glare guard—they're inexpensive but very helpful.

Smart Tip

Tip...

Not using a pick-and-pack service? A hand truck, otherwise known as a dolly, can be a back saver when you need to cart around large packages for shipping or storage. Dollies come with a variety of features, from safety straps to cushioning, and cost anywhere from $45 to $300.

The Office Supplies Mini Shopping List

Computer/copier/fax paper	$_____
Blank business cards	_____
Blank letterhead stationery and matching envelopes	_____
File folders	_____
Return address self-stamper or stickers	_____
Extra printer cartridges	_____
Mouse pad	_____
Miscellaneous office supplies (pencils, paper clips, etc.)	_____
Extra fax cartridges	_____
Total Office Supplies Expenditures	$_____

The Mail Order Maven's Office Checklist

Use this list as a shopping guide for equipping your office. It's been designed with the one-person home office in mind. If you've got partners or employees, or you just inherited a million dollars from a mysterious foundation with the stipulation that you spend at least half on office equipment, you may want to make modifications.

After you've done your shopping, fill in the price next to each item and add up the total. This will tell you about how much you can expect to spend on the equipment you need.

High-Priority

❏ Windows XP-based Pentium-class PC with SVGA monitor, modem, and CD-ROM drive (or Mac system) $_____

❏ Laser or inkjet printer _____

❏ Fax machine or fax software program _____

❏ Mail order software _____

❏ Word processing software _____

❏ Desktop publishing software _____

❏ Accounting software _____

❏ Phones, two to three lines with voice mail or... _____

❏ Answering machine _____

❏ Uninterruptible power supply (UPS) _____

❏ Back up system/external hard drive _____

❏ Digital camera _____

❏ Scanner _____

❏ Calculator _____

❏ Postage meter/scale _____

❏ Office/computer chair _____

❏ Office supplies (see "Office Supplies Mini Shopping List," p. 155) _____

Not on the Critical List

❏ Surge Protector _____

❏ Copier _____

❏ Postage meter _____

❏ Dolly _____

❏ Desk _____

❏ Filing cabinet _____

❏ Bookcase _____

Total Office Equipment and Furniture Expenditures $_____

Your Business Location and Your Employees

While office furniture and equipment, as discussed in the last chapter, will initially be part of your planning and budget, the reality of having and using such equipment means that you need a place from which to work. In many industries, location, location, location, is all about your customers finding you. In mail order, however, you do not need a busy high-traffic corner location or an office in the swanky part of town to impress your clients. Location, in this case, means, a place you can call home... and often that very place is right there in your home, literally.

The Home Office

Before you buy office furniture or any office goodies, make sure you have a place in your home that is

- relatively quiet,
- free from interruptions (you'll have to set up some rules of the house),
- has windows for fresh air,
- has outlets for your electronic needs, and
- has phone jacks, or places in which you can have some new ones installed by the phone company.

Your home office space should be a place in which you can devote your brain power to your business without your kids running through on their way to the backyard. You should have enough room for your technical assistants as well as shelves, bookcases, or other storage for your files. You should also find a location in which you can control the temperature to accommodate the changes of season—this eliminates attics in many homes. A dedicated office space is the optimal choice—however, if you do not have that extra den or bedroom to make your home office, you will need to corner off part of another room, one in which you can find such quiet for a large enough portion of the day/night to get your work down without interruption or a television in the background.

Make sure all wiring is safely tucked away and again, remember to set up ground rules with family members.

You should also add some personal touches and some items that make you comfortable since all work and no play, or relaxation, makes for a crabby entrepreneur.

The home office is convenient: You couldn't get any closer to your work unless you slept next to your computer and your telephone... and some people do (although it's not necessary).

The home office is economical: You don't need to spend money on leased space, extra utilities, transportation costs, or lunches down at the corner grill—although, like many homebased entrepreneurs, you may chose to eat out or pick up lunch your favorite nearby eateries (or a local deli) merely to get out of the house.

Kate W., in Overland Park, Kansas, bases her business in her home. She starts early and works late into the night, but even so, she's around for her family. In Roswell, Georgia, Caryn O. also maintains a home office, although most of her business operations, along with her 10 employees, call a large warehouse "home." "I keep a home office," the textiles merchandiser explains, "where I do my scanning [onto the company website]." Along with a great many other tasks. "In the morning, between getting my [daughter] off to school," Caryn says, "I'm on the internet answering e-mail. Then I'm off to work. Then I leave at a certain time to get my daughter off the bus. When I get home, I am back on the computer answering e-mail and scanning in or deleting fabrics from the website. And I'm always in contact with the people at the warehouse."

Bright Idea

Some homes, especially older ones, have walk-in closets that are large enough to turn into a cozy little office—some even have windows. If your closet is of the sliding-door, runs-along-one-wall variety, take out the clothes and stash them somewhere. Remove the doors, and you've got a dandy office nook! If you decide to turn your closet into an office, make sure it has adequate ventilation and light.

Trucks and Neighbors

As mentioned earlier, you need to be aware of the zoning laws in your area—and, if necessary, obtain a variance for running a home business. The major concern of homebased business owners, in this regard, is having a slew of trucks pulling in and out of the driveway. It is, therefore, important to work from an outside warehouse if dealing with large items that can't just fit in your backseat or a van. Also, do your best not to call attention to yourself, even if you have a variance to do business. Neighbors can give you a hard time, so keep the business low key and focus on the neighborly hellos.

The Tax Man

A big advantage to the home office is the ability to wear two hats—to be at home with your family and be at work at the same time. Another advantage is the ability to count your home office as a tax write-off. The IRS will graciously allow you to deduct money from your income taxes if you're using a portion of your home as your income-producing workspace. You can deduct the percentage of expenses equivalent to the percentage of space your home office occupies. If, for example, you're using one room in an eight-room house, you can deduct one-eighth of your rent or mortgage plus one-eighth of your utility bills.

There is, of course, an "if" involved here. You can only use this deduction *if* you are using a space in your home solely as your office. If you have turned your spare bedroom into your office and you don't use it for anything but conducting your business, then you qualify. If, however, your office is tucked into a corner of the kitchen, and you're still feeding people in there, you don't qualify for the home office deduction (unless you can convince the IRS that you order Chinese food every night and the refrigerator is actually a file cabinet.) This goes for other home deductions as well. You can pro-rate your electric bill and other bills for the business portion used within the home. Be sure you are as exact as possible in your calculations when figuring such deductions.

Organized and Efficient

If you prefer to have your coffee and croissant—and your office—in your home, it's important to remember that you're still a professional. Your work quarters, like yourself, should be organized and efficient. Of course, organized does not meet some arbitrary standard. It means being able to find things in your work environment. Some people work very well with piles on their desks while others maintain clear desks and have everything filed in filing cabinets. Whatever works best for you is the solution.

It's also important to note that while putting your office space together that you arrange everything in such a way that you can utilize it to your advantage.

Appropriate a desk or a table large enough to hold your computer, keyboard, phone, pencil holder, stapler, etc., and still have enough room left to spread out your working papers. Don't skimp on elbow room.

Files and Storage

Your main realms of activity will be advertising, order processing, administration, and shipping. Make sure you have enough space to store currently running and already-tried ads and catalogs, as well as files for current and potential advertising venues, manufacturers, suppliers, and customer service issues. Whether you use the fanciest hanging file folders in mahogany drawers or simple manila ones in cardboard boxes, you must be able to access this information quickly and easily. It's no fun digging through the back of the clothes closet or running out to the garage every time somebody calls with a question.

You'll also need enough space to package your products for shipping. It doesn't matter if it's the kitchen table or a special workstation in your office, so long as there's adequate room to spread out your materials and wrap that package professionally.

Also, don't forget your catalogs, brochures, or other mail-out materials! You will need easily accessible boxes or shelves where you can keep these items safe, clean, and tidy at all times.

The Home Office Worksheet

Use this handy worksheet to locate and design your home office.

List three possible locations in your home for your office, which should include a work area for you and enough space for your desk, computer, and telephone:

1. _____

2. _____

3. _____

Make a physical survey of each location:

○ Are phone and electrical outlets placed so that your equipment can easily access them? Or will you be faced with unsightly, unsafe cords snaking across the carpet?

○ Measure your space. Will your current desk or table (or the one you have your eye on) fit?

○ Do you have adequate lighting? If not, can you create or import it?

○ Is there proper ventilation?

○ What is the noise factor?

○ Is there room to spread out your work?

○ Optional: How close is it to the coffeemaker? Refrigerator? (This can be either a plus or minus, depending on your current jitter factor and waistline.)

Next, list three possible home locations for your inventory:

1. _____

2. _____

3. _____

Again, make a survey of each location:

○ Is it climate-controlled? Will you need climate control?

○ Is there adequate lighting, ventilation and space for you to easily access your inventory?

The Home Office Worksheet, continued

○ Will you need to construct special shelving or add other storage space? If so, make notes here:

_____

_____

Finally, take a look at your packing and shipping space options. Make a list:

1. _____

2. _____

3. _____

Ask yourself:

❏ Will you have an adequate, well-lit work space?

❏ Is there room to stash and easily access packing, gift-wrapping, and shipping materials and tools?

Growing Pains

As your business grows, you may decide to move into a commercial office space. Because the mail order business doesn't rely on client traffic or a prestige address, any area that appeals to you and your pocketbook is up for grabs. Rents in high-traffic areas like malls or trendy downtown shopping districts can be astronomical, so don't set your sights on them. Instead, try going the office/warehouse route in an industrial park. If product storage, rather than room for people, is your only problem, you might consider keeping your home office and renting space from a self-storage facility, as Kate, the team logo merchandiser, has done.

Beth H., the gluten-free foods specialist, houses her company, along with her ten employees, in an industrial park. The site features office space with an adjacent warehouse.

If storage is not a concern for you, but you want an office away from home, you might look for commercial space in other areas—but not in the retail arena. You don't need the high visibility, or the higher rent that goes with it.

Freeze or Melt

The biggest factor in your decision whether to have a home or away office—other than you and your family's personal preferences and lifestyle—will be inventory storage. Take these questions into consideration:

- How large will your products be?
- How diverse are they?
- Will they require special handling or storage?
- Can they survive in a spare bedroom or the garage, or will they need controlled conditions?

If you're selling foods from New England's shores, for example, you won't get very far storing Maine lobster or cod in the garage (unless it's an unheated one in the dead of winter). You'll need refrigeration. If you're selling candles in New Orleans, you may want to think twice about storing them in your garage in the summer (unless you're going for the naturally melted look).

Prestige Address

You've decided on a home office. Now what about your address? Mail order mavens have mixed views on this issue. Some feel that since customers do occasionally decide to pay a surprise visit, it's best to rent a post office box and preserve your privacy. Others believe that a post office box instead of a street address gives customers the idea that you're a fly-by-night operation.

One way to maintain your privacy and keep a "real" address is to rent a box from a company like Mail Boxes Etc. You use the rental facility's physical address and add a "suite" number to distinguish your box from those of the facility's other patrons. Your customers, however, won't know the difference.

The only drawback to this system, of course, is that you have to pop over to the facility every time you want your mail, whereas if you stick to your home address, the postman brings it to your door. (Mail centers will provide you with a key so you can check your box after hours.)

Another plus for the mail center option: When you have inventory shipped to you, UPS will quote and guarantee delivery dates if you have packages sent to a "business" address. But if they come to your home office, they consider it a residential delivery and will not guarantee dates.

Your Cargo Bay

Commercial mail order facilities usually range in floor size from 2,000 to 5,000 square feet and are divided into office and inventory storage spaces. Obviously, the more storage space you have, the more inventory you can house. But don't overextend your "cargo bay" and skimp on the area allocated to humans—you'll still need a command center for your shipping, receiving, order processing, and administrative work.

Whether your office is in an artist's loft, over a bagel bakery, or in an industrial park, you'll need the same basic setup as in a home office, with plenty of room for all those files, plus your desk, chair, minimalist furniture for guests, and a desk and chair for any employee(s) you may hire. Also, let's not forget the electronics. Whether in a home or commercial office, your computer should occupy a place of honor, away from dirt and extreme cold or heat. Ditto for your printer and fax machine.

In a commercial office, you'll also want that altarpiece of American offices, the coffeemaker. In addition, if you can provide a tidbit or two—a plate of cookies, for example, when you know those rare visitors (like manufacturers' reps) are arriving—you'll go a long way toward cementing ties. Everyone appreciates a treat! Many office facilities, of all types, have some of the kitchen amenities.

An alternate option is to lease space with another business. Often, companies buy more space than they need in anticipation of future expansion. While, you may also anticipate expansion down the road, you can lease part of the larger space during your formative years. This way, you'll share costs such as electricity. Of course, if you have enough funding, you could go the opposite route and be the tenant with plenty of room, renting some of your excess space out to a young up-and-coming company until growth determines that you will need the entire space. Either way, make sure it is in the lease that sub-leasing is okay with the landlord.

Alternative Officing

If commercial office space is not your bag, you might consider a less conventional approach. You can rent a house or an apartment (providing you check the zoning laws first). If you're already living in an apartment, you may choose to rent another unit in the same building to use as your office. You can walk to work. In fact, the landlord may give you a package deal—or a finder's fee! Don't be surprised, however if this idea doesn't fly—zoning laws not withstanding, many building owners, managers and tenants do not want a business operating out of their apartment complex.

Leases

If you do opt for any types of commercial office space, make sure you have an attorney review the lease carefully. Choose someone who is familiar with leases in your state or city, rather than hiring your wife's cousin who is a divorce attorney.

There is no such thing as a "standard lease" despite what a landlord may tell you. Every lease can be negotiated and each has its own fine print. Make sure all common areas are discussed in advance and make sure you know what you are responsible for as a tenant of the building. Also, make sure you have an out after x amount of time. You will also need to know if you can sub-lease and what the parameters are for doing so. Additionally, you will need to know what the future holds in terms of rent hikes—how much and how often. These need to be in conjunction with state and local laws, so review them with your attorney as well.

Hiring Employees

Depending on how much growth you envision for your business, you may never need employees. Some small businesses do very well with one person at the helm, utilizing a fulfillment house and a call center. These are not employees, but services for which you will be paying. An employee, full-time or part-time, works directly for you.

Employees bring with them as many cons as pros. When you hire help, you're no longer a swinging single. You've got added responsibilities. Suddenly there's payroll to meet, workers' compensation insurance to pay, state and federal employee taxes to pay, and work to delegate.

Some people are born employers, finding it easy to teach someone else the ropes and then hand over the reins. Others never feel very comfortable telling someone else what to do or how to do it.

One of the many perks of the mail order business is that you can accomplish a great deal without ever hiring anyone. You can easily start out as a one-person show, handling all the tasks of your fledgling company yourself. You won't need help immediately. Then, as your company flourishes, you may find that:

- you need more hours in a day,
- you need science to make great strides in the field of cloning, or
- you need to hire help.

One Singular Sensation

Most of the work in a mail order business can be more or less compartmentalized into three areas: sales and marketing; order processing and fulfillment; and general management and administration. As a newbie mail order operator, you will probably have all three areas handled by one person: you. You'll have to be, as the song says, one singular sensation—capable of wearing a lot of hats and tap dancing your way through every routine in your company. You'll need to:

- Conceive and direct extensive marketing campaigns that will garner sales
- Design and produce ads, brochures, catalogs, or other direct-mail pieces
- Write ad, brochure, or catalog copy
- Manage order taking
- Fulfill orders
- Keep the books
- Rent and maintain mailing lists
- Handle customer service
- Deal with manufacturers and suppliers
- Seek out new inventory where no mail order maven has gone before

However, as your company grows, you may eventually discover that you can't do it all yourself. When you reach the point where you're walking around with coffee jitters and bags under your eyes from multitasking, you may want to outsource some of your responsibilities. You can, for example, contract with:

- A copywriter and a graphic designer to do advertising and catalog development
- A fulfillment house to warehouse your products and process orders
- A list maintenance service to keep your mailing database in pristine condition

Again, these are not employees. It is when the tasks that you do begin to get over-whelming, that you will want to bring someone in to help on a regular basis. Hence, your first employee(s).

Typically, order taking, fulfillment, customer service, promotion and advertising, and maintaining data (which ranges from bookkeeping to handling the mailing list), are the primary areas in which mail order entrepreneurs typically take on help. Often, you will start with someone part time and then move to a full-timer.

Caution: Before Hiring Anyone!

You can't hire someone until you know exactly what he or she will be doing and how much you will be paying the individual to do it. You will need to sit down and carefully map out the scenario for bringing another person into your home or office. Here is a list of some of the areas you will wan to consider while drawing up a job outline:

- What tasks will he or she perform?
- What equipment will this person need?

- What space do you have available?

- Do you want him or her to work independently or closely with you? (This depends on your reason for hiring the person and your style of work.)

- Are you looking solely for an assistant or someone to start taking on additional responsibilities as he or she becomes more comfortable in the business?

- What background/training and technical skills should this person have?

- What rules and regulations need be in place? This includes breaks, lunch hours, rules of the house/office, parking, etc. You need to set up some basic parameters in advance. If someone comes to work drunk or has illegal narcotics on them, will this person be fired immediately? What constitutes grounds for dismissal?

- Does he or she get a vacation? Sick days? Overtime pay? (Be cognizant of the labor laws in your state—read them in advance!)

It's important that you put most of this on paper and have a copy to give to your employee(s). There are numerous lawsuits every day whereby employees are suing their bosses or former bosses. The more that you have in writing (signed by the employee, stating that he or she has read the material), the better off you will be.

Also, keep in mind that when interviewing someone, and discussing their hiring, you are not allowed to ask personal questions, such as age (other than whether or not the applicant is over 18) marital status, sexual preference, and so on. Likewise, you need to make it clear, in writing, that you are an equal opportunity employer, meaning you do not discriminate by race, religion, or sex.

Hiring the right people can help you move your business forward. Hiring the wrong people can put you out of business. Screen potential employees carefully, call references, and check their backgrounds. There are background-checking services available today that—through the use of technology—are able to assist you in screening employees. It's worth your while to have background checks done on employees so that you do not run into trouble later. Places such as Personnel Profiles at www.personnelprofiles.com and InfoCublic at www.infocublic.com among several service providers that can let you know about the background, credit history and, in some cases drug history, of your future employees. More details can be found in the Appendix.

Money

The final aspect, and typically the first one that comes up when determining whether or not to hire help, is money. First, can you afford to pay someone on a regular basis? If so, can you afford the going rate, whatever that may be in your market or region of the country? Clearly, someone in a major market such as New York City or Los Angeles may earn more per hour than someone in a small town. Know what people are getting and be competitive. To entice good employees, you can offer benefits. This

Good Questions

Not only does the job applicant prepare for an interview—the interviewer should also be prepared. You want to know which questions you want to ask and what answers you are seeking. The idea is to get an overall feel for the applicant's past experience, attitude, aptitude, and personality. You may want to find out what he or she hopes to do in the future (goals or aspirations). Questions that ask how the person will react in various situations can give you an idea of whether or not the person can handle situations that require quick decision making.

A resume may show that someone has been a cashier for five years, but it may not show whether or not the individual has the people skills you would like from someone taking orders and handling customer service. You need to evaluate skills and the personality/character of the individual.

is determined based on what you can afford. Medical and health benefits can be costly for one employee, but may be worthwhile if you can get someone who can truly help you in the long run to maximize your business. Other incentives may include flexible hours or freebies if you have an appealing product. Mail order entrepreneurs selling video games, for example, may have an easier time attracting an employee who is a gamer by simply throwing in some freebies—to be used after work hours.

Rules and Regulations

Businesses are, by law, required to have employer identification numbers and to file and pay necessary taxes, workers compensation, social security (FICA), and so on. Here is a short list of what you need to know before hiring employees.

1. You need to obtain an EIN (employer identification number).

2. You must register with your state's labor department.

3. A payroll system must be in place for withholding taxes, which need to be paid on schedule.

4. You'll need to inquire about—and (depending on the number of employees) get - workers' compensation insurance.

5. There will be required notices pertaining to safety and employee law. Make sure you are aware of all safety requirements, especially if employees are helping you with packaging and shipping.

6. You should have software, or simply a notebook, in which to keep all employee data.

7. You will need to run background checks and make sure all of your employees are of working age, legal citizens, have proper working papers, and social security numbers.

8. Finally, you will need to file *IRS Form 940-EZ* each year and all other related tax forms applicable to your state.

Start by contacting the department of labor in your state and the nearest IRS office to make sure you have all of the necessary paperwork. Discuss all of this with your account and/or attorney prior to getting started.

Your Helpers

We are going the archetype route here and giving you a thumbnail sketch of the different team members you may want to hire. Keep in mind, however, that these are sketches. Your company will be as individual as you are, and the people you choose to hire will also be individuals. If you do your hiring right, using your analytical and intuitive skills and communicating your enthusiasm for the company (plus providing incentives), your employees will be more than worker bees—they'll be team members, every bit as creative and dedicated to your company as you are.

Sales and Marketing

Your sales and marketing people may arguably form the most important areas of the firm. Why? Because they'll be responsible for planning advertising campaigns, designing ads, catalogs, and other printed materials, compiling and maintaining lists, and actually selling your merchandise to customers.

Here are the sales and marketing areas for which you may want to either hire someone or look for a freelancer to contract (who would not be full-time employee):

- **Planning and management.** These are your hybrid pocket-protector/market innovators, responsible for analyzing the market, developing a marketing plan, and supervising the plan's implementation. They'll do this by creating surveys, analyzing statistical data from government and private research sources, charting the courses of customers' spending habits, analyzing trends, and testing all campaigns. Often, you can hire someone as needed by seeking out a consultant in the area. Make sure he or she has a good track record and hire very carefully since results here are not always as tangible as finding someone who sold 500,000 widgets single-handedly.

- **Graphic design.** These are your artistic types, the ones with the weird postcards and clip art tacked all over their work areas and the really fun ideas for designing your materials and giving them that visual edge. They also do all the production stuff, working with photos, clip art, and original graphics, combining them with your copy in layout programs to create documents that will be output en masse at a print shop. This may not require a full-timer—possibly a part-time person (always on the books so you don't get yourself into hot water).

- **Customer service.** These people should be excellent at problem solving, yet mellow enough to take cranky people in stride without dishing it back. They also need to be sharp enough to think on their feet because they'll handle customer complaints, returns, and other problems. They should have the authority to make decisions about what to replace or repair and whom to reimburse. This may require a full timer depending on the size of your orders—someone whom you see with future possibilities in the business.

- **Sales.** Friendly! In most mail order operations, sales refers to the inside salespeople who actually take orders over the phone and—don't forget!—do cross-selling and up-selling. These people often find their jobs overlapping with those of the customer service reps because they sometimes field complaints, so they should also be trained in how to handle various customer service issues as well.

The ideal setup would be to have at least one employee for each of the four areas described above. If that is not yet possible because of your budget, then hire in order of your most pressing needs, which is usually sales. Cross-training someone to be helpful in various aspects of the business can be beneficial to both you and your employee.

Order Processing and Fulfillment

This is a key aspect of any mail order business. If you decide not to use a fulfillment service, you may need to bring in help to handle this important function in-house. Remember, if your customers don't get the product they thought they were ordering, or they don't get it when they expect it, or it arrives smashed or dented—or any other nasty permutation of the above—your company will not go very far, despite a brilliant marketing campaign. In this area, you may want to hire:

- **A warehouse manager.** This is your inventory and shipping expert, the one in the comfortable khakis with the pencil tucked behind his or her ear and the omnipresent clipboard (and computer printouts). Your manager will schedule workers, assign duties, keep a log of shipped merchandise and incoming returns, and—under your aegis—hire and train staff. This needs to be someone who is ready to handle a full-time position with a fair amount of responsibilities. In addition, you'll want someone with whom you feel you will have good communication.

- **Packers and shippers.** These are your T-shirt-and-sneaker types, bobbing along to music on their iPods (if you don't mind). The job is to make sure everything arrives in one piece and looking like a special gift. For this job, you can typically look for students or other part timers. Some may stick around a while, but most won't.

Administration and Management

Now we arrive at the internal operations branch of your mail order business, the people concerned with all those accounting, record keeping, and personnel matters. Here's who you'll be looking at:

- **Accounting manager.** This button-down type will handle supply and inventory invoices, make sure large orders handled by contract are paid to you in a timely manner, and make sure your bills are paid to others on time. Your accounting genius will also handle customers' bounced checks and charge-backs (remember, this is when the customer returns something paid for by credit card), and balance your books. Look for someone with a good numbers background who is ready to work full time and perhaps learn the business.

- **Record keeper.** Here's another archetypal button-downer, responsible for maintaining accurate ledgers of customer purchases, archiving retired paperwork, and scanning existing paperwork for errors. This person will work with your accounting manager but might also report in some degree to your marketing manager.

- **Human resources or personnel.** Whichever name you call it, the person in this department is your no-nonsense, by-the-book (but fun) type who looks out for the health, welfare, and morale of your employees. This person oversees health insurance administration, advertises your employment opportunities, and sometimes hires staff, and devises and administers employee benefits like movie tickets and ride-sharing plans. (Choose someone with fun ideas!) Your personnel manager is also responsible for payroll, including keeping track of those sick and vacation days. For a small but growing mail order business, a one-person personnel department will usually do the trick—and initially, the one person will probably be you. Typically you won't need to fill this position until you have been around a while and built up the business significantly.

> **Bright Idea**
>
> How about a college intern as an advertising or marketing whiz, copywriter, or graphic designer? You'll benefit from the student's fresh ideas and not having to pay very much money; the student will benefit from the resume-building, on-the-job experience. Talk with local colleges about their intern programs and see how you can qualify.

▲

Your Kind of People

Now that we've got all the archetype, stereotype, boilerplate personnel stuff out of the way, let's go back to what we said earlier about hiring your kind of people, your very own invaluable team members—people who are individuals.

Moms and Dads

When Caryn, the fabric merchandiser, began her hiring program, she decided to make her company as personal for her ten employees as it is for her. "My company is made up of moms and dads," the Georgia resident says in no uncertain terms. "My family is always number one—that's the most important thing over anything. I felt that the one thing I could give to other people was to allow them the same thing that I allow myself: for their family to be number one. So if I have a mom or dad whose kid wants them at a school event or is sick, or their spouse is getting an award and they want to be there—they can do it.

"Yes, they'll be missed at work," Caryn admits, "but somebody else will take over for them and take up the slack. That's the kind of people I want working for me because those are the values I think are so important."

Moms and Teens

Beth, the gluten-free foods provider, also employs a staff of ten—and among them, who else but moms? "What happens," the former cooking teacher explains, "is that most of the people are not full-time. They're part-time, so we rotate. We employ moms in the morning until about three in the afternoon. Then we have coverage from maybe one to five with people who don't have to get home right away to their families."

Who are these afternoon people? They're teens, recruited from the high school right around the corner from Beth's office. "It's perfect," the Connecticut mom says, "because when they're off from school, they want to pick up some extra money, and the moms aren't available because they're home with the kids.

"I recruited almost every one of the moms from my son's class," Beth reports. "Little by little, they each ended up knowing other people [who spread the word]. There are four or five of us who have kids in the same class."

That same family feeling has helped Beth recruit and retain her teens, too. She started out by contacting the high school guidance office. "We had a really great crop of kids," the former food writer says. "If one person was leaving or one person came to work for us, they would bring a friend. So, for a long time, we were able to keep going with just friends of friends."

After a while, however, everybody went off to college. "We started to run out of friends of friends," Beth explains. "But we don't have a lot of summer openings because our kids come back then."

Of course, you need to make sure that teens have their working papers—states have different laws regarding hiring teens, some starting at 14 years of age.

Holiday Help

You may want to start, as Beth has, with part-time help, someone to work four hours in the morning or afternoon, or perhaps two or three days a week. Or you might want to start off with somebody full-time. Some mail order mavens take on help during their busiest season and take all the reins back in their own hands the rest of the year.

Kate W., with two and a half years of operation under her belt, had in October already interviewed temporary help for the coming holiday season rush. "Last holiday season, I thought we were busy," the football fan says, "and that's the volume we did this summer. With 15,000-plus catalogs out there this year, I really expect to have the holidays be a lot busier. I don't like to do the computer stuff, so I'll either do the phones or the packing. There's too much for one person to do in a day."

Whether you hire full-time, part-time, or seasonally, there are no rules except the ones you make—which is another of the wonderful perks that come with running your own business. Well, actually there are some rules, those imposed by the IRS, which means hiring people must be on the books.

All Together Now

Another alternative to hiring employees is to put your family to work, if they are so inclined to help out. We've already seen how some of the mail order mavens we interviewed used family computer gurus to set up and maintain websites. Why not take your family operations even further?

Teenage children can help out with data entry and can certainly pack and ship products. So can a willing spouse. When you have on-call help in the family, you have the advantage of no employee taxes or insurance, although—at least in the case of teens—you'll probably still have to pay your workers. Helping mom or dad or a spouse with the family business gives everybody a warm, fuzzy feeling of pitching in and can be a great togetherness booster.

That's certainly what Caryn has found. "You come into my house," the Atlanta-area merchandiser says, "and walk into the room that's my home office, we've got 50 to 70 fabric bolts in there at any one time and samples, and the kids are matching things up. My kids have even gotten involved in their own way, one with crafts, one with other things. We all get into it; we all talk about this stuff and about new ideas all the time."

The Sampler

Hire new team members as you need them, but not until they're really a necessity. There's nothing worse for you as an employer—or for your employee—than a position without enough to do. It leads to boredom, anxiety, and financial pressures. But when you really and truly need someone, go ahead and hire.

"We have one person now who just handles samples," says Caryn. "That's a new department. When we got on the internet, there were so many customers who wanted samples because they saw them on [our website]. We were so inundated with sample requests that now we've got a full-time position."

Caryn didn't start out with a sample request filler or any of her other nine employees. "We started small," the Roswell, Georgia, mom recalls. "Actually, my first employee was the person I hired to take care of my son, whom I brought to work with me.

Insuring Your Gems

Once you find those gems of employees, you'll need to think about caring for them. Workers' compensation insurance laws vary from state to state; check with your insurance agent for details in your area. Workers' comp covers you for any illness or injury your employees might incur that is directly related to employment with you. Although your employee may be working in your home, your homeowner's insurance probably won't pay for a problem incurred there, on the grounds that it's actually a workers' compensation case. Rather than making yourself a nervous wreck over all this (creating your own mental health claim), check with your insurance agent (and check the labor laws) and then make an informed decision. As soon as you bring other people into your place of work, whether it's your home or an office, you need to take precautions against liability. Today, more and more people are finding unique reasons for filing lawsuits, so don't be one of those folks who believes it can't happen to them. The dry cleaning business in Washington, D.C., surely did not think that they could possibly be sued for $65,000 for ruining one pair of pants, but someone tried. Fortunately the dry cleaner won and did not have to pay—nonetheless, take precautions, first with insurance, then against potential liability.

More on protecting yourself against customer lawsuits later. For employees, make sure everything is spelled out and have company rules and regulations in writing—even in a casual work atmosphere, matters come up that need to be addressed, such as family leave, time off, etc. Upon hiring, be professional and hand out anything from a comprehensive employee manual to a one-page sheet that can be read by each new hire—and be sure to have them sign that they received it and read it.

10

Pushing the Envelope, Part I: Direct-Mail Advertising

In this chapter, we explore what might well be the most fun, exciting, creative, and most demanding part of mail order: pushing the envelope (or catalog, brochure, or other direct-mail piece). As a mail order maven, a great deal of your resources will go into designing and implementing advertising campaigns to take your sales to the limits and beyond.

▲

Be prepared. Many mail order entrepreneurs estimate that they spend 25 percent of their startup budget on acquiring mailing lists and developing advertising materials, and 10 to 15 percent of their annual expenses on maintaining these efforts.

The ultimate goal of mail order advertising is not just to inform your customers of the quality or value of your product or service; but to inspire immediate action—to get the person to go on to your website, dial a phone number, or pick up a pen and paper and order now.

How are you going to achieve this? Through just about any medium you choose: catalogs, fliers, brochures, sales letters, print ads in magazines and other publications, the internet, radio, and television. We've divvied all of this up into two chapters. This first chapter on advertising deals with the direct-mail methods—the catalogs, fliers, and other materials you send winging through the postal system. We'll delve into the mechanics and magic of advertising in magazines and on television, radio, and the internet in the next chapter: Pushing the Envelope, Part II. In that chapter, we'll also talk about other ways of promoting and marketing your business, some of which can be very cost effective.

Line Dancing

All direct-marketing ads follow one of two formats: the one-step or the two-step. Although these sound like Texas line dances for which you have to be light on your feet and well-coordinated, they're actually very simple. The one-step ad encourages potential customers to order immediately, while the two-step ad introduces the product or catalog (step 1) and asks the prospect to contact you for more information, like a catalog or brochure (which you then send as step 2). The modern version of step two can be to go to the computer and punch up your website.

Why would you want one type of ad instead of the other? Several reasons. You'd choose the one-step when:

- You're advertising one or a few products as opposed to an entire catalog.
- The product(s) can be easily described and understood.
- Potential customers won't need further enticement or encouragement to purchase the product(s).

Take a look at the sample one-step display ad on page 178. Using a hypothetical company, Chocoholic Central, you can see that this is an ad designed to offer one product with simple variations, which are described with a few "brush strokes" of typescript. Part of the ad is an order form that the customer can mail back with a check or with their credit card information. The middle of the order form says "Order Today in Time for the Holidays!" to further encourage that immediate order. You should note that we've also encouraged telephone orders with a prominent toll-free number and given customers the option of ordering through the internet with the website address.

The Mail Order Two-Step

So when do you use the two-step ad? When you want to:

- introduce a line of products or your catalog
- sell products that cannot be easily explained in a small ad
- develop a list of interested prospects to which you will send that expensive catalog.

Check out the sample two-step display ad on page 179. Instead of advertising one particular product, it generates interest in Chocoholic Central's entire product line and entices the potential customer to order a catalog or go to the website for a virtual catalog. This method is particularly effective because you only send catalogs to people who have already expressed an interest in your products. This can also help you develop your mailing list.

The two-step ad is usually used in print media rather than electronic venues like radio, television, and the internet.

Best Product in the Galaxy

Now that you understand the difference between a one-step, a two-step, and a waltz, you'll want to tailor your advertising to your target audience. Yes, we know we've already discussed this, but it bears repeating. Targeting your audience is the most important step in using your advertising budget wisely.

You don't want to target just any old consumers—you want the ones most likely to purchase your product. And to get to these people, you've got to do your homework. Start with the same questions about your target audience that you answered when you did your market research.

Once you've evaluated your potential customers, you've got to be able to reach them. It doesn't matter if you have the most exciting product in the galaxy—if nobody in the galaxy knows about it, it isn't going to sell. So spend some quality time evaluating how to reach your people. If you're selling travel services, you'll want to advertise on The Travel Channel, within the pages of *Travel & Leisure* magazine, and/or on Orbitz or one of the popular travel websites because that's where travel-oriented people go for information and entertainment. If you're selling baby clothes, you'll get more orders for your advertising dollar by placing your ads in magazines aimed at parents rather than in general women's magazines or websites that attract college students, most of whom are not yet parents. Focus your advertising on the specific

For the Chocolate Lover In Your Life

Why just eat the candy when you can eat the box, too?

That's right, now you can enjoy a selection of edible chocolate delights inside one of our luscious dark Belgian chocolate boxes embellished with marzipan roses and edible gold leaf!

Choose from one of four elegant, edible sizes:

		Quantity	Total Cost
4-inch by 4-inch square	$20.00	_____	_____
6-inch by 6-inch square	$28.00	_____	_____
8-inch by 8-inch square	$40.00	_____	_____
6-inch-diameter heart	$42.00	_____	_____

Florida residents add 6% sales tax	_____
Shipping & handling	3.95
Total	_____

Order Today in Time for the Holidays!

Name _____

Address _____

City _____ State _____ Zip _____

Phone ( ) _____

☐ Check ☐ Visa ☐ MasterCard ☐ Discover Card ☐ American Express

Card # _____ Exp. ____ / ____

Signature _____

(as shown on card)

Or Call Us Toll-Free at (800) 555-4000 to Place Your Order!

Chocoholic Central

123 Cocoa Court

Truffle Bay, FL 30000

www.ChocoholiccCentral.com

And may all your dreams be sweet!   Code V11

audience most likely to buy your products: parents. Since parenting magazines have a smaller circulation than their general women's counterparts, your ad costs will be cheaper, but you'll connect with the people you want to reach. Remember, advertising in a magazine with a 100,000 circulation that reaches 10,000 people in your target audience will probably cost much more than advertising in a magazine that has a 30,000 circulation, of which 20,000 are in your target group. In the second scenario, you're getting more bang for your advertising buck.

When your ad costs come down, your profits go up, and, as Martha Stewart would say, "That's a good thing."

Reality List

Targeting means more than choosing your audience with care. It also means carefully selecting, and compiling, your mailing list. The absolute best list you could possibly choose would consist of people guaranteed to buy at least one of everything in your line on a weekly basis. Since that list probably exists only in the realm of fantasy, your absolute best "reality list" is one composed of people who have already purchased similar merchandise at similar prices by mail order. So if you're selling books on rose gardening, you'll want to target people who've already bought mail order books on gardening—and specifically on rose gardening. If you're selling angel figurines, you'll want to target people who have already bought angelic collectibles through the mail. People have specific interests, and once they've decided what those are, they're generally hooked.

You may not be able to pinpoint all those rose gardeners or angelic types quite that specifically, but the closer you can come—say, by identifying people who like gardening (or, even better, flower gardening)—the better list you'll have.

Mailing Lists Revisited

A mailing list can make or break a direct-mail campaign, and a good list can have a greater impact than doubling your ad budget.

You can target your audience more effectively with a mailing list than with any other medium. Suppose you decide to go with an alternative and advertise on television, perhaps during "I Love Lucy" reruns or "The X-Files" or the "Tonight Show." Although each will have its own demographic profile, you'll get a fairly indiscriminate selection of viewers. You have no way of knowing if they're confirmed mail order buyers or if they routinely refuse all direct mail. You don't know if your audience is made up of teenagers, seniors, young singles, or older married couples.

Ah, but when you rent a good mailing list from a reputable place, you've got your audience targeted to a T. You can choose Midwestern women who've bought bridal gowns through the mail or Northeastern men who like mail order tools and earn more than $50,000 a year.

Common Threads

As we've discussed, in the mailing list world, there are two types of lists: the compiled list and the buyer, or response, list. A compiled list is made up of people who belong to certain groups or organizations—for example, members of alumni organizations or car clubs, members of professional organizations, or even people who have attended certain types of seminars or workshops. A compiled list can also be made up of people

Who, What, and Where

Remember the old reporters' adage of always asking who, what, when, where, why, and how? Use the same questions to home in on your target customers and refine your advertising goals:

- ○ Who are my potential customers?
- ○ What can I offer that they would be interested in buying?
- ○ Where can I find these potential customers?
- ○ Why should they buy from me instead of from their present source?
- ○ When (how fast) can I provide my products to them?
- ○ How can I persuade them to do business with me?

with specific demographic characteristics in common—those living in Manhattan or those who make more than $40,000 a year. You get the picture. The main point to remember with compiled lists is that the people on them are not necessarily traditional mail order purchasers—buying through catalogs or from mailings. However, today, it is becoming more and more likely that you will target e-mail shoppers (who are actually mail order customers, they just don't realize it).

Now, the other type of list—the buyer list—is the one you want to shoot for. Why? Because the people on it are already known mail order buyers. They might be buyers of cookbooks or auto parts or dog toys, but the idea here is that since they've already purchased a product related to yours through the mail, they're more likely to be interested in yours. This is why, once you start making sales, you need to compile a list of all of your purchasers—they are your very own buyers list and the people you most want to reach out to with new offerings. After all, not only have they purchased items via mail order, but they've bought from you!

This does not mean you should never use compiled lists. It does mean, however, that you should use them carefully. As a newbie, your best bet is to stay away from them altogether. Stack all the cards you can in your favor: Use buyer lists.

The Formula

Like any good mad scientist, the savvy mail order maven also has a magic formula for working with lists. That formula is RFM: Recency, Frequency, and Money. RFM helps you identify the best lists by asking three questions: How recently have the peo-

▲

Lists Galore

Wondering just how many lists are out there and how selective they can be? Check out these offerings from various list owners and brokers who advertised in just one recent issue of *Catalog Age* magazine:

- ○ Amateur and professional jewelers
- ○ Avid book readers
- ○ Boating enthusiasts
- ○ Career women
- ○ Cat and dog owners
- ○ Gardeners
- ○ Grandparents who buy gifts for their grandchildren
- ○ Health-conscious Hispanics
- ○ High-end travelers (those who spend big bucks)
- ○ Hikers and campers
- ○ Home workshop enthusiasts
- ○ Medical professionals
- ○ Offshore fishermen
- ○ Video producers

ple on the list ordered something by mail? How frequently do they order? How much money do they spend?

Besides the all-important RFM factor, demographics are crucial in choosing your list. You need to consider income, age, gender, education, type of residence, occupation, and use of credit cards in making purchases. If you're selling romance novels, you would probably choose a girls-only list, because most men wouldn't be interested. Got it? Good.

Another list selection factor is psychographics. This is the categorization of people by psychological profile. Political conservatives, for instance, are more likely than liberals, to be hunters. So if you're selling hunting gear, you might try mailing to Republicans. If a list owner or broker says he's got a psychographic profile, ask for it. Check out the profiles listed to see if they match your prospective buyers.

Yet another factor to consider is who else has been renting the same list and how often. This can tell you who your competitors are and how successful they have been with it. If you've got a travel service and you find that another travel service has rented the same list four times in the past year, you can figure they're having good luck with it—which means you probably will, too.

1,2,3, Testing

Mail order mavens do a lot of testing to determine which products are viable and at what prices, which mailing lists are the best, and which ads or other sales materials are most effective. It's extremely difficult to determine the effect of most traditional forms of advertising, but because mail order is a direct-response venue that goes right to the customer, you get—for better or worse—immediate results.

You can find out within a matter of weeks what's working for you and what isn't. Then, if something isn't working, you can tweak it, or scrap it, or scrape it into another form. Testing requires accurate record keeping and number crunching.

You may not like the prospect of analyzing all those figures, but if you don't constantly test and evaluate your ads, you're cutting yourself off from a major avenue to mail order success. Here are the three main elements you'll want to test:

1. Advertising mediums. Which sells better for you, display ads in magazines or radio ads on local stations?

2 Venues within an advertising medium. By placing the same ad in two magazines with similar readerships, you can determine which one brings in the most orders. You can use this method to test two lists, two television stations, or two of any other venue. However, don't judge too quickly. Any one-time trial could be an aberration.

3. Elements within an ad. You can test almost any element of an ad, including copy, graphics, and price. Some mail order mavens even test to see response rates based on color of envelopes by sending several colors and determining which color got the greatest response. Again, don't judge too quickly.

Use a program such as Microsoft Excel or, if you have mail order software, a section of the program for statistical research—or even graph paper—and chart your various statistical information. Then review it very carefully.

Price Testing

Here's how testing actually works. Let's say you're selling a maternity jumper. You've already decided to use a four-part sales letter (mailing envelope, letter, order card, and business-reply envelope). You plan on mailing out

Smart Tip *Tip...*

Exercise patience. You can't accurately analyze test results until all your orders have come in.

35,000 pieces. But first you want to find out which selling price—$45, $49, or $52—will generate the most revenue.

You decide to rent a mailing list from *Impending Motherhood* magazine because this is your target audience. You call your list broker and tell him you plan on a final list of 35,000 names but first you want to do a test with 9,000 names—3,000 for each of your "price points," or potential prices. He puts together three lists of moms-to-be with 3,000 nth names on each list. (As we explained in Chapter 6, nth name selection means taking a random sampling by using every seventh name, or every tenth name, or whichever number you choose). This eliminates any alphabetical or geographic glitch with the way the list is organized. If you don't use the nth name selection, your first 9,000 names might net you every customer in the Northeast or everyone with a surname from A through D.

Key Code Roundup

Meanwhile, back at your office, you make up three sets of your sales piece, with each set exactly the same—except for two critical differences:

1. Each set has a different price point: $45, $49 or $52.
2. Each set is marked with a different key code (also called a source code, remember?).

Key codes—your own secret ones—will tell you which set your customers have responded to. For example, the bottom left-hand corner of the order card for the $45 set bears the code "IMJP45." "IM" stands for *Impending Motherhood*, "JP" means jumper, and "45," of course, indicates the $45 price. The key code for the $49 set is IMJP49, and the code for the $52 set is IMJP52.

You can design your source codes any way that makes sense to you. If you look again at the sample one-step and two-step display ads on pages 178 and 179, you'll see key codes printed beneath the gift boxes. One says V11 and the other reads CL11, which tells us that we placed one in the November issue (11th month) of *Victoria* magazine and the other in the November issue of *Country Living* magazine.

Back to the maternity jumpers. After you design your codes, you record the numbers in your codebook, along with a description of your advertising campaign, for future reference.

That done, you send a copy of your sales package to the list broker so that it can be approved by the *Impending Motherhood* people. They give it the go-ahead and send you the three sets of names you rented, printed on pressure sensitive (peel-and-stick) labels. You peel and stick, mail out your materials, and wait for your orders to arrive.

Every morning as you open the orders that have arrived in the mail, you use the key codes printed on the order forms to count how many you've received in each price point. When customers call in with phone orders, you ask them to read the source

Maternity Jumper Key Code Chart

Key Code	Price Point	Phone Orders	Mail Orders	Total Orders	Response (Percent of 3,000)	Gross Sales*
IMJP45	$45	33	30	63	2.1	$2,835
IMPJ49	$49	31	29	60	2.0	$2,940
IMPJ52	$52	24	21	45	1.5	$2,340

We calculated gross sales by multiplying the total orders by the price point.

code off the order form for you. You record all this information in your software program or in a ledger.

At the eight-week point, your response will have tapered off and you'll be ready to compare results. Take a look at the Maternity Jumper Key Code Chart. As you can see, the $45 price brought in more orders, but you've made more money by charging $49 per jumper. So when you mail off your 35,000 sales letters, you'll use the $49 price on all of them.

The Big Picture

Testing is extremely important in the mail order business, but like most things in life, it's also important to practice moderation. You can get so carried away with testing that you lose sight of the big picture—which is, of course, making sales. Don't worry about testing the tiniest things, like the size of your stamp or the color of ink, at least not until you've tweaked all the more important elements.

So what are these important elements?

- Your copy (what your ad or sales piece says and how it says it)
- Your offer (free catalog, free gift, money-back guarantee, 30-day trial, etc.)
- Your price
- Your list
- Your format (catalog, sales letter, brochure, internet ads, television ads, etc.)

Sales Letters

The two main forms of direct mail are sales letters and catalogs. You can design all sorts of variations on these themes, from postcards and "greeting" cards to fliers, brochures, and coupon mailers. Among the most venerable, most popular, and most effective is the sales letter, so let's start off with it.

A sales letter is not just a letter—it's a package comprising several components:

- The letter itself
- The envelope it arrives in
- The order form or reply card
- The reply envelope it comes back to you in

Your sales letter needs to instantly capture your potential customers' attention—preferably as soon as they've got the envelope in their hands—so that they'll open that envelope. (For more on envelopes see "The Envelope, Please" on page 188.) Then, when they do, it must again instantly capture their attention and then hold that attention—so that they'll read it through. Besides interest and attention, the main thing to aim for in your sales letter is the sense that you're writing to each potential customer personally.

Try reading all those sales letters that land in your mailbox. What do they have in common? For one thing, they start off with something that immediately hooks your attention. Maybe it's a description of the offer, enticing you to read on with tidbits of the information you'll get when you buy that book or newsletter. Maybe it's a description of the benefits of using the product, like roses the size of cabbages or more miles to the gallon. Some letters use the flattery approach, assuring you that they have targeted you because you are known for your green thumb or mechanical ability. Others might start off with a question, like "How would you like to…?" or "Wouldn't the world be a better place if everybody…?"

Bells and Whistles

Mail order newbies are often confused about the difference between features and benefits. Your product's features are the bells and whistles it comes with. The benefits are the things it does for you. For instance, the features of a spiffy little sports car would be a convertible top, a five-speed transmission, and a stereo/CD player/coffeemaker. The benefits would be that it gets you where you want to go in the blink of an eye, makes you feel young and sexy, and, of course, attracts attention.

When you write your sales or ad copy, you want to describe the features, but you also want to be sure to tell your customers about the benefits. These, after all, are the reasons they buy.

Try the same approaches in your letter. Experiment until you hit on something that sounds good to you and matches your particular product or service.

Then go on to the body of your letter. Again, analyze the ones you have received. What makes some letters hold your attention longer than others? Notice that they spend a lot of time describing the product or service. You will want to do the same thing. Emphasize the benefits of your product or service throughout your body copy, repeating those benefits as often as you can using different descriptions so they stick in your potential customer's mind.

Smart Tip

Tip...

Have a trusted friend or family member proofread your sales letter. Sometimes it's almost impossible to detect minor typos in your own work, and computer spelling and grammar checks, while helpful, will not pick up a misspelled word that actually spells another word.

If you've got testimonials, use them. They lend credibility to your product and company, and they add another dimension to your copy. It's not just you who thinks your product is great—it's real people, just like your prospect. The sample on page 190 shows you what testimonials typically sound like, how they're formatted, and how you might include them as a separate sheet with your sales letter or other materials. (For more information about using testimonials, see "Sure-Fire Techniques" on page 198 and "Just Ask" on page 200.)

After the main body of your letter, tell your customer what to do to obtain your terrific product. If you're offering a discount or a freebie with a time element, this is the place to mention it. (The advantage of using a time element, like "must be received by June 14th" is that it lights a fire under your customer—who won't want to put off ordering and risk losing out on whatever goodie you're offering.) This is the action part of the letter, so make it very straightforward and to the point.

The Personal Touch

Check out the sample sales letter on page 189. Then take a look at these sales tips:

- Design the most enticing gift, discount, or free offer you can, and make it prominent in your letter.
- Grab prospects' attention with something they want. Relate it to either the freebie or how your product or service benefits them.
- Use time-proven winning words like "secret" and "free." Everybody wants to know a secret, and everybody wants something for free!
- Don't write for thousands of prospective customers—write to just one, as though you're speaking to him or her personally.
- Save the flowery prose for that poetry contest. Instead, use everyday language

that appeals to the average person. In fact, try to use the language that matters to your customers. If, for example, you are selling video games, use the language of "gamers." Use the words and phrases that will appeal to your target market—your tone and phrasing will likely be different for college students then it would be for seniors. Speak the language of the buyers.

- Don't focus only on the features of your product or service; describe the benefits.

- Try letters with indented paragraphs, underlined words, and two colors; they pack more of a punch and outperform plain letters.

Beware!

Don't make the common mail order mistake of failing to correspond with your customers on a frequent basis. Tell those repeat customers how much you appreciate them. Let potential and one-time customers know what they're missing—and that you miss their business. The more your customers hear from you, the more often they'll order.

- Use gimmicks like boldface type, underlining, and italics sparingly. If you use them too frequently or for no particular reason, they become annoying.

- Keep your letter clear, clean, free of grammar and style errors, and no more than two pages long—even shorter for a young audience from the MTV sound bite generation. Have someone you trust as a spelling, punctuation, and grammar star check your work before you commit to a print run.

- Relax and enjoy yourself and try many variations until you come up with something that grabs you—then test market it among friends, family, and even do a sample test run. It's always better to get feedback by sending a letter to 100 people (asking for honest feedback for a 15 percent discount) than sending a mediocre letter out to all 10,000 people on your list.

The Envelope, Please

The envelope is your invitation to your customers, the outer trapping that entices them into your virtual store. What can you do to encourage them to open the envelope and step in? Make it as intriguing as possible. Some mail order mavens suggest using an envelope that looks handwritten, which can lend a personal touch. Others go for the official/open immediately look, hoping the customer will think it's from the IRS and rip it open right away. This is a dangerous tactic since most people dread such a letter and, while they are glad that it is not the IRS, they will toss it because they feel that they are being duped. Some aim for envelopes in bright, can't-miss colors, while others simply design an attractive envelope. You can also try the old "free gift" approach, but if you do, you'd better be giving away something or people will feel cheated.

What works for one company won't necessarily work for another, because each mail order entrepreneur's target market, merchandise, theme, and ambience are

Chocoholic Central

Hi Susan!

I'd like to offer you a very special invitation *with a free gift*.

I've chosen you to receive this offer because I know you value the little things that make life special, especially for the ones you love—things like delicious, delectable milk chocolate, dark chocolate, and hazelnut treats.

> *Imagine how special those scrumptious treats would be tucked inside a box that is handmade of fine Belgian chocolate and embellished with marzipan flowers and edible gold leaf! Yes, a treat so special that they can eat the box it comes in!*

> *Slip a heartfelt message inside that chocolate box and add sweets for the sweet tooths in your life.*

Because I'm so anxious for you to try my chocolate boxes, I'm inviting you to choose any one from my selection of four chocolate boxes and receive it for *10% off!* And when you order, I'll send you a rose-and-chocolate scented sachet to tuck into a drawer, in your car, or under your pillow for sweet dreams every night of the year!

I hope you'll take advantage of this special offer. **I can't offer it for long, but I can promise that you'll fall in love with these chocolate gems—and so will those cherished people who receive them.** If you're not pleased for any reason, just send back the box in its special wrapping, and I'll cheerfully refund your money.

Just fill out the enclosed reply form and pop it in the mail to me. Don't take too long! Because of the upcoming holidays, my offer must end December 1st.

Very best,

Arianna Arelson

Arianna Arelson, President & Founder of Chocoholic Central

P.S. I've enclosed a page with some letters we've received from other customers like you who have given chocolate boxes in creative and heartwarming ways. Take a look!

123 Cocoa Court, Truffle Bay, FL 30000

(800) 555-4000   **www.ChocoholicCentral.com**

Testimonials

*Here's what some of our customers have told us about
our elegant, edible chocolate boxes:*

"I gave one of your chocolate boxes to my daughter for her 16th birthday with her grandmother's gold locket tucked inside. She says it's the best gift she's ever received. And all her friends want to know where I got the box!"

—*Carolee Carter*
Memphis, TN

"Every year I try to think up something special for the girls in my bridge club for Christmas. Well, last year I gave them a half a dozen of your chocolates in one of your chocolate boxes. You should have seen their faces—sheer delight!"

—*Mrs. Myrtle Dunagin*
Lawrence, KS

"I saw your ad in one of my girlfriend's magazines and knew she'd been looking at it. So when it came time to propose, I put the engagement ring inside the heart-shaped chocolate box. She went nuts over that box and said it was the most romantic thing she'd ever seen. (P.S. She insisted on saving the box. It's been in our refrigerator for six months now, along with a piece of wedding cake.)"

—*James Amado*
Tucson, AZ

unique (or should be). But whatever your company's style, you should consider the outer envelope a canvas on which to work your mail order magic. Check out these tips and tricks for creating catchy envelopes:

- Use oversized envelopes that will stand out from the crowd in a stack of mail. Don't overdo it or you may find your mailing getting destroyed when crammed into mailboxes.
- Scatter colorful graphics over the envelope.
- Use both sides of the envelope as your canvas—not just the address.
- Design the envelope to look like a fancy invitation.

As with everything else, you need to design your envelope to fit your products and image. Balloons all over the envelope will entice young parents more than businessmen. An envelope that looks like a sports collectible will appeal to sports fan and a sci-fi look will appeal to sci-fi fans. Know your clientele.

If you include a free gift, make it of the paper variety, such as a free coupon or special discount card. Bulky envelopes, or envelopes that appear suspicious, will be stopped by the very security-conscious postal police.

The Participation Effect

Another quirky thing about direct mail (which is also a quirky thing about human nature in general) is that people are far more likely to respond to an offer for which they have to actively do something. In other words, people like direct-mail offers in which they're asked, for example, to paste a "Yes" or "No" sticker on the reply card. That's why all those Publishers Clearing House packets are full of stickers and reply cards and tear-offs. They work. Call it the participation effect.

Of course, these gimmicks cost money. But if you can afford them, and they fit your company's style, by all means use them. If not, think about how else you might incorporate the same idea into your order form or reply card. If you're offering a free gift with the order, for instance, you might let them choose the color or style they want by checking a box on your form.

Gimmick or not, the main purpose of the order form or reply card is to encourage orders. So make the form clear, easy to understand, and easy to fill out. Check out the sample order form/reply card on page 193.

Make It Easy

Here's another area where it pays to make things easy: Adding a self-addressed return envelope makes ordering simple for your customer, especially when you provide a different-sized envelope (a smaller one to fit your reply card, for instance). Having your customer stick the form in the envelope contributes to the participation effect we've already discussed.

Some mail order mavens swear that you get a better response if you use a business-reply envelope (one with postage prepaid by you). Others say this doesn't matter. Do your homework and investigate how your closest competition handles this. Run a few tests and then decide for yourself. But postage prepaid or not, be sure to include that self-addressed reply envelope.

Brochures

A brochure is basically a baby catalog, the perfect vehicle for the mail order newbie who can't afford a big, glossy publication—and possibly doesn't have enough products

▲

to fill one. But a brochure should not be cheesy. Like the catalog, it must still convey the impression that your company is an established, high-quality operation.

Your brochure doesn't have to be a full-color photographic masterpiece. With the wondrous array of desktop publishing software available and a generous application of imagination, you can turn line art and paper into a classy brochure. But you should meld your knowledge of your products and your potential customers with your market research and your own judgment before making a final decision on whether to use full-color.

If you design your brochure so that it fits in a No. 10 (business-sized) envelope, you can make it the perfect companion for your sales letter. If you're sending the brochure out on its own without an accompanying letter, try a size that will make it stand out from all the No. 10 envelopes in the mailbox. How about 8 inches by 5 inches? Choose whatever size fits your brochure layout and your budget.

Consider sending your multifold brochures as self-mailers, folded and tabbed (sealed at each end with those half-moon-shaped stickers), instead of stuffing them into envelopes. Affix your address labels on one side, and you've saved yourself the cost of envelopes!

Catalogs

Now let us return to what mail order newbies often think of as the Cadillac of the direct-marketing world, the catalog. It's fun, it's (frequently) glossy, and it can be lucrative—but it can also be incredibly expensive and a wonderful way to lose your proverbial shirt. Before you decide to go with a catalog, do every bit of your homework, think carefully, and plan thoroughly.

Catalogs come in lots of sizes and you don't have to start with a big one. You don't even

Order Form/Reply Card

Yes! Send My Garden Art Today!

Please mark the Garden Art statues you'd like to receive:

		Quantity	Total Cost
❏ Frog Prince	$20.00	_____	_____
❏ Garden Fairy	$28.00	_____	_____
❏ Daisy Cherub	$40.00	_____	_____
❏ Dancing Cricket	$42.00	_____	_____

Florida residents add 6% sales tax _____

Shipping & handling _____7.00_____

Total _____

Name _____

Address _____

City _____ State_____ ZIP _____

Phone ( ) _____

☐ Check ☐ Visa ☐ MasterCard ☐ Discover Card ☐ American Express

Card # _____ Exp. _____ / __

Signature _____
(as shown on card)

Your order entitles you to a free decorative watering-can planter!

Please check the appropriate box below to indicate your color preference:

❏ Classic Copper
❏ Perfect Periwinkle
❏ Rustic Tin
❏ Wagon Red

The Dancing Daisy Garden
123 Iris St., Clematis, FL 30000, (800) 555-2200

▲

A Few Formalities

Don't forget that if you plan to sell your ideas, recipes, or formulas in the form of brochures or pamphlets, you'll want to copyright your material. You can copyright cartoon characters, sculptures, paintings, plays, maps, songs, scripts, photographs, and poems as well.

To copyright your material on your own, simply include a copyright notice on it. Three elements make up the copyright notice:

1. The word "copyright," the copyright symbol "©" or the abbreviation "copr."

2. The name of the owner of the copyright (that's you).

3. The year of first publication.

Here's what a copyright notice should look like: *Copyright © 2002 by John Doe*

To officially get your copyright, you need to file with the U.S. government. For information, visit the U.S. Copyright Office, which is part of Library of Congress, at www.copyright.gov.

---

have to start with a "real" catalog—as we said in the previous section, you can start with a brochure and work your way up to a catalog.

Many mail order entrepreneurs, focusing on their online sales and their e-catalogs, use a small catalog to drive business to their website. This may mean putting three, five, or ten top-selling, most appealing items on a few pages and letting recipients know that there is much more to be found on the site. Since web business has exploded in the past five to ten years, the catalog is often used as a way to promote products but also to advertise your web presence. It's not uncommon for people today to browse a physical catalog and then go to the website to order, or find additional items. Either way, you are introducing yourself via the mail, making a sale via the mail (or in this case e-mail), and shipping through the mail—so, it's mail order all the way, but the modern way.

Catalogs, whether they are drawing people to your website or serving as your mail sales vehicle, should have a central theme. If you've done your homework and developed a target audience, this won't be difficult. Beyond your general premise, however, you'll need to create something for the buyer to tie into. For example, you've already come up with your theme: gift chocolates or auto supplies for the home mechanic. Once you've got that theme, don't deviate, but add something timely—gift chocolates for the holiday season or auto supplies for the dad who's a car lover—the perfect gift for Father's Day. Providing reasons for people to buy something gives

Brochure Page

Raisa Magic Mane Conditioner

8-oz bottle makes any mane soft, silky, and easy to braid. Perfect for show days, parades, or just hangin' out in the barn.

RM3353 $8.95

Lucky Shoe

We all know it takes more than luck to win a show. But it doesn't hurt to have this handsome sterling silver horseshoe to hang on the wall at home or in the stable. Measures 12" x 4" and comes gift boxed for giving. (But you can order one for yourself, too!)

RM3358 $21.50

"I've tried mane conditioners before and thought they were all the same. But one bottle of your Raisa Magic Mane Conditioner and I changed my mind! So did my horse, Abbey. We won our first dressage show the first time we used it. Thank you!"

—Vicki Valiant
Burbank, CA

Order Toll-Free (800) 555-MANE

Mon.–Fri. 7 A.M. to 6 P.M. and Weekends 9 A.M. to 5 P.M.

or use the handy order form on page X.

your target audience an excuse to spend money. Is it back to school or the start of football season? Maintain your theme and work in a timely element so that there's a reason why your catalog is suddenly showing up in their mailbox.

Technicolor Dream

Contrary to what you might think, your catalog doesn't have to be a Technicolor photographer's dream unless you're selling gifts, food, jewelry, or home furnishings. If you're selling auto parts, for instance, your customers aren't likely to be more bowled over by a full-color photo of a spark plug than by a black-and-white one or a line drawing. It's what you do with your copy, your layout, and the theme and mission of your company that counts.

In other words, if your theme is horse-care goods and your mission is to provide quality products at reasonable prices for horse lovers who don't have time to shop, then make those things evident in all your catalog copy. The benefits you're selling are more time with the horse and the ability to purchase products that aren't available in your local stores—since many people don't have horse-related stores in their neighborhood.

If your products call for color photos, you can sometimes get manufacturers to supply color shots of products, which you can pop into your catalog. But take care with these. If you end up with a hodgepodge of different styles, your layout—and your company—will look messy and disorganized.

As in the sales letter and brochure, keep your catalog personal. Some catalogs go for two or three items per page and describe each item in detail—which makes them read like interesting and instructive little magazine articles. Other catalogs pack up to a half-dozen products on a page with clever, concise copy to describe each. The format you choose

Brochure Personal Letter

Dear Friend,

I've been in love with horses ever since I can remember. I think you probably have, too! After years of wishin' and hopin' and savin', I was finally able to buy Molly, my beautiful Swedish Warmblood. Molly and I have been a team for six years now. We show at dressage meets about once a month and train at our local stable every other evening.

It's a lifestyle I love, but between working full-time, caring for my family, and training and hangin' out with Molly, I found that I had no time to shop for all the horse care products that we really need.

That's why I started **The Horsey Set,** to bring quality horse care (and horse fun) products to people who love their carrot-munching friends but don't have the time to shop for them.

I hope you find the things you and your horse want and need within these pages. Please let me know. I want to hear from you!

Happy riding,

Darcy

Darcy Daniels

P.S. All **The Horsey Set** products carry a 30-day, risk-free guarantee. If for any reason you're not pleased with an item, just send it back, and I'll gladly refund your money.

That's something you can hang your hat on!

will depend on the size of your catalog, the number of products you're offering, and the style of your catalog.

They'll also expect your copy to be factual. They're relying on you to convey how the product looks, sounds, feels, smells, or tastes. If you don't report accurately, buyers are not going to believe you—or buy from you—a second time. As an added bonus, with accurate product information, you'll get far fewer returns.

Easy Ordering

One of the most important elements of your catalog is the order form. Once you've done all the work of choosing your merchandise, deciding on prices, designing graphics, writing copy, and laying it all out, you want to make it as easy as possible for your customers to place orders. This is the all important "action" step in the process. Make it simple for your customers to take action. The order form must be easy to find and easy to fill out. Most mail order mavens print it on heavier paper stock and have it bound into the center of the catalog.

It should also be easy for customers to order by phone or e-mail. Don't make them hunt all over the catalog for your phone number. Print the phone number and e-mail address in easy to read letters and numbers, and run it across the bottom of every other page. Make sure you've got your telephone number and website on your order form, too. Also, if you also plan to accept faxed orders, don't forget that fax number!

Sure-Fire Techniques

We've seen what direct mail looks like and how to design your own pieces for optimum effect. Now let's take a look at some sure-fire techniques for winning customers:

- *Give away freebies.* Remember, everybody likes to get something for free. Everybody appreciates a gift. Depending on your style, budget and target market, you can give away something substantial (but inexpensive) or a mere trinket. If you're selling baby clothes, how about a free bib? For books, you can make your gift a simple bookmark. If you choose something your customers will use often and then imprint it with your company's name, you'll have given away not only a gift but also free advertising for yourself.

Order Form Checklist

Your order form is one of the most important parts of your catalog. Keep in mind that it must be easy to use. If it looks like an IRS form, your customer may flinch and file it away. Look over the order forms in all the catalogs you've accumulated and borrow the best from each. Then follow this checklist to make sure the one you've designed contains these essential elements:

1. Your company's name and address, phone number, and web address for ordering, and customer service phone number (if different)

2. A place for your customer's name, address, and daytime and evening phone numbers so you can easily contact the person if there's a problem with the order.

3. Space for your customer to clearly write. Make sure you've got enough lines for an average order, plus a few more. Extra spaces encourage extra orders! Include:
   - ❍ Item number
   - ❍ Page number where the item is found
   - ❍ Quantity
   - ❍ Item description (includes size and color)
   - ❍ Price per item
   - ❍ Item price total (if the customer orders more than one of each item)
   - ❍ Monogramming, imprinting, or other personalizing service fee (if applicable)
   - ❍ Gift box or wrapping fee (if applicable)

4. Space for an alternate mailing address if item ordered is a gift the customer wants sent directly to the recipient (if this applies to your products)

5. Subtotal (total price of items)

6. Your discount policy (if you have one—for instance, for large orders)

7. Sales tax, clearly described

8. Shipping charges, clearly spelled out

9. Total price of order

10. Payment method. For credit cards, leave clearly identified spaces for your customer to write in the card type, number, expiration date, and the name as shown on the card.

11. Your return policy, clearly spelled out

12. Don't forget the thank you!

Note: The back of the order form is a good place to add any other information you think your customer should know, like how to order by fax or by internet, how to reach customer service, how to purchase a gift certificate, and how to find out more about guarantees or warranties. You can also add a space on the back of the order form for your repeat customers to fill in a change of address. This is also a terrific spot for your customer to fill in the name and address of a friend who might like to receive your catalog, perhaps giving the customer a 10 percent discount on his or her next order. Take advantage of this opportunity to add a free name to your mailing list!

Just Ask

By now you're thinking: "I know I should include testimonials in my advertising, but how do I get them?" There are several ways, all beginning with the word "Ask." When customers write to compliment you on your products, services, or company, ask if you can use excerpts from those letters as testimonials. When customers call with compliments, ask if you can write out what they've said and send it to them for a signature so their comments can be used in your sales materials. Some companies actively solicit customer comments by sending out questionnaires and then asking permission from selected customers to use their responses as testimonials.

Don't be shy. Your customers are helping you, but at the same time, you're giving them that little spot in the limelight. You're forging a relationship!

- *Offer a money-back guarantee.* Your returned merchandise rate will be lower than you might think because most people don't have the time or energy to send something back. This is not, of course, an excuse for sending shoddy products. Instead, it's a way to help your customers over the hurdle of sending their money to someone they do not know for something they haven't actually seen. And don't forget that if you offer a money-back guarantee, you have to honor it—it's the law.

- *Time-date your offers.* Make your offer good only for a limited time. Say something like, "If you respond within the next 30 days, you will receive a free _____" or "This offer is good only through _____." This encourages your customers to order now instead of in the nebulous future. When you combine a time-dated offer with a money-back guarantee, you will increase your responses. Another way to get fast responses is to offer only a limited quantity of your product. You can also make a special offer, giving a certain discount or freebie to people who respond to one particular ad or mailing, or giving an additional goodie to the first X number of people who respond.

- *Write riveting headlines.* Your direct-mail piece must compete with scads of advertisements crammed into your customers' mailboxes. Your pitch may be terrific, your product and price may be unbeatable, but if you don't catch their eyes with your opening number—your headline—they're never going to know how special your offer is. Winning headlines generally come in three basic styles: the ego appeal, as in "You have been selected" or "You're invited"; the greed appeal, as in "Free gift inside"; and the news appeal, as in "A new discovery..." Penning your headline before you write your copy will help you focus on what basic need or desire your product satisfies and what appeal your copy should make. Keep in mind however, that a glut of e-mail marketers have used these headlines before, so if you can be

original and treat your customers with some level of intelligence—not trying to fool them—you may be better off. For example, "Horse Care Products Delivered Right to Your Door" is more appealing to your target audience than "You May Be A Sweepstakes Winner!" Since you've come this far to hone in on your target audience, why not make your headline appealing to them as well? "Chocolate So Good, You'll Want to Eat the Box" is more catchy to the chocolate lover than "Open Immediately, Vital Information," which sounds like a government report and will typically be tossed.

- *Offer testimonials from satisfied customers.* Don't overdo it, however. Five testimonials make the point, twenty won't be read—in fact, the more you include, the more likely people will begin to think they are bogus (even though by law they can't be).

- *Accent with artwork.* Illustrations and photos attract attention. If you use a caption under a picture, make sure it has sales value. People will read captions even when they don't have time to read the rest of the piece.

- *Give them a kick with catchwords.* Certain words trigger emotional responses. Some of the most persuasive in the language, especially when it comes to advertising materials, are: "new," "free," "how to," "love," and "discover."

- *Help customers respond quickly.* Accept credit cards and toll-free calls. It's much easier for your customer to fill in a credit card number on a form, enter it on your website, or call and give it to you over the phone than to sit down and write out and send a check.

- *Offer corporate billing.* This means billing means you bill the customer's company (which, of course, only works with business-to-business products).

- *Remember the participation effect.* Give your customers something to stick, paste, tear off, or insert. If you can't afford these gimmicks, consider something like the seemingly handwritten note that implores the customer to "Read this only if you've decided not to buy."

11

Pushing the Envelope, Part II:

Advertising, Promotion, and Marketing

Mail order is—more than anything else—the fascinating business of advertising. So much so, in fact, that we've devoted another entire chapter to the subject. Here, we explore the advertising possibilities beyond those of direct mail, from print ads and radio to television and the internet.

We'll also take a look at promotion and marketing, which are means of generating attention to your business without always leading with revenue.

Display Ads

Print ads are terrific vehicles for getting your message to your target market, and they come in one of two styles: classified and display. We're going to talk magazines only because newspapers—while a good read and a good source of bin liners, creative wrapping paper, and packing material—do not make good mail order advertising venues. The reason for this is two-fold: Most newspapers have a very limited geographic range, and their readership is too broad to allow for target marketing.

So with magazines in mind, let's start off with display ads, which usually feature some sort of graphics combined with the printed word and are found throughout a publication (as opposed to classified ads, which consist solely of the printed word and are found only in the classifieds section).

Niche Publications

If you've done your homework and chosen a niche you're familiar with and enjoy, you probably already know which publications will work for you—they're the ones your target audience reads and the ones you probably read, too. These are the best places to start because you already understand at least part of the demographics and psychographics of their readers. If you are selling vampire collectibles and your target market is vampire fans, you'd probably drive your stake, or ad, into *Country Vampire*, *Vampire Today*, or *Fashion Vamp* magazine.

> **Tip...**
>
> **Smart Tip**
> While it's important to choose print media (and mailing lists) geared toward your particular audience, it also pays to be creative. Sometimes you can do extremely well with an audience segment that doesn't at first appear to be the best choice. Men's colognes, for instance, sell well in women's magazines. Why? Women like to shop for their men.

Pick up those issues on your coffee table or nightstand. Study them carefully. Do mail order ads do well here? Compare the number of "traditional" ads with the number of mail order ads. If a mail order makes up a significant portion, you can figure that other mail order companies are experiencing success with the publication—which means it's a good place to be.

Check for repeated ads featuring products similar to yours. If you're selling a carburetor tune-up kit, see who else is selling the same kind of kit or other auto maintenance merchandise. Look for similar types of ads. Some competition is good. If you see ads for other

Backwards Calendar

Most laypersons (which no longer includes you) don't realize how much time is involved between the production of a magazine and its publication date. Magazines require that ads be submitted at least two months before publication. What this means is that to place a holiday ad in the October, November, and December issues of a niche magazine for your target readers, you need to start working backwards. To start the ad running in October for the upcoming holiday season, you'll need to get it to the advertising department in August—and give yourself a little leeway in case something needs to be changed. An art director may call you to let you know that a certain color isn't looking as good as you had hoped. You want to see the ad before it runs to make sure it looks just right. To get it into the hands of the magazine in August, you'll need to start working on the ad in June and July—that's right, Christmas in July! There is a long lead-time when working on advertisements, especially those for magazines.

Call the advertising rep and ask about due dates, then work backwards on your calendar.

auto parts, but none for carburetor tune-up kits, that may mean that you have found a good place in which to advertise. However, if all of the other ads are for car paint or similar products to improve the outside appearance of the car, then perhaps the magazine is specializing on car exterior's only. Again, study the magazine carefully.

Once you determine that you've found a magazine that you like, go to a library and look at six months to one year of back issues or spend a few dollars and order them online. Online may be the easier way to do it, because many libraries may not have the back issues of niche magazines and may archive only major national publications such as *Newsweek* or *Psychology Today*.

But don't imagine you know it all. There may be other vampire publications you have yet to discover. That's why you'll turn to the Standard Rate and Data Service, otherwise known as SRDS. (See the Appendix for contact information.) SRDS publishes directories that list more consumer and trade publications than you might imagine ever existed, along with a short description of each one and its editorial content, facts on what sort of people read it, and a breakdown of its circulation figures.

From SRDS' plethora of information, choose a list of possible publications in which to place your ads. Then call the advertising department of each magazine and ask the rep to send you a media kit. Media kits contain sample issues, detailed information about editorial content, a breakdown of reader demographics, the publication's ad

▲

Questions to Ask Before Buying a Print Ad

As a consumer, and that's what you are when ad shopping, you need to ask the right questions such as:

○ What is the magazine's circulation?

○ What are the demographics of the readers?

○ How often is the magazine published?

○ How is it distributed? (Newsstand? Subscription? At special functions? All of the above?)

○ What are the rates for different sized ads and for what is the rate for running the ad several times? Typically, there is a discount rate for running an ad more than once.

○ Are there special theme issues or special sections? Do these have different rates?

○ How far in advance does the ad need to be handed in?

○ Will they send you a copy of the ad to proof before they go to print?

rates, and an audited circulation statement. This is a sworn statement from the publisher, verified by an outside source, that the magazine has the actual circulation claimed in its circulation figures. Another great source for magazines is *Bacon's Magazine Directory*, which is in the reference section of most libraries and serves as a guide to 13,000 business, consumer, trade, and professional magazines arranged by topic. It includes circulation, advertising rates, contact names, and contact information.

Media Buying Services

In the early going, you may want to hand pick specific media sources. However, as with most things today, there are companies that can and will "do it for you." In this case, media buying services can be a big plus, especially once you get busier filling orders and have less time to place each ad individually.

A media buying service is an agency that specializes in purchasing time and space for advertising in the mainstream media. Such a service typically purchases broadcast time, print space, indoor space, outdoor space, internet space, and other types of commercial advertising. They should work within your budget and determine the amount of advertising and the right combination of online and offline advertising that will work best for your business and will reach your target market.

Since they buy in bulk for various business, media buying services can typically get better rates than you would get on your own. The American Marketing Society's Marketing Power (www.marketingpower.com/content17777. php), is an example of a media buying service. You can find plenty by Googling the phrase "media buying service" and exploring the various possibilities, or by networking, since

Smart Tip

Know your media ABCs! There are two primary circulation audit sources, the Audit Bureau of Circulation or ABC (www.accessabc.com), and the Business Publications Audit Worldwide or BPA (www.bpaww.com).

many mail order professionals (as well as entrepreneurs in other businesses) use these services. This can be particularly beneficial if you are doing a significant amount of advertising. While you are paying the media buying service, you are saving significant money on the ads themselves, so often, you are coming out ahead. Additionally, since you are not limited to a region or state, they can help you spread out geographically, saving you some valuable time spent researching other markets.

Also, good media buying services should help you monitor your advertising.

Before signing up with a media buying service, meet, or talk by phone, with representatives from a few places and see what they can do for you, how much it will cost and whether or not they are providing some personalized services. For example, can they seek out magazines targeted for your product or do they only work with x number of publications? Good services should be able to focus on your needs. Compare and contrast a few before making a final decision.

Size Matters

Now that you've decided which magazines in which to advertise, you'll have to decide what size ad to run. Magazines generally sell space, the areas reserved for ads, in standard sizes and formats. The costs for these spaces, especially in widely recognized general-interest publications, can just about take away the breath of an unsuspecting newbie. But don't get alarmed—we'll explore ways to save money on advertising in Chapter 12.

Naturally, the larger your ad, the more attention it's likely to get. But as they say, size isn't everything, and you can get excellent results with a small ad if your copy, graphics, target market, and choice of magazine all meld in the right mix.

One school of thought is to start with the smallest ad that pulls in money and gradually increase your ad size as long as it continues to pay for itself. How do you know what small size to start with? Try the smallest one that lets you say what you need to say. A one-step ad, for instance, will take up more space than a two-step because you'll

Magazine Ad Space

A standard magazine page is 7 inches by 10 inches, with each page divided into three columns. Each column is 140 lines deep, or 14 lines per inch. While you typically purchase space by the column, in some cases you can buy by the line. If this is your preference, check the magazine's rate card or ask the ad rep.

Type of Ad	Number of Columns	Other
Full page	3	
Two-thirds of page	2	
One-third of page	1	Can also be one-third of page square (instead of running vertically)
One-sixth of page	One-half	
One-twelfth of page	One-quarter	

need extra room for the order form. How do you know when the size no longer pays its own way? By testing. You knew that! (If you didn't, go back to the cost per order calculations in Chapter 5 for a quick review.)

The other school of thought dictates that once you've determined what size ad works for you—by studying other ads, by intuition, and by testing—leave it alone. Don't mess with success unless your products, product line, or company theme change enough to warrant a modification.

Smart Tip

Tip...

How many magazines should you advertise in? Let your budget be your guide. Place ads in as many publications as you can afford. The more exposure you have, the more money you'll make. But if you can only afford one at first, that's fine, too.

Getting in Position

Ad size is not the only parameter in buying space. There's also the issue of positioning, or where in the magazine your ad gets placed. The chart on page 209 will give you an idea of industry position-think. Most magazines charge extra for the really hot positions. A back cover, for instance, while always a full-page size, costs more than a full-page ad elsewhere in the book because it's considered a prime position.

Some magazines will let you choose the positioning for your smaller ad; others more

Magazine Ad Position

Ad Position	Desirability
Inside front cover	☆
Back cover	☆
Front half of magazine or "book"	☆
Back half of book	
Top half of page	☆
Bottom half of page	
Outside of page	☆
Inside of page	
Closer to editorial content	☆
Before editorial content	☆

Note: ☆ indicates preferred position.

or less stick it in wherever it fits on a page. It often depends on how squeezed they are for time when you place your ad, so it pays to place your ads as early as possible. Also, the more often you advertise, the better relationship you develop with the sales and production people and the more likely they'll be to work with you on what you want.

This can also be a place where a media buying service can be of help. They may do a lot of advertising with the magazine and carry more weight than you do as an individual.

Fresh Gourmet Coffee

Your next ad decision should by this time have a familiar ring: color or black and white? The answer should also have a familiar ring: Nobody can decide for you. While it's generally true that color pulls more responses than black and white, you may not need color for your particular products. And since color costs more, if you don't need it, don't pay for it—at least not until you can more easily afford it.

As we've already explored, you'll also have to decide for yourself whether to use photos, line drawings, or no illustrations at all. Some very successful ads use nothing but type and perhaps a logo if you have one. When you think about graphics, think about what you want that illustration to do. Are you just decorating that costly ad space or are you using the illustration to make a point? If it's just décor, dump it. With

Apples and Oranges

Use the old bean when you test magazine ads. To make sure you're not unfairly skewing your results, follow these guidelines:

○ *Don't compare apples and oranges.* Make sure the magazines in which you're testing ads cater to the same audience. As we've pointed out, you can't compare the results from a maternity dress ad in *Impending Motherhood* with one placed in *Sports Illustrated*.

○ *Don't place test ads in different monthly issues.* If you're selling gifts, for instance, and you place one ad in the December issue of Magazine A and one in the January issue of Magazine B, you can't make a true comparison, because people will naturally buy more gifts before Christmas than after.

all the fun and fancy fonts and borders available through even inexpensive desktop publishing programs, you can do all sorts of decorating tricks without pictures.

If you decide to go with graphics, think about what point you want the illustration to make. If your product makes an impact with a full-monty mug shot—for instance, a fine art print or a piece of furniture—let it stand alone. Pictures may be worth a thousand words, but they can be costly. You'll have to decide if you need a photo to make a point or not. In some cases, a good illustration can do the trick. Remember, your ad is trying to tell the reader something about the product—what it is and why it is of benefit to them. Therefore, an ad needs to be eye-catching but effective at selling your product(s) and your business.

Another thing to keep in mind when considering graphics is that if you're advertising technical products that aren't too exciting in photo form in the first place, an illustration can often bring out aspects that aren't readily apparent in a photograph. A good graphic artist can play up the fancy trackball on a computer mouse, for instance, and even give the mouse a mousier look for a touch of humor that will get your ad noticed.

Start observing the advertising world around you with a professional eye (you are a professional now) and you'll begin to see that even those expensive television ads are going for the line art look. For your own products, the best advice—again—is to study your competitors' ads, use your best instincts, and test. You'll find out quickly enough what works.

Rough Guide

The mail order entrepreneurs we interviewed for this book write their own copy and design their own catalogs. Some do their own artwork. Doing it yourself saves money, and after all, nobody knows your products and your market like you do. If you're a newbie, however, you could be shooting yourself in the foot.

Industry experts suggest that you make a draft of your copy and design and then take your work to an advertising pro for polishing. As you learn more, you can eliminate this step, if you like.

How much can you expect to pay an ad agency? Prices vary, depending on which agency you use and what services you outsource. As a rough guide, let's figure you're going to go with a smaller agency. Smaller firms like the business brought to them by startup entrepreneurs, while big-name firms with offices in three states will usually only work with mega-corporate clients that have million-dollar ad budgets.

When you go with a smaller agency, creative services (such as developing a logo for your company or designing an ad) generally cost around $75 to $100 an hour, while production services (anything from entering copy into the computer to market research and media placement) may run extra. The length of time needed to design or place an ad depends on what you bring to the table—like how much design and research you've already done and the size of the project—and how quick and creative the agency's pros are. The best way to find out how long it will take for your ad to be designed and/or placed is to ask—along with some other important questions:

- Does the agency have mail order experience?
- What other projects have they turned out? Ask to see a few samples.

From the Drawing Board

You've designed a brilliant display ad and purchased space in a magazine. Now how do you get it from your desktop publishing program to the production department? Most publications like to have the ad copied from your computer onto a CD and then sent to them, or e-mailed directly. Many magazines will accept e-mailed ads, as long as they've been designed using a particular format. Very few magazines will now require the good old-fashioned ad that's been pasted up with film negatives and cardboard.

If you use an ad agency, you won't need to worry about any of this. If you're doing it yourself, ask the magazine for its specifications and guidelines while you're negotiating for ad space.

- What were the success rates of the ads you're reviewing?
- What fees does the agency estimate for your project?
- In what time frame can you expect your ad to be finished?
- Don't forget to check references!

If your advertising budget is tight but you need professional help, try hiring an amateur with a learner's permit or a freelancer with graphic art and advertising experience. Post a notice for advertising or graphic arts students at a local college. Students are usually hungry for not only money but also professional experience for their portfolios, and possibly course credits. They frequently have brilliant ideas.

You can also contact other local businesses that are advertising in your area and find out who did their ads. Many small business owners use freelancers, while other have a cousin, brother, sister, or neighbor who has some copywriting experience. Remember, the copy is as important as the graphic design or artwork. You may find a couple of people who, together, can help draw and write your ad for a couple hundred dollars—or you may barter, since you also have goods that they may enjoy.

Classified Ads

The major appeal of classified ads for the mail order maven is that they're far less expensive than display ads. Add to that the bonus of simplicity—there's no layout to design, no graphics to worry about, and no choice of fonts to obsess over. Add another bonus—defined interest. People who peck around in the classifieds are often there because they're looking for something in that particular classification: vacation destinations or collectibles or money-earning opportunities or whatever. So when they see your ad, they already have an expressed interest in what you're selling. By contrast, people who see your display ad have generally just happened onto it; it was on the page they were reading, but they weren't specifically looking for what you're advertising.

The downsides of classified ads are that you've got an extremely limited space in which to make your pitch, you have nothing with which to catch your prospect's eye except words that graphically look just like everybody else's, and you've got a much smaller audience to work with. Far fewer people read the classified sections than the editorial ones. Additionally, some mail order products just can't be sold effectively through the classifieds. High-ticket items, products or services that require lots of explanation, and products that don't lend themselves to two-step ads don't make good classified candidates.

So, aside from cost, why would you want to run a classified ad?

- It's an inexpensive proving ground. You can test new products for relative pennies and, if the response warrants it, step up to a display ad.

- It's a good way to build your mailing list. For each response you get, you also get a name to send a direct-mail kit or catalog, and to add to those all-important back-end profits.

Weed Out Words

You write the classified ad in basically the same way you write your direct-mail pieces and your display ad: attention-getting headline, riveting copy, the call to action, your address (with the ad's key code discreetly imbedded), or phone number. Use as few words as possible, because you are charged by the word. Let's say you're selling a how-to book for crafters and go over each step:

1. *Your attention-getting headline.* "Earn Money with Your Crafts!" People are always interested in making money. It's a proven attention-getter. As an added bonus, you have filled in the target audience for your ad: crafters. And crafters, like most artists, like recognition, so you've got their attention on two counts here. Magazines will usually print your headline in bold at no extra charge, so remember to ask.

2. *Your riveting copy.* Here's where you need to get your idea across as succinctly as possible: think TV Guide-style program write-ups. For example, "New book tells you how. Results guaranteed." You've got that magic word "new" and that other magic word "guaranteed."

3. *Your call to action.* Remember, this is where you tell your potential customer exactly what to do and when to take advantage of your offer: "Write today for full details!"

4. *Your address and key code.* "Craft Faire, 123 Rose Cottage, Dept. A, Camellia, FL 30000."

Here's your ad in 23 simple words:

Earn Money with Crafts!

New book tells how. Results guaranteed. Write today for full details!
Craft Faire, 123-A Rose Cottage, Camellia, FL 30000.

Remember to weed out all extraneous words. If you look back at our step-by-step process, you'll see that we originally had a couple of extra words, "Earn money with your crafts" and "New book tells you how. In the final version, we deleted "your" and "you." We also deleted "Dept". and included the A (our key code) as part of the street address. The ad still makes sense, and at $10 a word, we've just saved ourselves $30!

▲

The Write Length

Now that we've told you to keep your ad as short as possible, let's gum things up a little by adding that according to industry wisdom, the more words you use to describe your product, the better the ad will pull… up to a point. Like the display ad, you'll eventually reach a stage where longer isn't any better. How do you find this? By testing. Start off with the shortest possible ad, gradually increase it by 50 percent, and then 100 percent, and see how each size works. You'll soon find out the "write length" to use!

As always, the best way to learn to write classified ads is by studying your competition. Look through the magazines you plan to advertise in. How many ads do you see repeated? Those are the ones to emulate. If they're still there month after month, it's because they're making money.

Your Website

Your website is your virtual catalog, with several advantages that we'll get to shortly. Web design, like designing an ad, can be done by you or by a professional web designer, or as a combined effort by you working with a designer. If you are not comfortable with the technical end of producing a site, you can lay out exactly what you want on paper and have someone make it happen. For a few thousand dollars, a good

---

Frequency

How often *should* you run your print ads? For classifieds, the answer is: As often as possible. "Consistency is important," says Lisa Tober, an account executive with *Woman's Day* magazine. When readers look at classified ads, they may not want to order at the moment, and they assume they'll find your ad in the next issue, when they'll be ready. If it's not there, you've just lost a customer.

Display ads also rely on consistency, but with the added expense, you may want to schedule yours only for higher-pulling months, which are during the holiday season for most mail order gift items. Traditionally, magazine sales fall off during the summer months (everybody's at the beach reading tacky novels), but your products may do best during these times. It's up to you to do some research and then decide!

web designer can put together a site that meets your needs with a few pages of products and a shopping cart for buying and then ordering.

Shop around for web designers. Since almost every business has a website, it's not too difficult today to get names of web designers —ask at local business associations, ask other business owners, and even look at the bottom of home pages—most websites list the company that designed them. The key is to get a website built that you would like, not someone else's vision. So that it does not become too costly, get all of the fees in advance. Find out what is included and what will require additional fees and use that as a guideline. Most new entrepreneurs do not need a very elaborate site. As mentioned earlier, Patty from www.instantphotoframes.com, did her site by herself at first and then had it revamped by a pro after five years of successful sales. "I knew we could do even better," says Patty, explaining why she had it spruced up.

Your Web Look

Deciding on the right look for your website should include a few basic elements. First, what tone and style are you trying to present? Are you selling high-end products? Toys for teens? Sports memorabilia? You'll want the site to convey the right message to your audience. This means the type font, photos/graphics, and wording all need to reflect your products.

To get ideas, you'll want to view numerous other sites designed to sell products and see what you like, in terms of style and layout. Keep in mind that as people bounce from one site to another, they want to get information quickly, without having to scroll down to find out what the site is all about. They want wording and phrases that are straightforward, clear and concise, not convoluted sales talk or buzz words. Too many business-oriented websites go on and on with sentences about finding solution strategies for measuring productivity, and leveraging your key position to meet a greater demand in the overall marketplace… whatever that means. If you want people to stop and read, make sure that what you're saying makes sense.

A web catalog is your key to sales, so you want to show your products with clear photographs and accompany them with well-written, *brief* descriptions. While some products are self-explanatory, others require a longer explanation. For such products, you'll want to have a place where readers can click to find out more. This way, you can show more products on a catalog page and allow people who are interested in a certain item to get more information by going to a separate page, called a landing page. This is the page between the initial first look at the product and moving on to the shopping cart. Amazon.com always takes you to such a page when you click on a long list of books—this allows you to read a description of the book, perhaps see a sample chapter or table of contents and even see what other readers had to say. If you are selling something like microwaves, for example, it's hard for someone to simply buy one from a brief look and a two-line description. That's why you offer more information, such as the features of the product, on the landing page, which then leads to the shopping cart.

What is especially wonderful about a web catalog is that you can make changes instantly—something you cannot do once you've mailed out catalogs to 10,000 people. For example, if you have a new product, you can post it immediately or if you want to put something on sale you can do that too. If someone finds a typo, you can correct it.

The immediacy of the web is unparalleled, and within minutes your changes are seen worldwide.

Some Do's and Don'ts for Web Pages

DO: Make yourself accessible and reachable—too many websites remain anonymous and in this day and age of identity theft, people are leery of shopping at sites with no address, phone number, or "about us" describing the company. Also, make the "Contact us" link very easy to find.

DON'T: Overdo it with bells and whistles. Slow-loading graphics, long intros, and other hi-tech features will lose many possible buyers who can click off of your site in a nano-second. Sites need to load quickly and these extras slows them down.

DO: Give your products some room on the page so that they are not crowded together. The eye can only capture so much at one time.

DON'T: Use weird color patterns. White backgrounds, slightly off-white, light gray, or a very light toned-down blue are most common because they are easy on the eyes and show up clearly on all sorts of different monitors. Remember, just because it looks good on your computer doesn't mean it will look good on another monitor—chances are it won't. Also, remember, some white (or empty) space is a good thing. If the site is chaotic, people give up trying to find things.

DO: Update the site often with products, special sales, surveys, and even some content. Keep the site fresh and people will keep coming back. Unlike the traditional catalogs that have to reprint for each season, you can alter your site by making changes every day.

DON'T: Make navigation difficult. If people have to click more than twice to find something, they're more apt to leave. Make sure every product is easy to find and things like "customer service" and "about us," are also easy to locate. Include a sitemap and check often to make sure you don't have any dead links.

DO: Trade links with similar—not directly competitive—businesses. Check them out first. You can even sell advertising space.

DON'T: Sell advertising that deletes from your products or brand. Some banner ads are so prominent that they outshine the site itself.

Communicating with Web Shoppers

Web shopping can be interactive. "Communicate with people," stresses fabric supplier Caryn O. "Let them know about yourself. Let them know what you represent." Caryn spends a lot of time on her site, sharing not only her wares but her business and life philosophies with her member customers. "My members come to my site daily," she says. "They look for new fabrics every day. They can't wait to see what's new. I'm always thinking of new things to do and what I can do differently. I'm constantly changing, and I get lots of compliments on the new additions. People love that.

"If people come to a website and see the same things over and over, they're not going to keep coming back. They're going to wait longer and longer, maybe instead of [visiting every] week, now it's [once a] month. You need people to come daily."

Getting customers to visit your site daily is something you can easily accomplish. With a traditional catalog, you cast your merchandise not in stone but on paper, which after all the time and expenses of production, printing, and mailing is about as easy to change as stone. With a web catalog, however, you can make changes daily (or even hourly) if you like, adapting your site to your customers' desires and spending patterns.

Web customers can register their preferences for various types of merchandise, and you can use that knowledge to cross-sell or up-sell them the things you know they want. Amazon.com, for example, notes the types of books customers enjoy—mystery, romance, cooking, etc.—and suggests material in those subject areas every time they log on. It's a great way to make those dedicated customers feel remembered and understood.

Amazon.com also offers customers the option of signing up for e-newsletters on their favorite types of books and then sends mini-reviews of new or popular books every few days—with, of course, the option to purchase the book.

No Spamming

Keep in mind that people who shop the e-commerce way don't like hype. They expect to be informed and entertained, but they don't want to be electronically shouted at, patronized, or pandered to. (Which you shouldn't do to your paper customers, either.) Sending requested e-mail updates is good business and fun interacting, but "spamming," or sending e-junk mail, is definitely poor "netiquette" and will not win friends and influence customers. What will? The same elements that win you paper customers—honesty, integrity, fairness, service, and respect. Show your

> **Bright Idea**
>
> Hold a contest, suggests Robert Peters of I-1 Internet Group. Put a guest book on your site and advertise that every 100th shopper gets 10 percent off on their next purchase. It creates interest and good will and builds your mailing list.

web customers they're important by how you treat them. Offer discounts, freebies, and any other perks you can think up.

More tips for winning and keeping internet mail order customers:

- Give your customers easy ordering access. Don't force them to wade through page after page before finding your "order form." Also, while you DO want to get some information on your customers, don't ask tons of questions—let them buy the product without jumping hurdles.

- Provide alternative ordering methods for customers who are leery about ordering by credit card. Offer these folks order forms they can print out and fax or mail to you. And of course, offer your phone number so they can order by phone if they choose.

- Check and answer your e-mail on a daily basis. Don't let virtual customers languish any more than you would phone or mail customers.

- Update your site frequently. "If something's sold," Caryn says, "get it right off. Don't let it sit there and get people upset because they can't order it."

- Offer customers information and entertainment. These elements will draw them in, hold their attention, and make them feel you're a part of their world and they're a part of yours. If you're selling travel products, for instance, post an article on the best vacation spots for the season or ten tips for traveling inexpensively. If you're selling coffee, post fun tips on the different blends available.

- Check out competitors' sites, just as you check out competitors' other advertising materials. Borrow the best of what they are doing, then do it better.

Breakthrough!

The internet offers breakthrough possibilities for computer-oriented entrepreneurs," says the NMOA's John Schulte. The entrepreneurs we interviewed certainly agree.

"Our mail order has just exploded because of the internet," Caryn, the fabric retailer explains. "It's just amazing. A lot of our customers who used to deal with us through the mail now also use the internet because it's so much easier."

Mary M., the romantic gifts purveyor, has decided to go all the way with her online store. "We're not even going into production with another paper catalog," the St. Louis resident says. "We're focusing on the website. From all the statistics I've researched, it's growing by leaps and bounds."

Cigars and Golfers

Just having a catalog on the web does not mean having customers. You have to go out and find them, just as you do with a paper catalog. There are all sorts of advertising techniques you can use, says Roy Fletcher of Fletcher Consulting in Pembroke Pines, Florida. Perhaps the simplest is a banner exchange program, in which you make an advertising trade with another website. You put your banner on your exchange partner's site and you let that company put its banner on yours. What's a banner? It's a small ad that pops up on a site's home page, or on any page for that matter. When potential customers click on the banner, they're magically transported to your site to shop.

Here again, you need to think of your target market. Choose sites whose customers will be interested in your products or services. While you don't want to mix apples and oranges—trying to put a banner for your horse products on a site that sells dolls, for example—you can get creative. "You might, for instance, put a banner for your upscale cigars site on a site that caters to upscale golfers," says Fletcher.

The Flow of Traffic

Another good web advertising tactic is what's known as an affiliate program. This works like a banner exchange, except that there are fees involved. You put your banner on somebody else's site and you pay them per click, say 15 cents for every customer who clicks onto your site. Or you can arrange to pay a percentage of sales, say 8 or 10 percent of each transaction that results from a customer clicking onto your site from that banner.

This is possible through technology that basically acts as a traffic cop, Fletcher says. It tracks banner sales and generates monthly reports for each party, you and your affiliate program partner, so that you both know exactly how much money you're due.

Promoting Your Site

"If you build it they will come." While this was the key phrase in the wonderful 1989 film "Field of Dreams," it will not work for websites. You need to draw potential customers to your site and then keep them coming back. Advertising is one means of drawing attention to your site, as well as having the site featured on all printed materials, from catalogs to business cards. There's more, however that you can do. For example, on search engines like Yahoo or Google, you can pay to move up, so that when someone is looking for your type of products, your online catalog will move up on the long, long list that appears. You can also improve your ranking by optimizing your site. Each search engine will give you ways in which you can improve your positioning. Some of the basics include using keywords appropriately—this means listing a host of words (or two or three word phrases) that you think people could type in to get to your site. Then use them in your copy and on your site. Don't just use them randomly throughout the site, or the search engine police will catch on and you won't move up. Keywords can be especially effective in the first couple of paragraphs. Also having keywords in your meta tags (the little tag that comes up when you go to a link before you click on it) can also be advantageous. You should also include a sitemap, indexed if possible, and a logical structure that the computerized "spyder" as it's called (that's what searches through your website) can find everything easily. Of course, more hits from unique visitors will also move you up in the rankings, but that comes from promoting the site.

Patty, from www.instantphotoframes.com, had other means of promoting her website. "I contribute to a lot of other (non-competing) sites that include party planning, which is my area of expertise. I write articles… and that's a great way to promote anything, because content is important on a websites and many sites are in need of such content," explains Patty, who will write for the other sites in exchanges for a mention of her site and a link. Since Patty has already written her own party planning books, and owns the rights to them, she sometimes pulls excerpts from the books. In other cases, she writes a short article or even offers expert advice. "As a mail order business owner, it's important to use your expertise and spread it around. If you've got a really neat product and it can be used in any consumer situation, that's a good thing. Websites are searching all over for content, sometimes it only has to be a little tidbit," adds Patty.

Another manner in which Patty promotes her site is by having it listed in directories, and there are numerous online directories. Most online directories are free, while some charge a nominal fee—if the directory is well known enough (and gets enough visitors), it can be worth spending some bucks.

Keep Them Coming Back

Once you have drawn visitors to your site, you'll want to keep them coming back. One way to maintain an interest in your brand and website is by starting an online newsletter and encouraging people to sign up from your site. Such newsletters can be very effective if you provide some quality content along with advertising and promotion. People will keep reading if you are giving them something to look at besides advertising.

Promote your newest products around the content (which can be a couple of paragraphs) and send newsletters every couple of weeks or once a month.

You can also offer cost effective incentives, such as discounts on products or services, free downloads or specific perks that would appeal to your target audience.

Another popular trend is word-of-mouth marketing. In fact, you can learn about such marketing from the Word of Mouth Marketing Association at www.womma.org. The key to generating this type of marketing is to present something that your viewers will want to send to their friends. For example, including image-appropriate e-cards on your website or in your e-newsletters will then prompt users to send them to their friends. The same holds true with lists, recipes, or anything that people like to share. Once they get it and forward to a friend with your company name on it, you've effectively started the chain reaction that is word-of-mouth marketing.

Free Offline Advertising

You can get terrific free advertising by getting your company or products written up in magazines. Most publications have one or more sections devoted to new products in their target market, and they always need something to fill those spaces. Why not your something?

What you need to do first is prepare a press release, a one- or two-page article about your product(s) accompanied by a photo or two. Here's how you do it:

- *Make sure your product is a quality one.* Editors take their duties seriously and won't publish news on merchandise or services that sound shaky or shoddy.

- *Do your homework.* Don't send your release to every magazine in the known world. Choose magazines that cater to your target audience—and don't forget trade publications. If you are selling clothing or jewelry, for instance, include fashion industry magazines on the list of places to send your press release.

- *Call each magazine to find out which editor to send your release to.* Be sure to get correct name spellings and titles. You can request details, such as if the editor has any special press release preferences (such as mail or e-mail) . Keep your conversation short and professional, but friendly. You may be making a valuable contact!

- *Use the standard press release format.* Start your press release with a catchy lead tailored to your target magazines and follow it up with a concise, fact-driven release. Double-space your material and keep it in an easy-to-read font and type size. Keep it short. Three paragraphs should do it: One on your new product (or product news) and why it is unique, special, and newsworthy; a second paragraph with the basic facts behind the new product or innovative concept that you want them to write a story about; and a third paragraph on your company, often called a boilerplate, which is a three or four sentence overview of your business that you can reuse on various press releases.

Remember, keep it concise. Editors are incredibly busy people. If your release is too long, you'll lose their interest.

- Don't get too carried away with blowing your own horn. Overblown claims make you sound amateurish.
- Send reprint-quality slides of your merchandise. Many smaller magazines have very limited photo budgets, so any artwork they can use is a terrific bonus.
- Personalize your mailing. Send a cover letter with your press release, addressed to the editors you've already talked to, reminding them of who you are, and stating that you think their readers will find your products of interest.
- Follow up. Wait a few weeks. Then call or e-mail to make sure the editors have received your release and find out if they have any questions.
- Be persistent. If your first release doesn't garner coverage, send another one and then another in a regular publicity program. But don't send the same release over and over. You don't want to bore the editors to death. Vary your lead, your story, and your products.

Radio

In the beginning, it's probably best to stick to direct-mail and print advertising. But as your company grows, you might want to expand to other advertising venues—radio, for instance. Local stations, not just in your town but all over the country, make excellent vehicles, and time (which is the radio equivalent of magazine space) is more affordable than you might think—as low as $6.50 per spot.

Get copies of the SRDS radio directories and do your homework. Choose stations whose listeners are demographically and psychographically matched to your target audience. If you're selling nose and navel rings, for instance, you're not going to do all that well with golden oldies stations whose listeners are into Paul Anka or Tom Jones. You're seeking the stations playing the latest in hip-hop or Top 40.

Radio time is divided into five periods, of which the most expensive are morning drive time, 6 to 10 A.M., and evening drive time, 3 to 7 P.M., when you've got all those captive audiences trapped in their cars on the freeway. The other periods are 10 A.M. to 3 P.M., 7 P.M. to midnight, and the night owl zone of midnight to 6 A.M. Surprisingly enough, the dead zones are often much better advertising times for mail order products. Nobody knows for certain why this is so—maybe insomniacs have more time to write down your company's name and address and mail away for things, or they might be desperate for something to think about besides the sleep they're losing, or perhaps they just like to order by mail. The point is, it works.

Of course, the idea here is to get free advertising. Therefore, look for talk radio stations seeking guests with expertise on various topics. Since most stations need to fill a lot of guest slots, you may very well be able to use your expertise to fill interview air time. Put together one page that serves as your bio, including your credits and expertise on the subject, plus a little information on your business. Have this ready to mail, e-mail, or fax to station managers, program directors, or producers of the individual talk shows. Call first and ask to whom you should send.

The other advantage is that some stations will accept P.I. deals for payment. This has nothing to do with private investigators; it means per inquiry. In a P.I. deal, you pay nothing up front for the cost of advertising. Instead, you pay the station a percentage of the profits you make on each inquiry you receive from your on-air ad.

You'll have to convince the station that your advertising can pull in enough money to make this worth its while, but smaller stations, especially ones with open time in the dead hours, are good candidates.

Television

Well, we've all seen the one-shot television commercials for "Greatest Polkas of All Time CD Collection—just $19.95 plus shipping and handling!" Those commercials air over and over again, one product after another, because they work. As with radio, television is probably not the best venue for the newbie. Why not? For one thing, television works best for one-shots, which we do not recommend, and for another, it's an expensive venue. But as with radio, when your company grows, you might want to give it a try.

The Fringe Zone

The television day is divided into four parts:

- Daytime: from dawn until 4 P.M.
- Early fringe: from 4 to 8 P.M. and all day on weekends
- Prime time (the most expensive): from 8 to 11 P.M. (7 to 10 P.M. for central time zone stations)
- Late fringe: from 11 P.M. to dawn.

Like radio, the most expensive time is not necessarily the best for mail order advertising. In fact, the late fringe can be an ideal source of advertising revenue for mail order entrepreneurs.

As with any other advertising medium, target your market. Check out SRDS and *TV Guide*. Network television doesn't give

> **Bright Idea**
>
> Once you've got that magazine coverage, take advantage of it. Include "as seen in *Vampire Today* (or whichever) magazine" in your sales materials. This is another type of testimonial and gives you loads of credibility.

you as much demographic and psychographic range for local programming as radio does, but with the ever-expanding reach of cable networks, you should be able to find a vehicle that complements your audience and products.

Local TV stations will often produce your ad for you. Let them! Give them your guidelines or copy, which should run along the same lines as a print ad. Remember that you can show the benefits of your product better with television than with just about any other medium, so take advantage of it.

If you choose to advertise on TV, you should be aware that television has a built-in mail order price threshold. Most products sell best at a top range of $24.95. But check out your competition. Most products sold on TV go for $19.95. Why? Because that's what sells!

Not unlike radio, there are many talk shows that need guests—especially on local stations and the numerous cable network affiliates. As cable networks add more and more channels, such as Sci-Fi 4 or 5 or ESPN 7, 8 or 9, the need to fill time increases, opening up more slots on talk shows. This is where your press releases and introductory letters to station managers and television producers come in handy. Unlike radio, however, they can't interview you by phone, so it does matter how you dress and how you look. Therefore, you need to watch talk show guests carefully and see what they wear and how they handle their appearances on air. You need to learn how to talk to both the host of the show and the audience, sit up straight, not fidget and present yourself as a confident expert—with an occasional smile. A little media training can go a long way.

Public Relations

Even though you may never come face to face with the customers who view your advertisements, public relations is an important consideration. Good public relations can get your company's name out to people who may not otherwise hear of you and can also keep your current customers thinking fondly of you so they'll continue ordering.

There are all sorts of low-cost public relations techniques you can use. Try some of the following:

- *Volunteer* as a guest speaker at the meetings of local associations or clubs that serve your target audience. If you're selling chocolates, talk to women's groups, cooking classes, and even kids' clubs about the history of chocolate. If you bring samples, you will probably make customers for life. If you've got a business-to-business company, talk to local business groups. Remember, word-of-mouth marketing is a powerful advertising tool—get creative!

- *Join organizations* that match your target audience and volunteer for things that will get your company recognized—and thought well of. Most people respect volunteers within an organization and consider them experts in the organization's area of interest. Volunteering can heighten your company's credibility.

- *Go green.* Use recycled materials as often as possible and stress this fact in your catalog or other printed materials and when you talk to people. Explain that your company helps the environment by conserving fossil fuels, too: When people shop by mail, they're not out running all over town burning smog-producing gasoline.

Bright Idea

Have everyone in your audience sign a guest register when you give talks at local club or association meetings. They'll be flattered, and you'll have more names for your in-house mailing list. Ask permission to send them your e-mail newsletter.

- *Offer your products* as prizes for charity events. You can also align with charities to sponsor activities and help make their fundraisers successful, while also getting your name out to the public.

Use your imagination! If your niche is horse products, can you supply ribbons for show winners? If it's gardening, can you sponsor a yard beautification program? Whatever you can do to get your name in front of the public in favorable ways will add to your company's image—and your income.

Before signing up with any pricey public relations agencies, see what you can come up with on your own or seek out some advice or consulting work from someone in the field. PR can be costly, so you may want to do it yourself in the early going, and there are plenty of public relations books available.

Helping Others

Helping others while you help yourself is good for the soul and also a great public relations strategy. Caryn, the fabric merchandiser, has made advocating her customers' businesses a fundamental part of her website. Members' wares, along with contact information, are displayed on the site free of charge. "We try to encourage our members to support each other," Caryn says. "We try to get them business as well. We're very big [on the concept that] we'll do better if you do better, and we'll do anything to help you do better."

Caryn receives frequent calls from grateful members thanking her for directing business their way. "We're just happy to help," the Roswell, Georgia, entrepreneur says. "The thing people forget is that when you help somebody else, it truly comes back to you. If you continue to help other companies, when they need products, who do they come back to?"

12

The Check is in the Mail: Money Management

Whether you're a chronic number cruncher or a finance-phobic, you'll want to give your company periodic financial checkups. The reason is that if there's a problem, you'll find out before it becomes critical. For instance, if you discover that your income barely covers your printing and operating expenses, you can change the size of your ads or the number of catalogs you mail out. Conversely, if orders are pouring in on your website, but you're falling behind in getting products out to customers, you may want to spend a few dollars to get some helpers.

"With this type of business," Kate W., the team logo merchandiser says, "you have to keep a close eye on your cash flow because it's a very expensive venture. You have to know what's making you money and what's not. If a certain type of advertising isn't making any money, you need to know that before you continue to do it for another two months."

Financial checkups don't have to be negative. After all, they can indicate how well you're doing—which may be even better than you expected. If you've been saving for a new printer or a software upgrade, or if you're hoping to take on an employee, you can judge how close you are to achieving your goal.

The key to financial comfort is not waiting for an annual checkup, but monitoring your spending on a regular basis and taking time for a monthly checkup. This way, you never fall too far out of the financial loop.

Making a Statement

An income statement, also called a profit-and-loss statement, charts the revenues and operating costs of your business over a specific period of time, usually a month. Check out the income statement on page 229 for our hypothetical mail order company, Chocoholic Central. To date, the owner of Chocoholic Central does not yet draw a salary from this new business, but relies on a percentage of the net profit for income.

You'll want to tailor your income statement to your particular business. To make the statement really accurate, you'll need to prorate annually payments such as a business licenses or a once a year tax-time accounting fee, and include those figures into your monthly statement. Therefore, if you pay $1,200 annually for insurance, divide this figure by 12 and list the resulting $100 as your monthly insurance expense.

Use the worksheet on page 230 to create your own income statement. You'll be surprised at how much fun finances can be!

Coming Up with a Response

You know how to figure your cost per order on a print or classified ad. (If you don't, go back to Chapter 5). You know how to conduct a test mailing of a catalog or other direct-mail piece, sending to, say, 3,000 or 5,000 names before committing yourself to a huge run of 20,000 or more. (Chapter 10, remember?) But how do you determine how much

Sample Income Statement 1

Chocoholic Central

INCOME STATEMENT
For the Month of October 2007

Monthly Income	
Gross sales	$6,400
Cost of sales*	1,600
Gross Monthly Income	**$4,800**
Monthly Expenses	
Rent	$N/A
Box rental	20
Phone/utilities	840
Call center	N/A
Electronic card processing	55
Employees	N/A
Miscellaneous postage	20
Licenses	8
Legal services	70
Accounting services	50
Office supplies	30
Shipping supplies	70
Insurance	100
Dues and subscriptions	40
Web hosting	35
Internet service provider	20
Loan repayment	N/A
Miscellaneous	25
Total Monthly Expenses	**$1,383**
Net Monthly Profit	**$3,417**

Cost of sales is the company's advertising and mailing costs.

▲

Monthly Income Statement Worksheet

For the Month of _____

Monthly Income	
Gross sales	$
Cost of sales*	
Gross Monthly Income	$
Monthly Expenses	
Rent	$
Mailbox rental	
Phone/utilities	
Call center	
Electronic card processing	
Employees	
Miscellaneous postage	
Licenses	
Legal services	
Accounting services	
Office supplies	
Shipping supplies	
Insurance	
Subscriptions/dues	
Web hosting	
Internet service provider	
Loan repayment	
Miscellaneous	
Total Monthly Expenses	$
Net Monthly Profit	$

of a response—and how much money—a mail order product is likely to bring in? More specifically, at what point will you break even and begin seeing a profit?

We took the question to John Schulte of the National Mail Order Association, who kindly provided us with an "Advanced Break-Even Worksheet" (starting on page 237) and a detailed explanation of how it is used. It may bear a resemblance to those annual forms from the IRS, but it's a lot more fun—and a lot easier to work with. Make lots of copies of the worksheet to use with different product pricing variables. Use your first one to work out the break-even point for the hypothetical mail order proposition Schulte uses to explain the step-by-step calculations on the worksheet. (See the "Advanced Break-Even Worksheet Instructions," starting on page 239.)

Smart Tip

Tip...

The National Mail Order Association (NMOA) is a valuable asset to any mail order newbie, as attested by many of the people we interviewed for this book. Don't hesitate to call on the organization for help. You can visit the NMOA at www.nmoa.org.

What's an average response? There is no easy answer to that one, Schulte says. Response rates depend on a number of factors, including the type and quality of your mailing list, the kind of product or service you're offering, the time of year, and the type of customer you have targeted. If you're selling big-ticket items like $100,000 tractors, for instance, you might be delighted with a one-tenth of 1 percent response. If you're selling the mega-toy of the year during the holiday season, you could expect a much higher response.

Hey, Big Spender

As a mail order entrepreneur, you need to keep your costs pared to the bone to make a profit. So whether you're inquiring about print advertising space, printing or letter-shop services, copywriting, graphics, or vendors' products, the key is to negotiate. Don't accept the first price someone quotes you. Ask for a better deal and, surprisingly enough, you'll often get it.

Besides bargaining, shop around. Get quotes from several printers or list brokers or call centers. Evaluate not only price but also factors like the estimated amount of time needed to complete a project and company qualifications. Don't be afraid to ask questions. Nobody expects you to be an expert on everything, especially in the early stages of your business career.

You may be able to get a head start on finding the best prices for different services from an unlikely source. "When you purchase a bulk mail permit, the postal service provides a whole packet of information. Based on [our] ZIP code, they gave us a directory of companies that do a number of services. Through that directory, we interviewed several companies and found [a print shop] that was conveniently located and had the best price," explains Kate W.

There are many things you can do to wisely manage your money in the print ad arena. Try these ideas:

- *Off-season rates.* Like tropical islands or ski resorts, some magazines have off-seasons, when their advertising volume takes a downturn. And like those vacation destinations, these publications will often give you a better-than-normal rate for advertising during the lull. Of course, you have to make sure your own seasonal curve will bear the cost. If you're selling suntan oil in January, this might not be worth the proposed savings.

- *Flying standby.* Sometimes magazines, like airlines, find at the eleventh hour before going to press that they don't have all their space sold. Since blank space looks bad, the usual solution is to fill it with public service ads like the ones you see for the Red Cross or the Humane Society. This is good karma but bad for the books. You can save the day by offering to purchase space at a standby rate, for which you may get as much as 50 percent off the usual rate. You'll have to inform the magazine ahead of time that you'd like this arrangement so its salespeople will know to call you, and you'll need to be able to have an ad ready at a moment's notice. (Sometimes you can have one on standby already at the magazine.) It helps to have established a good relationship with the magazine. But what a savings!

- *Mail order, P.I.* You remember the PI (per inquiry) from our review of radio advertising in Chapter 11, right? Well, it can work for print ads, too. In a PI arrangement, the magazine runs your ad "for free." In exchange, you give it a percentage of whatever money you make off inquiries from that ad. Sometimes the inquiries come to you, and you do all the book work and send the magazine its share every month (or whenever you've agreed). Sometimes the inquiries go to the magazine, which takes its portion off the top and sends the balance to you.

- *Frequent flier.* Magazines will usually give you a discount for advertising frequently. The size of the discount depends on whether you advertise every month, or three, four, or six times a year. This can be a terrific deal, but do not commit to it until you've done your testing and ascertained that the ad is working.

- *Cooperative Advertising.* This involves products you sell and the manufacturers of those products. If, for example, you are a distributor of a popular toy, then work a deal whereby you will feature the toy in your ad and split the cost of the ad with the manufacturer.

- *Spread discount.* In the magazine industry, a "spread" isn't a low-fat butter substitute; it's an ad (or an article) with two or more pages. While this is probably

Rating Ad Rates

One way to determine the cost-effectiveness of advertising in a particular publication is by calculating an efficiency ratio between the circulation and ad rates. This ratio is your cost per thousand, or CPM (M being the Roman numeral for thousand). A CPM is simply the cost of advertising divided by the magazine's circulation in thousands. If the circulation is 30,000 and the rate for a full-page ad is $600, you'd divide $600 by 30 and arrive at a CPM of $20.

Then you'd compare this with another potential advertising candidate, say, one with a circulation of 50,000 and a full-page ad rate of $700. Dividing $700 by 50, you'd have a CPM of $14.

If one magazine's CPM is considerably lower than the other's, and you can only afford to advertise in one of them, you've got a good place to start your decision-making process. But you'll still need to take all those demographics into consideration. If the cheaper magazine doesn't address your target market, think twice!

---

not an option for you as a newbie, you may get to the point where you can afford to purchase a spread. The good news here is that while spreads are terribly expensive, magazines will often give you a discount of up to—you guessed it—50 percent.

- *Cash it in.* Many magazines will give you a 2 percent discount if you pay within 10 days of placing your ad. To find out if this is offered, you'll have to examine the magazine's rate card or SRDS listing. If you see an early-payment discount, take it. Just deduct the discount amount when you send in your paid-within-10-days check.

- *Cash in on advertorials.* Many magazines include in your advertising contract, or let you pay a little extra, to be part of an advertorial, which looks like an article but is really an ad. The magazine is required to mention that it is an ad, but not all readers pay that close attention. What they see is a short article about your business, sometimes as part of a

Smart Tip

Looking for ways to increase your income? Set a goal for your average sale amount per order. When you reach that average, set a new goal. This strategy helps you determine what you need to do to increase sales. If your average order is $50, for instance, and you're selling chocolates, you might come up with special promotions to boost the average to, say, $75 per order.

▲

larger section featuring similar businesses. Inquire about whether the magazine runs advertorials or what one might cost if you're already an advertiser.

When you go wheeling and dealing, remember that magazines usually don't like to admit that they give any of these special deals. You may not find most of them on the rate card, so you'll have to get to know the ad reps and ask. When you do, be firm but friendly—not pushy. Keep in mind that you're establishing relationships here, ones that ideally will take you far into the future, earning tidy sums for your company and for the magazine. Let the ad reps know that you're a serious businessperson and that, as one, you're looking for a deal. They'll respect your position. Make sure you respect theirs, and don't forget to say "Thank you."

The Tax Man Cometh

Once you earn all that money with your cleverly negotiated ads, someone else will be queuing up for a piece of the action: Uncle Sam. You should engage an accountant to help you figure out what you need to pay and what you can deduct. You probably won't need one for your daily or monthly concerns, but it's well worth the expense to have someone in the know at the reins when April 15 rolls around and for those rare

The Trick Shot

Clever mail order entrepreneurs come up with all sorts of tricks to keep costs down. "We cut our photography expenses in half," Kate W. says, "yet we doubled the number of photographs."

In Kate's first catalog, she featured group photos of her products on nearly every page, which required long, complicated photo shoots of her inanimate models. "There was a lot of artistic stuff," the team logo merchandiser says. "You had to put things so they all looked good together. Rather than setting down a coffee mug—one piece—and photographing it, we had to completely design and lay out everything."

The result was that her labor costs were astronomical. The following year, the tenor—and the expense—of the photo shoot changed. "We used about half the group-shot pictures from last year," Kate explains, "and then we did a lot of single product inserts. When you're only shooting one product, you can get 10 or 12 done in an hour vs. one every three hours. You learn that if you're going to bring costs down, you have to change your original ideas."

but Panicsville questions that come up now and then.

Your tax deductions should be about the same as those for any other small or home-based business. These deductions include all normal office expenses plus interest, taxes, insurance, and depreciation (this is where the accountant comes in handy). You can deduct the percentage of your home that's used as an office, provided that you are using it solely as an office. The total amount of the deduction is limited by the gross income you derive from business activity minus all your other legitimate business expenses, apart from those related to the home office. Review business expenses with a professional—he or she will likely find some deductions that you missed (and axe some that you thought you could claim). In the end, however, you'll feel more secure knowing that a professional helped you handle your taxes.

> **Tip...**
>
> **Smart Tip**
>
> You can call the IRS with questions from just about anywhere in the country using the convenient toll-free number listed in your local White Pages. You can also ask Uncle Sam questions through the IRS's website at www.irs.gov.

More Deductions

What else can you deduct? Business-related phone calls, the cost of business equipment and supplies (again, so long as you're truly using them solely for your business), subscriptions to professional and trade journals, and auto expenses. Deductible auto expenses accrue when you drive your trusty vehicle in the course of doing business or seeking business. In other words, you're chalking up deductible mileage when you motor out to vendors' or manufacturers' offices to pick up samples and when you take a spin upstate to attend a trade show.

It's wise to keep a log of your business miles. Keep track as you go, then look at the latest mileage allowable by the IRS. It's no fun to have to backtrack at tax time and guesstimate how many miles you drove to how many clients' locations during the year.

Let Me Entertain You

You can deduct entertainment expenses, such as wining and dining a vendor during the course of a meeting or hosting potential customers at a coffee hour. Keep a log of all these expenses as well, especially if they come to less than $75 a pop. Keep in mind that if you're entertaining at home, have your vendors or customers sign a guest book.

You must have a business-related purpose for entertaining, such as a sales presentation. General goodwill toward your potential customers or vendors does not make it, so be sure your log contains the reason for the partying, and don't get carried away. The IRS looks for excessive numbers in specific areas, and entertaining to the hilt may be one of them.

Planes, Trains, and Automobiles

Business travel is also deductible, as long as your travel is strictly for business purposes. If not, you can pro-rate the business portion of the trip and then not include the part in which you took the family on vacation. Typically, common sense should win out when determining what is and isn't factored into the equation.

Deductions include airfares, train tickets, rental car mileage, and so on. You can also deduct hotel and meal expenses. Since the IRS allows deductions for any trip you take to expand your awareness and expertise in your field of business, it makes sense to also take advantage of any conferences or seminars you can attend.

Advanced Break-Even Worksheet

Date:_____

Key Code:_____

Product or Service: _____

1. Selling price of product or service $_____

2. Variable costs of filling an order:

    a. Wholesale cost of product or service $_____

    b. Royalty $_____

    c. Handling expense $_____

    d. Postage and shipping expense $_____

    e. Premium, include handling and shipping $_____

    f. Use tax, if any (#1 x _____%) $_____

    g. Credit card processing charge
      (#1 x _____% transaction fee) $_____

    Total Cost of Filling the Order $_____

3. Administrative overhead

    a. Rent, utilities, maintenance, credit checks,
      collections, etc. (_____% of #1) $_____

    Total Administrative Cost $_____

4. Estimated percentage of returns, refunds, or cancellations   _____%

5. Expense in handling returns:

    a. Return postage and handling (#2c + #2d) $_____

    b. Refurbishing returned merchandise (_____% of #2a) $_____

    Total Cost of Handling Returns $_____

Advanced Break-Even Worksheet, continued

6. Chargeable cost of returns (_____% of #5 total) $_____

7. Estimated bad debt percentage   _____%

8. Chargeable cost of bad debts (#1 x #7) $_____

9. **Total Variable Costs (#2 + #3 + #6 + #8)** $_____

10. Unit profit after deducting variable costs (#1 - #9) $_____

11. Return factor (100% - #4)   _____%

12. Unit profit per order (#10 x #11) $_____

13. Credit for returned merchandise (_____% of #2a) $_____

14. Net profit per order (#12 + #13) $_____

15. Cost of mailing per 1,000 $_____

16. Number of orders per 1,000 mailings needed to break even:

    Mailing cost (#15) divided by net profit (#14) $_____

Source: The National Mail Order Association

Advanced Break-Even Worksheet
Instructions

Let's take a look at a hypothetical mail order proposition and go through the various steps to see what costs must be included to determine how many orders per thousand you must get to break even.* First, the worksheet should carry the date, the name of the proposition, and the key code for that particular mailing. You'll need this information for future reference.

1. We start with the retail selling price of the merchandise or service. In this case, let's say we're selling the Green Thumb Gardening Book for $25 with ten days' free examination and a premium, a "seed planting gauge," included as an extra incentive to examine the book. The customer gets to keep the planting gauge whether he buys or returns the book. Fill in $25 under item #1.

2. Here we enter #2a, the wholesale cost of the book (including shipping carton), which is $6. This gives us a good markup of more than 400 percent. For one-shot mailings, a larger selling margin is necessary, especially on lower-cost items.

   The next consideration is royalty, item #2b. If you're selling a book or an item on which a royalty or commission needs to be paid to the author, manufacturer, or inventor, this expense should be included as a part of the total cost of the merchandise or service. In this hypothetical case, there is no royalty because the book is purchased from another publisher.

   The handling expense, item #2c, includes the opening of the mail, data entry, and processing the order for fulfillment. This amounts to 95 cents. Postage and shipping expense (#2d) is 60 cents. As we included a premium in this offer (the planting gauge), we must add its cost (30 cents) as part of the expense of filling the order (item #2e). If your state has a use tax, this must also be added (#2f). For this example, we will not be adding a use tax. In most cases, you will also have to add a credit card processing expense, as most people use their credit cards for orders. Let's take 3 percent (including transaction fee) as an example. Multiply item #1 by 3 percent and you get 75 cents for #2g. Adding all the expenses under #2, it costs $8.60 to fill an order.

3. But there are other costs that must be included. How about administrative costs, which include rent, light, heat, use of equipment, maintenance, credit checks, collection follow-up, office supplies, and the like? Many firms make a flat charge of 10 to 20 percent of the retail price (#1) to cover these expenses. Let's use 10 percent of $25.00, or $2.50, and enter this under #3a as the total administrative cost.

4. The next question is what percentage of your customers will return the merchandise if sold on a free examination offer? Suppose we take 10 percent as an average and post this under item #4.

*All numbers used in this worksheet are hypothetical and do not relate to any actual known numbers.

Advanced Break-Even Worksheet
Instructions, continued

5. How much does it cost to handle returns? It certainly costs as much as it did to ship the books. So let's charge $1.55 (#2c plus #2d) for item #5a. (Of course, some customers will pay the shipping for returning the merchandise but let's not count on it.) Also consider that some of the books may be damaged in shipping, so let's allow 10 percent of the cost of the book (10 percent of #2a), 60 cents in this example, for refurbishing (#5b). This brings the total cost of handling returns (item #5) to $2.15 per order.

6. As we are figuring that 10 percent of the orders will be returned, refunded, or canceled (item #4), the total cost of handling returns will be 10 percent of $2.15 (item #5), or 21.5 cents per order. Let's just say 21 cents.

7. Bad debts (money owed from customers who never pay up) are another expense that must be considered. This percentage will vary from about 5 to 25 percent, depending on the proposition, the way the offer is presented, and the list used. Let's take 10 percent as an average figure and enter it here.

8. So our bad debt cost is 10 percent (item #7) times $25.00 (item #1). This amounts to $2.50 that must be allowed for the cost of bad debts. Enter $2.50 for item #8.

9. The total variable costs are item #2 ($8.60) plus item #3 ($2.50), item #6 ($ .21) and item #8 ($2.50), amounting to $13.81.

10. After deducting the total variable costs of $13.81 (item #9) from the selling price of $25 (item #1), we're left with a unit profit of $11.19.

11. But there is a return factor of 10 percent (item #4) that must be accounted for. Deducting item #4, or 10 percent, from 100 percent leaves 90 percent of the unit profit. Post 90 percent for item #11.

12. Taking 90 percent (item #11) of $11.19 (item #10) leaves a unit profit of $10.07 per order. Post this amount for item #12.

13. Any merchandise that is returned after examination will be put back into your inventory to liquidate or perhaps be sent back to the manufacturer. This represents a credit against the original cost of the merchandise. Since we estimate the returns to be 10 percent (item #4), we would have a credit of 10 percent of our cost (item #2a, $6), or 60 cents.

14. Adding the unit profit per order (item #12) to the credit for returned merchandise (item #13), we have a net profit per order of $10.67.

15. Suppose the cost of your mailing package—carrier envelope, letter, circular, order form, reply envelope, mailing list, lettershop labor, postage, etc.—amounts to $100 per thousand. What about creative and production charges such as editorial preparation, artwork, advertising, consultation, copy, engravings, and typesetting that must be paid for?

Advanced Break-Even Worksheet
Instructions, continued

You have the choice of charging these expenses against the test mailing or amortizing them over your projected mailing possibilities. If you charge it all in one lump sum against the test, it will show a distorted picture. This could kill the test before you give it a chance. It's better to spread this part of the cost over the total quantity of a projected mailing. If the creative and production charges amount to $1,000 and you figure you can mail to 2 million names if the test is successful, you could charge 50 cents per thousand names against the cost of the mailing. If the test is a flop, you'll have to absorb the expense anyway, so why not give it a reasonable chance to come through? Enter $100.50 ($100 plus 50 cents) under item #15.

16. Dividing the cost of mailing 1,000 letters (item #15), $100.50, by the net profit per order (item #14), $10.67, tells us that you need 9.4 orders, or .94 percent per thousand, to break even.

Suppose your break-even point on a test mailing is 9.4 orders or .94 percent, less than a 1 percent response. How many orders more than 9.4 per thousand should you get to justify going ahead with a larger mailing? That depends on whether there's the potential to win long-term customers or if this is a one-shot deal. If you are selling merchandise that provides some kind of residual income, such as vitamins or another product that people reorder regularly, you may be happy with just breaking even to bring in new customers and having future sales make up your profit. But with one-shot propositions, you should look for some kind of return on investment, since you're taking a bigger risk with your money—and that means getting enough orders to take you past your break-even point.

To give you an idea of how the money grows when you get just a few orders more than what's needed to break even, we've laid out an illustrative scenario. For this example, we will get one-third more orders than our break-even point of 9.4. This would give us a total of 12.5 orders per thousand, or 3.1 orders more than the break-even point. (This is a 1.25 percent response.)

With 3.1 orders more than the break-even point and a unit profit of $10.67 per order, the net profit would be $33.08 per thousand (3.1 x $10.67). On a 100,000 mailing, the net profit would be $3,308. On 500,000 it would be $16,540. And on 1,000,000 it would $33,080.

A word of caution! The time that elapses between the date of a test mailing and the date of the final mailing may affect your results. For example, a test made in January that pulls 12.5 orders per thousand might pull only 9.4 or less if mailed in June. So test in the slow months, if possible, and mail in the good months to eliminate unprofitable mailings.

Source: The National Mail Order Association

Happy Mailings
or Empty
Envelopes?

Most people succeed in the mail order business by following the tried-and-true business methods of persistence and plain old-fashioned hard work, with a healthy dose of optimism sprinkled throughout. If we have illustrated anything in this book, we hope it's that becoming a successful mail order entrepreneur involves a lot of work—rewarding and sometimes exhilarating work, but darn hard work nonetheless.

We also hope we've managed to convey that becoming a mail order maven is not the same as becoming an overnight success. It takes lots of market research, loads of planning, tons of testing and analysis, and an abundance of creativity to gain those repeat customers.

One of the other points that was hopefully clear throughout the book is that the people who have selected mail order as a career, whether it was through mailing catalogs or launching a successful website filled with goodies, in most cases, were passionate about their business ventures. Since mail order businesses most often start out at the grassroots level, from someone's home (and often remain there), it is a business with which you can feel very personally connected... and that makes it particularly rewarding.

Don't Look Back

When the mail order entrepreneurs interviewed for this book were asked for some words of advice for beginners, they gave—not surprisingly—some very thoughtful responses.

"I think in any type of mail order business, you want to identify a need and target your mailing," says Beth H., the gluten-free foods purveyor in Connecticut. "If you try to saturate a market that is very broad, you are just dooming yourself to failure. You really need to start small and remain focused. You need to know who your competition is. I think you have to have an excellent product and top-notch service. And you have to be consistent. If you can do all of those things, then I think you have a good shot at having a successful business."

"Ask everybody questions," adds Liz L., children's T-shirt designer in New York. "Find someone you know and like at your local post office. If you have any questions, they will help you, and I am sure every community has an office you can call with questions if your local post office can't handle something. Attend seminars at your local college. Join groups. Get involved and really get into your field. Read trade magazines."

In Kansas, Kate W., the university team logo merchandiser, also suggests reading. "Read, read, read," she says. "Read everything you can get your hands on before you start." In addition, she recommends having an interest in your target market. "If you're going to do it solo," Kate advises, "make sure it's something you have a genuine interest in. If I wasn't so loyal to [my niche] and excited about it every day, it would be really hard to put in the long hours consistently."

"Go very slowly," cautions Caryn O., the fabric supplier in Georgia. "Going too fast can put you out of business quickly. If you can't fill your customers' needs, you'll be shocked how quickly you can go out of business. It's just as detrimental as having no business. So go slow. It'll work out. Get it right. Get it down to a science. It gets easier and easier."

"I pride myself in customer service," says Patty, the party photo frames supplier from Minnesota. "I usually use drop shippers, but I keep some of the most popular frames on hand for those last minute callers who are in a panic and need something in a hurry. I'll wrap them myself and ship them out at the post office or at through UPS. Customer service in the mail order business is probably the most important thing you deal with. People write to me, thanking me for helping them out, telling me how I saved their life. If good customer service is not going to be a part of your strategy, then you better re-think it."

Yin and Yang

If you're the type of person who can handle the ups and downs of entrepreneurship in general and the yin and yang of creativity and number crunching that makes up the mail order maven's world, you'll probably thrive. If not, you may discover during your company's first year of life, or a little beyond, that the business isn't for you. You may feel that instead of happy mailings, you are experiencing empty envelopes.

Whether or not you're earning money, the success of your business is contingent on a happiness factor. Because of the amount of work and responsibility involved in running your own business, you may discover that you'd be just as happy—or more so—working for someone else, and that's okay. With everything you will have learned, you'll be a great candidate for a job.

None of the people interviewed for this book, from a brand-new newbie to a veteran with 15 years of experience, seem to have any intention of packing it in. Rather, they appear to delight in doing what they enjoy and helping others with the same interests.

"We share a lot," Caryn says. "We know so many of our members that you wouldn't believe it. We have customers all over the world. We've met some of the most wonderful people. It's really a fun thing."

Although the mail order entrepreneurs who so generously helped with this book serve different markets and have different levels of experience, they all have one important thing in common—a winning attitude. If you go into this business with the right stuff—a willingness to work hard and learn everything you can, the confidence to promote yourself and your business, and the drive to succeed—chances are, you will.

Appendix
Mail Order Resources

They say you can never be rich enough or thin enough. While these could be argued, we say you can never have enough resources. Therefore, we present for your consideration a wealth of resources for you to check into, check out, and harness as part of your own personal information blitz.

These resources are intended to get you started on your research. They are by no means the only ones out there. We have done our research, but businesses do tend to move, change, fold, and expand. As we have repeatedly stressed, do your homework. Get out there and do some investigating.

The best place to start? Surf the net, you'll find plenty of resources at your fingertips—check them out.

Advertising Rate Information

Standard Rate and Data Service (SRDS), 1700 Higgins Rd., Des Plaines, IL 60018-5605, (800) 851-7737, (847) 375-5000, www.srds.com

(Note: Most local public libraries carry copies of SRDS directories—an option if you don't want to invest in your own right away.)

▲

Associations

The Direct Marketing Association, 1120 Ave. of the Americas, New York, NY 10036-6700, (212) 768-7277, www.the-dma.org

Mailing Fulfillment Service Association, 1421 Prince St., Suite 410, Alexandria, VA 22314-2806, (703) 836-9200, www.mfsanet.org

National Mail Order Association, 2807 Polk St. N.E., Minneapolis, MN 55418-2954, (888) 496-7337 (for ordering books and reports only), (612) 788-1673, www.nmoa.org (The NMOA website lists numerous books and has links to a tremendous volume of information.)

Books

Building a Mail Order Business: A Complete Manual for Success, William A. Cohen, Ph.D., John Wiley & Sons.

The Direct Marketing Tool Kit For Small Business, John Shulte (available through NMOA).

Home-Based Mail Order: A Success Guide for Entrepreneurs, William J. Bond, McGraw-Hill.

How to Start a Home-Based Mail Order Business, 3rd edition (Home-Based Business Series) by Georganne Fiumara, Globe Pequot.

How to Get Rich on the Internet: America's 21 Top-Gun Internet Marketers Reveal Their Insider Secrets to Outrageous Internet Marketing Success! by Ted Ciuba, Morgan James Publishing, Ltd.

Mail-Order Success Secrets, Revised 2nd Edition: How to Create a $1,000,000-a-Year Business Starting from Scratch by Tyler G. Hicks, Prima Lifestyles.

Call Centers

All USA Communications, 10526 Cermak, #300, Westchester, IL 60154, (888) 413-0210, (708) 236-1200, www.allusa.net

Anser Services, 2761 Allied St., Green Bay, WI 54304, (800) 723-0000, www.anser.com

Answer Center America Inc., 5532 N. Broadway, Chicago, IL 60640, USA (800) 270-7030, www.answercenteramerica.com

AnswerNet Network, 345 Witherspoon St., Princeton, NJ 08542, 800-411-5777, www.answernet.com

Contact One Call Centers, 818 W. Miracle Mile Tucson, AZ 85705, (800) 278-3347, www.wetakecalls.com

Five9, Inc. U.S. 7901 Stoneridge Drive, Suite 200, Pleasanton, CA 94588 (925) 201-2000, Sales Office: (800) 553-8159, www.five9.com

The Northridge Group, Inc. 9700 West Higgins Road, Suite 820 Rosemont, IL 60018-4736, (847) 692-2288

Personalized Communications, 205 E Center St., Duncanville, TX 75116, (214) 361-6684, www.per-com.com

Credit Card Services

Bank of America, Merchant Services, Bank of America, N.A., WA5-505-01-40 P.O. Box 2485, Spokane, WA 99210-2485, (866) 538-3827, www.bankofamerica.com/small_business/merchant_card_processing/

CreditCards.com, 9200 Sunset Blvd., 6th Fl., Los Angeles, CA 90069, (888) 327-4748, (310) 724-6400, www.creditcards.com

Delivery Services

DHL, (800)-CALL-DHL, www.dhl-usa.com

FedEx, (800) GO-FEDEX, www.fedex.com

UPS, (800) PICK-UPS, www.ups.com

USPS, (800) THE-USPS, www.usps.gov

Helpful Government Websites

Bureau of the Census, www.census.gov

Federal Trade Commission, www.ftc.gov

The Food & Drug Administration, www.fda.org

Internal Revenue Service, www.irs.gov

U.S. Patent & Trademark Office. www.uspto.gov

U.S. Postal Service, www.usps.gov; for mail rate calculators: www.usps.gov/business/calcs.htm

(Note: Ask your local bulk-mail processing center—which you can locate by calling your nearest post office—for copies of Publication 95, Quick Service Guide and the Mailers Companion)

Magazines and Publications

Catalog Success, 1500 Spring Garden Street, Suite 1200, Philadelphia, PA 19130, www.catalogsuccess.com

Direct Marketing, 224 Seventh St., Garden City, NY 11530, (800) 229-6700, (516) 746-6700, www.directmag.com

MultiChannel Merchant magazine (formerly *Catalog Age* magazine), 203-358-4221, 11 River Bend Drive South, P.O. Box 4242, Stamford, CT 06907-0242, http://multichannelmerchant.com

Target Marketing, 1500 Spring Garden Street, 12th Floor, Philadelphia, PA 19130, (215) 238-5300, www.targetonline.com

(Note: Most magazines will send a sample issue for free if you call and ask.)

Mailing Lists

American List Counsel, 88 Orchard Rd. CN-5219, Princeton, NJ 08543, (800) ALC-LIST, (908) 874-4300, www.amlist.com

infoUSA, Inc. 5711 South 86th Circle, P.O. Box 27347, Omaha, NE 68127, (800) 321-0869, www.infousa.com

U.S. Data Corporation, 21820 Burbank Blvd., Suite 205, Woodland Hills, CA 91367, (888) 610-DATA (3282), local (818) 444-4590, wwwusadatacorp.net

USAData, Inc., 292 Madison Ave, 3rd Fl., New York, NY 10017, (800) 599-5030 or (212) 679-1411, www.usadata.com

(Note: Check into any issue of magazines like MultiChannel Merchant or Target Marketing—advertisements for list brokers, managers, and owners. Also, several organizations and associations offer list rentals.)

Mail Order Consultants

Direct Marketing Insights, Inc., 222 West Coleman Boulevard, Mt. Pleasant, SC 29464, (843) 884-1428, www.dminsights.com/mail_order_consultants.html

John Schulte & Associates, 2807 Polk St. N.E., Minneapolis, MN 55418-2954, (612) 788-1673, e-mail: schulte@nmoa.org

Richard Siedlecki, 4767 Lake Forest Dr. N.E., Atlanta, GA 30342, (404) 303-9900, e-mail: sied@mindspring.com

Mail Order Software

MACH2K from Data Management Associates, www.mach2k.com

Mail Order Manager (M.O.M.), from Dydacomp, www.dydacomp.com

Mail Order Software Plus from Datamann, www.datamann.com

Mail Order Wizard from, Haven Corp., www.havencorp.com

Mailware, from Core Technologies, www.mailware.com

RESPONSE from CoLinear, www.colinear.com

Harvey Software (shipping sofware) www.harveysoft.com

SparkList, from Sparklist, www.sparklist.com

(Note: Most software vendors will send you a free or nominally priced demo if you ask or you may be able to download a demo from their website.)

Mail Order Websites

American Computer Group (database services for direct marketers), www.mailorder.com

Audit Bureau of Circulations, www.accessabc.com

The Bridge (marketing research), www.mbc-thebridge.com/research

Find Answering Service, www.findanansweringservice.com

Media Central, www.mediacentral.com

Smart Business Supersite Catalog Page, www.smartbiz.com/sbs/cats/catalogs.htm

Seminars and Conferences

The Direct Marketing Association, 1120 Ave. of the Americas, New York, NY 10036-6700, (212) 768-7277, www.the-dma.org

National Mail Order Association, 2807 Polk St. N.E., Minneapolis, MN 55418-2954, (888) 496-7337 (for ordering books and reports only), (612) 788-1673, www.nmoa.org

(Note: Your local community college or university may also sponsor seminars and workshops.)

Shipping and Packaging Supplies

Anchor Box Co., 5889 S. Gessner Rd., Houston, TX 77036, (800) 522-8820, (713) 778-1500, www.anchorbox.com

Associated Bag Co., 400 Boden Rd., Milwaukee, WI 53207, (800) 926-6100, (414) 769-1000, www.associatedbag.com

Geopac, P.O. Box 3660, 521 Main Ave. S.W., Hickory, NC 28601, (828) 322-5258, www.geopac.com

PackagingSupplies.com, 16363 Pearl Road, Cleveland, OH 44136, (800) 536-3668, www.packagingsupplies.com

Uline, 2105 S. Lakeside Dr., Waukegan, IL 60085, (800) 958-5463, www.uline.com

Successful Mail Order Businesses

The Fabric Club, Caryn O'Keefe, P.O. Box 767670, Roswell, GA 30076, (800) FAB-CLUB, (404) 344-9432, www.fabricclub.com

The Gluten-Free Pantry, Beth Hillson, P.O. Box 840, Glastonbury, CT 06033, (800) 291-8386, (860) 633-3826, www.glutenfree.com

Just for Fans, Kate Wolford, 11936 W. 119th St., #105, Overland Park, KS 66213, (800) 934-FANS, (913) 681-3634, www.just4fans.com

Little Lizzie, Liz Landa, P.O. Box 593, Rhinebeck, NY 12572, (845) 876-8130, www.littlelizzie.com

Instant Photo Frames.com, Patty Sachs, Minneapolis, MN., 763-432-3395, www.instantphotoframes.com

Glossary

Action devices: items and techniques used in direct mail that help encourage positive responses, such as tokens or coupons.

Additional profit center: a method of earning money other than through sales to mail order customers, such as renting mailing lists to other direct marketers.

Advertising schedule: List of advertisements booked by media showing details of sizes, timing, and costs.

Audited circulation statement: a sworn statement from a magazine publisher, verified by an outside source, that discloses the magazine's circulation.

Back end: a mail order company's list of repeat customers.

Barcode sorter (BCS): a mail processing machine that reads barcodes on mail and automatically sorts the pieces.

Bulk mail: mail sent at discounted prices and according to special postal guidelines; also called standard mail.

Call center: a company that answers phones and takes orders from customers for a mail order business.

▲

Catalog house: a company that supplies preprinted catalogs and drop-shipped merchandise to mail order entrepreneurs.

Charge-back: the refunding of money for returned or disputed merchandise that was paid for by credit card.

Classified ad: a print advertisement without graphics found only in the classified section of a publication.

Clustering: grouping names according to geographic, demographic, or psychographic characteristics on a telemarketing list.

Compiled list: a mailing list composed of people in specific categories, e.g., doctors, lawyers, Manhattan residents.

Conversion rate: percentage of potential customers who, through direct mail solicitation, become buyers.

Cost per order: the cost of an advertisement divided by the number of orders received.

Cost per thousand (CPM): the cost of an advertisement divided by a magazine's circulation in thousands.

Cross-sell: to attempt to raise the total amount of a customer's order by suggesting the purchase of related products.

Demographics: data based on the characteristics of a population, measured by variables such as age, sex, marital status, family size, education, geographic location, and occupation.

Direct mail: see direct marketing.

Direct marketing: the use of printed materials such as sales letters, brochures, and catalogs to advertise products and services available for order via mail, telephone, fax, or e-mail; another term for mail order; also called direct mail and direct response.

Direct response: see direct marketing.

Display ad: a print advertisement that has graphics and can be placed almost anywhere in a publication.

Dropship: an arrangement in which a third party such as a manufacturer or a wholesaler sends products directly from its warehouse to the mail order retailer's customers

Early fringe: the television time slot from 4 to 8 P.M.

Evening drive time: the radio time slot from 3 to 7 P.M.

Focus group: a group of people gathered for the purpose of conducting market research.

Front end: a list of prospects to whom material has been mailed but who have not purchased products or services.

FTC: Federal Trade Commission.

Fulfillment: the process of filling and shipping mail orders; fulfillment often also includes taking the orders.

Fulfillment house: a company that fills and ships orders; fulfillment houses frequently also take orders by phone or mail.

General catalog: a catalog that sells a wide variety of merchandise.

Half-life: the time span between when an issue of a catalog is mailed out and when half the total number of orders expected from it are received; generally considered to be three or four months, depending on the type of merchandise and the target market.

Help if necessary: a stipulation in which a magazine reruns an ad at no additional charge until the advertiser garners a response.

In-house agency: an advertising agency formed and run by a company to address its own advertising needs.

Jobber: a wholesale-product distributor.

Key code: an identifying code made up of numbers and letters, or an address addition, such as "Dept. A," that is placed on all sales materials to indicate which advertisement or mail campaign a response originated from; also called a source code.

Late fringe: the television time slot from 11 P.M. to dawn.

Lettershop: a company that processes direct-mail pieces, performing services such as placing inserts, folding, stapling, sorting, and stamping.

List broker: a company or individual specializing in mailing-list rentals.

List management system: database system that manages customer and prospect lists, used to merge and purge duplicates between in-house lists and those obtained from outside sources.

Mailing list: a roster of names and addresses used by direct marketers.

Mail or Telephone Order Merchandise Rule: an FTC ruling that regulates direct-marketing practices.

Media kit: the package magazines send to potential advertisers that contains sample issues, an audited circulation statement and information about editorial content, reader demographics, and ad rates.

Merge/purge: to combine duplicate mailing list entries and remove invalid ones, such as those for people who have moved and provided no forwarding address.

Morning drive time: the radio time slot from 6 to 10 A.M.

Name acquisition: means of soliciting a response to obtain names and addresses for a mailing list.

Nixie: a mailing list address that has changed and for which no forwarding information has been provided.

Nth name selection: a random-sampling method of mailing list name selection in which every seventh or 10th name, for example, is used to compile a broad cross-section of names.

One-shot: a single mail order product marketed and sold by itself rather than as part of a line of products.

One-step: a print ad that incorporates an order form.

Overwrap: a second catalog cover made with cheaper paper than the rest of the book; used to test new products, advertise specials, or promote other materials.

Per inquiry (P.I.): a method of paying for advertising by giving the media source a percentage of the profits made on each inquiry the ad generates.

Pick and pack: a company that handles packing and shipping.

Piggyback products: sales materials from one mail order advertiser tucked in with the sales package of another advertiser.

Postal inspector: a direct-marketing regulator employed by the U.S. Postal Service and empowered to arrest those who engage in illegal mail order activities.

Proprietary rights: a company's right to manufacture a product.

Psychographics: a method of targeting mail order customers by psychological profile.

Qualified buyer: a customer who has already purchased products or services by mail order.

Questionnaire: form with specific questions (typically with answer choices) designed to solicit responses to specific questions.

Rate card: a card or sheet that lists a magazine's advertising prices.

Recency, Frequency, Money (RFM): a mailing list selection formula in which a list is evaluated according to how recently the people on it have ordered something by mail, how frequently they order, and how much money they spend.

Remnant: magazine ad space that remains unsold immediately prior to publication and is offered to advertisers at a discounted rate.

Repeat buyer: a customer who has purchased previously from your business.

Response list: a mailing list composed of people who have previously responded to specific mail order campaigns; for instance, people who buy gardening books or people who buy horse-care products.

Rollout: to mail out materials in a direct-marketing campaign after having done the initial test market mailing.

Sales conversion rate: number of sales in relation to number of calls, e-mails, or mail responses initiated or received.

Salting: the practice of inserting fictitious/dummy names and addresses into a mailing list so that the company renting the list to others can tell if it has been used illegally; also called seeding.

Select: a specific category, such as age, geographic region, or income bracket, by which names on a mailing list can be sorted and selected for mailings.

Self-mailer: a direct mail piece that is mailed without an envelope.

Source code: see key code.

Space: areas set aside by magazines or other publications for advertising.

Specialty catalog: a catalog that sells a specialized selection of goods.

Spread: an ad that covers two or more pages in a publication.

Standard mail: see bulk mail.

Standard Rate and Data Service (SRDS): a service that provides media information and rates on print, radio, television, and internet advertising sources.

Tear sheet: printed page from a publication to show that an ad was run.

Test market: trial for a new product or service offer sent to a specific market.

Two-step: a print advertisement that encourages customers to call or write for more information rather than allowing them to order directly from the ad.

Up-sell: to attempt to raise the total amount of a customer's order by suggesting the purchase of more than one of the same product.

Web optimization: ways to increase the visibility of your website and the ranking on search engines, including the use of keywords.

Index